Managing Business

Pla_____ _____ ___on

IDEA GROUP PUBLISHING

Hershey • London • Melbourne • Singapore

Acquisitions Editor:	Mehdi Khosrow-Pour
Senior Managing Editor:	Jan Travers
Managing Editor:	Amanda Appicello
Development Editor:	Michele Rossi
Copy Editor:	Ingrid Widitz
Typesetter:	Amanda Appicello
Cover Design:	Lisa Tosheff
Printed at:	Yurchak Printing Inc.

Published in the United States of America by
Idea Group Publishing (an imprint of Idea Group Inc.)
701 E. Chocolate Avenue, Suite 200
Hershey PA 17033
Tel: 717-533-8845
Fax: 717-533-8661
E-mail: cust@idea-group.com
Web site: http://www.idea-group.com

and in the United Kingdom by
Idea Group Publishing (an imprint of Idea Group Inc.)
3 Henrietta Street
Covent Garden
London WC2E 8LU
Tel: 44 20 7240 0856
Fax: 44 20 7379 3313
Web site: http://www.eurospan.co.uk

Library of Congress Cataloging-in-Publication Data

Managing business with SAP : planning, implementation and evaluation / Linda Lau, editor.
    p. cm.
Includes bibliographical references and index.
ISBN 1-59140-378-2 (hardcover) -- ISBN 1-59140-379-0 (pbk.) -- ISBN 1-59140-380-4 (ebook)
1. SAP R/3. 2. Business--Data processing. 3. Management information systems. I. Lau, Linda K., 1958-
  HF5548.4.R2M36 2004
  658'.05'57585--dc22

2004003750

British Cataloguing in Publication Data
A Cataloguing in Publication record for this book is available from the British Library.

All work contributed to this book is new, previously-unpublished material. The views expressed in this book are those of the authors, but not necessarily of the publisher.

Managing Business with SAP:
Planning, Implementation and Evaluation

Table of Contents

Preface

At a time when many major corporations, particularly in the technological field, are continuously laying off workers or outsourcing their IT services to overseas countries, SAP, Inc. and organizations using the SAP concepts and software applications, on the other hand, are in need of more IT professionals familiar with their systems. Although the popularity of SAP has reached an all time high, there are insufficient research and exploratory studies available in this field. Therefore, the primary objective of this book is to provide a comprehensive overview of this interesting area, and to address several of the important issues relating to the successful implementation and management of ERP/SAP systems.

This book is divided into three major sections. The first section consists of three chapters, which introduces the foundation for ERP and the SAP technology. John Loonam and Joe McDonagh of University of Dublin in Ireland begin the book with Chapter 1, entitled "Principles, Foundations, & Issues in Enterprise Systems". With the current trends towards globalization and virtual organizations, coupled with rapid and constant business and technological changes, enterprise systems have become increasingly important in integrating and consolidating information across the organizations. Therefore, this introductory chapter describes the core principles, foundations and issues of enterprise systems, reviews the evolutionary process of enterprise systems, identifies the generic software characteristics, and discusses the benefits and limitations of these systems. Based on a review of current enterprise systems implementation approaches, several challenges were also uncovered. This chapter concludes with suggestions to overcome these challenges.

The editor authored Chapter 2, entitled "An Overview of SAP Technology". Because this book focuses on the development and implementation of SAP systems, this chapter will describe the major activities conducted by SAP since its inception in 1972 and SAP's flagship software program, that is, the R/3 system, in detail. This will include the capabilities of the R/3 system, the three-tier client/server technology it employs, the hardware and software requirements, and several problems associated with its implementation. The two R/3 implementation tools – namely, the Accelerated SAP and the Ready to Run systems – are also described.

Because of the increasing demand for ERP/SAP professionals, many academic institutions of higher learning are redefining their business curricula and seeing the need to join alliances with ERP software vendors such as SAP, Inc. to incorporate ERP concepts into their business education. The purpose of the SAP University Alliance Program is to provide college students with a better understanding of the business processes and ERP systems integration using SAP technology, and to facilitate a cross-functional business curriculum using state-of-the-art information technology. Participating institutions are installed with the SAP systems so that students can obtain hands-on experience with the technical applications. Adequately and academically SAP-trained graduates are better equipped to make strategic financial and operational decisions, and will result in higher employability, increased entry-level salary, and greater choice of employers. Chapter 3, entitled "Integrating SAP Across the Business Curriculum," is authored by Jane Fedorowicz, Ulric J. (Joe) Gelinas, Jr., George Hachey, and Catherine Usoff of Bentley College in Massachusetts, USA. The authors explain how academicians can successfully integrate knowledge of the SAP R/3 systems into the undergraduate and graduate college courses. They also suggest that this knowledge integration is a far better learning and instructional technique than the creation of standalone courses covering ERP concepts. They conclude the chapter with the process of training faculty to develop and test curriculum materials and to coordinate the integration effort with each other in the college.

The second section of the book describes the impacts and challenges of ERP systems. Chapter 4, entitled "The Impact of Agile SAP on the Supply Chain," is written by Sue Conger of the University of Dallas in Texas, USA. Most Fortune 500 corporations have integrated their business functions with at least one or more ERP software applications to improve the organization's agility. While the problems associated with ERP deployment are easily identified, the concepts of agility as applied to ERP deployment have been ignored in the literature review. Therefore, the primary objective of this chapter is to determine the impact of agile ERP software deployment on organizational agility. The author indicated that agile deployment has competitive benefits both for the software vendor and for the licensing business organization, and she used a case study to support her research findings. This chapter concludes with several recommendations and trends for companies intending to deploy SAP software applications.

Chapter 5, entitled "B2E SAP Portals: Employee Self-Service Case Study," is written by Andrew Stein and Paul Hawking of Victoria University of Technology in Australia, and David C. Wyld of Southeastern Louisiana University in Louisiana, USA. Currently, most, if not all, major corporations have already implemented ERP systems into their operations. Lately, the "second wave" of functionality in ERP systems targets small and medium-sized organizations, resulting in the development of the business-to-employee (B2E) model, yielding relatively quick gains with low associated risks. One such "second wave" product is the Employee Self Service (ESS), a solution that enables Australian employees' access to the corporate human resource information system. This chapter summarizes the research findings of Human Resources (HR) in modern organizations and the development of an HR ESS portal in a major Australian organization.

Joe McDonagh of the University of Dublin in Ireland authored Chapter 6, entitled "Enterprise Systems and the Challenge of Integrated Change: A Focus on Occupational Communities". Many organizations rushed to implement ERP systems, without having a clear understanding of the difficulties in achieving the benefits promised by such integration. This chapter critiques the nature of this dilemma and in particular, explores the role of occupational communities in its perpetuation through time. Specifically, one of the difficulties encountered is that the requisite knowledge and expertise are widely dispersed among diverse occupational communities.

The last section of this book addresses the issues and challenges of the actual implementation and management of ERP/SAP systems. The benefits of implementing successful ERP systems can never be overestimated. Many of these benefits are outlined in Chapter 7, entitled "A Successful ERP Implementation Plan: Issues and Challenges," which is authored by the book's editor. This chapter also describes several critical issues that managers must consider before making the final decision to integrate all the business functions in the organization. These issues are categorized under fundamental issues, people, the organizational change process, and the different approaches to implementing ERP. The chapter concludes with a flow chart, depicting many of the activities that must be included in an ERP implementation plan. There is a general consensus among IT researchers that, among numerous factors, user involvement and total support from corporate management are essential for the successful implementation of ERP systems.

Chapter 8, entitled "Benefit Realisation with SAP: A Case Study," is written by Graham Blick and Mohammed Quaddus of Curtin University of Technology, Australia. An ERP integration can be both time consuming and costly, but a successful implementation will result in tremendous cost savings and increased productivity. One such example is the successful implementation of SAP systems at the Water Corporation of Western Australia. This article identifies the "benefit realization strategy and realization process" as the key success factor for this implementation. Therefore, this chapter will describe the benefit realization structure and process, how SAP was successfully implemented, the benefits realization, and its impact. Finally, the chapter concludes with future directions for the company.

Colin G. Ash and Janice M. Burn of Cowan University, Australia, wrote Chapter 9, entitled "The e-ERP Transformation Matrix". In this chapter, the authors developed a model of e-business transformation (eBT) for ERP implementation based on a longitudinal multiple case study analysis of SAP sites. First, the authors identified the three research models (B2B interaction, e-business change, and virtual organizing) and the three different stages of e-business growth (integration, differentiation, and demonstration of value propositions). After a pilot case study of five Australian SAP sites was conducted, 11 international organizations in various industries were studied over a four-year period. The collected data were then analyzed to develop the proposed eBT model. By integrating the three e-business growth models and the three stages of e-business development, the proposed eBT matrix model focuses on achieving the benefits of B2B interaction from virtual organizing through e-ERP and the facilitators of e-business change. In conclusion, the proposed model suggests that successful e-business transformation with ERP systems occurs when business-to-business (B2B) value propositions are realized through the integration and differentiation of technologies used to support new business models to deliver products and services online. Further, the proposed model also indicated that employee self-service and empowerment are important components in building extensive relationship with e-alliances. Finally, corporate management are encouraged to use the proposed matrix model to guide them in strategizing the organizational transformation.

Chapter 10, entitled "ERP II & Change Management: The Real Struggle for ERP Systems Practices," is written by Paul Hawking and Andrew Stein of Victoria University of Technology in Australia, Susan Foster of Monash University in Australia, and David Wyld of Southeastern Louisiana University in

Louisiana, USA. One of the major issues encountered in system implementation is user involvement and change management. This chapter explores the change management practices of Australian companies, and identifies the critical success factors and barriers associated with implementing change management strategies. Thirty-five major Australian organizations with single or multiple ERP system implementations were surveyed.

The research findings indicated that many participants considered change management to be crucial to successful ERP implementations; unfortunately, the change management process was not properly managed in their organizations. The main success factor to change management was the provision of adequate resources, while the main obstacle is the lack of vertical communication throughout the organization.

Chapter 11, entitled "SAP R/3 Implementation Approaches: A Study in Brazilian Companies," is authored by Ronaldo Zwicker and Cesar Alexandre de Souza of the University of São Paulo (FEA) in Brazil. The authors describe the two different ways of "going-live" with ERP systems (big-bang vs small-bangs) and the advantages and disadvantages of implementation in phases. Based on a survey conducted on 53 Brazilian organizations that had implemented SAP R/3, the authors concluded that system configurations, resource allocation, project management, and the project's risks are all affected by the implementation approach used.

Cesar Alexandre de Souza and Ronaldo Zwicker continued their research on the management of ERP systems, and documented their findings in Chapter 12, entitled "ERP Systems Management: A Comparison of Large Sized Brazilian Companies". Currently, most, if not all, large and medium sized corporations have implemented some form of ERP systems. In this chapter, the authors investigate aspects involved in ERP systems management, such as the current dynamics of the organizational information technology (IT) use and the growing concern with IT area costs, and examine how these aspects can transform the role of IT areas within the organizations. The authors also hope to expand the knowledge about key issues related to the management of such aspects. The authors first proposed a model of successful implementation based on the current literature review of IT implementation. They then analyzed two large Brazilian companies using the case analysis approach and compared their research findings to the proposed model. The authors conclude the chapter with several important observations.

Chapter 13, entitled "A Critical Success Factor's Relevance Model for SAP Implementation Projects," is written by José Esteves, Universidad Politécnica Catalunya, Spain, and Joan Pastor of the Universidad Internacional de

Catalunya, Barcelona, in Spain. The primary objective of this chapter is to present a unified model of Critical Success Factors (CSFs) for ERP implementation projects, and to analyze the relevance of these CSFs along the typical phases of a SAP implementation project. The authors achieved this objective by using both the Accelerated SAP (ASAP) implementation methodology and the Process Quality Management method to derive a matrix of CSFs versus ASAP processes, and then evaluate the CSFs relevance along the five ASAP phases. The authors are hoping that these findings will help managers to develop better strategies for supervising and controlling SAP or other similar ERP implementation projects.

In Chapter 14, "A Comparative Analysis of Major ERP Life Cycle Implementation, Management and Support Issues in Queensland Government," She-I Chang and Guy G. Gable of Queensland University of Technology, Australia, conducted a study on the major issues involved in an ongoing ERP life cycle implementation, management, and support. The researchers administered a survey to a group of ERP system project participants in five state government agencies who are experienced with the SAP Financials applications.

Finally, the book concludes with Chapter 15, "Organizational Knowledge Sharing in ERP Implementation: Lessons from Industry." In general, end users of ERP systems need to have a broader range of knowledge, which includes not only the basic business knowledge that are required to complete their tasks and responsibilities, but also the knowledge of how their work integrate with other business functions and divisions in the organization. Therefore, it is essential that ERP users are able to share their knowledge with their peers. In this chapter, Mary C. Jones from the University of North Texas, USA, and R. Leon Price from the University of Oklahoma, USA, attempt to examine how end users can share organizational knowledge in ERP implementation. They examine knowledge sharing factors such as facilitation of knowledge sharing on the team; change management/training; and transition of IPS (integration partner staff) knowledge. The authors collected data from three firms in the petroleum industry using interviews, analyzed the qualitative data, and present their research findings in this chapter.

Acknowledgments

The editor would like to express her sincere thanks to everyone involved in the development and production of this book. First, I would like to thank all the authors who have written chapters for this book. Their significant intellectual contributions and professional support have made it possible for me to put together this book. My deepest appreciation goes to several reviewers, who took the time to review chapter proposals and chapter manuscripts in a timely manner. They provided constructive and comprehensive reviews, with critical comments, valuable suggestions, feedback, and insights to the authors.

Finally, I would like to acknowledge the help and hard work of the staff at Idea Group Publishing. They were actively involved in this endeavor from day one: from the inception of the book proposal, to the collation and review, and finally, to the publication of this book. Special thanks and my enormous appreciation to senior managing editor Jan Travers, managing editor Amanda Appicello, and development editor Michele Rossi, for their ongoing and tedious work of putting the book together. Thanks to Jennifer Sundstrom, who worked on the promotion and marketing of the book. And, lastly, thanks to Mehdi Khosrow-Pour, for his encouragement to take on this daunting project.

Linda K. Lau
Longwood University, USA

Section I

Introduction to ERP and SAP Technology

Chapter I

Principles, Foundations & Issues in Enterprise Systems

John Loonam
University of Dublin, Ireland

Joe McDonagh
University of Dublin, Ireland

Abstract

The objective of this chapter is to provide a detailed review of the core principles, foundations and issues of enterprise systems (ES). Since the late 1990s, enterprise systems have promised to seamlessly integrate information flowing through the organisation. They claim to lay redundant many of the integration problems associated with legacy systems. These promises are timely considering the current trends of globalisation, virtual organisations, and constant business and technological changes, features of many strategy agendas. In an effort to better understand the nature of these packages this chapter reviews the ES evolutionary process, and generic software characteristics are also identified, followed by system benefits and limitations. A review of current approaches to ES implementation allows for a critique of system outcomes and identification of challenges facing today's ES implementations. The chapter concludes with suggestions for overcoming some of these challenges.

Introduction

Organisations have introduced enterprise systems in order to reduce problems associated with legacy systems, cope with year 2000 challenges, offer the firm greater competitive advantages, compete globally, and to assist the company achieve a single "integrated" technological platform. With organisations stressing the need for greater supply chain integration, these systems offer the first glimmer of hope to achieve such integration. Continued technological advances "extend" current ES packages along the supply chain, with future systems focusing on the penultimate goal, that is, inter-enterprise integration.

However, all is not as it appears. Reviewing the ES literature reveals problems with the implementation of such systems. Apart from the technological challenges associated with their introduction, a deeper cord has been struck; that is, the challenge of attaining greater organisational integration. Studies have revealed up to 60% dissatisfaction from ES implementations, with the primary reason for such poor performance emerging from the failure to properly consider organisational and human issues. Undoubtedly, for better returns on ES investments, organisations need to pay as much attention to organisational and human issues as to technical issues.

This chapter starts with an historical overview of the information technology field. The evolution to ES packages is then presented, reviewing their emergence, nature and future trends. Benefits and limitations of such systems are then considered before a review of current approaches to ES implementation. ES outcomes are reviewed, followed by a critique of some challenges facing the field. The chapter concludes with suggestions for overcoming some of these challenges.

Foundations of Enterprise Systems

In addressing the historical context of enterprise systems, it is firstly important to review the nature of information technology (IT). According to Ward and Griffiths (1996), IT has experienced three eras[1] since its deployment in organisations. The use of computers in business only started in the mid-1950s and early 1960s with the development of mainframe computing. Early computer systems were based on centralised stand-alone machines, which were used principally for data processing. The 1970s witnessed the arrival of the micro-computer, offering increasing decentralised computing capabilities along with standardised software packages. Throughout the 70s organisations also became aware of the strategic potential afforded by information technology (Ein-Dor & Segev, 1978) and its ability to leverage greater organisational competitive advantages (McFarlan, 1984). The 1980s saw the emergence of end-user computing, which would assist in disseminating information throughout the entire enterprise. Throughout the 1990s, the concept of business process reengineering[2] and enterprise systems emerged with the belief that together they would address many of the integration challenges confronting organisations.

This brief overview of the history of information technology illustrates the evolutionary nature of the IT field, that is, its move from centralised computing to end-user computing. This transition grew out of the need for greater organisational-wide IT integration. Initially centralised IT systems from the 1960s and 1970s were deployed by organisations to assist in single application functionality, such as manufacturing or accounting systems. However, from the 1980s onwards, added pressures from IT systems to deliver greater strategic and competitive advantages meant that typical business applications had grown exponentially[3] (Slee & Slovin, 1997). What started out as "islands of automation" (McKenney & McFarlan, 1982), that is, applications running separately from each other, by the 1980s were often put into a single system in order to manage and centralise data better. This event is often referred to as technical integration, or alternatively as "spaghetti integration" (Slee & Slovin, 1997).

This type of "spaghetti integration" created its own problems. Connecting different functional areas was not easy, and required huge amounts of programmed computer code in order to allow the different functional databases to "talk to one another". In turn, this amount of programming often resulted in system errors, inconsistent information flows, and perhaps most worrying from an organisational perspective, the need for huge resource commitments[4]. By the late 1980s and early 1990s organisations were therefore experiencing large IT integration problems. Something new, less costly and less labour-intensive was needed.

In response, software vendors began to launch single application tools that could host a number of different functional areas from a shared database. These new software packages became known as Enterprise Resource Planning systems (ERP) (Lopes[5], 1992). The objective of these packages was to bring all IT needs of the company under the umbrella of a single software system. In other words these packages promised "seamless integration"[6] for adopting companies (Davenport, 2000a). In addressing the principles and foundations of these large integrative packages, it is firstly important to examine their evolutionary trial.

Evolution of Enterprise Systems

While ES packages are only a recent phenomenon, that is, only featuring seriously in business and academic press from the late 1990s, they do have a past. It has been suggested that ES packages are an extension of Material Requirements Planning (MRP) and Manufacturing Resource Planning (MRPII) packages, with enhanced and greater functionality (Yusuf & Little, 1998). In addressing these systems, we find that MRP packages date back to the 1960s. In simplest terms, MRP systems involved the calculation of quantities of materials and the times they were required in order to improve operations within manufacturing organisations. MRPII systems were to extend upon this concept during the 1970s, and encompassed new functionality like sales planning, capacity management and scheduling (Klaus et al., 2000). However, during the 1980s companies began to realise that profitability and customer satisfaction were objectives for the entire enterprise, extending beyond manufacturing, and encompassing functions such as finance, sales and distribution, and human resources. This gave rise to the concept of computer integrated manufacturing (CIM), which is regarded as the next evolutionary step on the road towards ES (Klaus et al., 2000, p. 144). By the early 1990s, with continued growth in package functionality and the need for greater organisational integration, ES packages began to emerge.

To understand enterprise systems clearly, it is important to define them. Davenport suggests that they are software packages that promise to deliver seamless integration across enterprises embracing both suppliers and customers (Davenport, 2000a). Yet the actual definition of an ES rests somewhat uncomfortably within academic literature. Many studies, for example, use the term Enterprise Resource Planning (ERP) to define what we call Enterprise Systems. However, the justification for using the ES definition is supported by other researchers in the field. Klaus et al., for example, after conducting research on some of the leading academics and experts in the ES field, found that many of their respondents believed that the ERP concept was too archaic and conjured up connotations of ES' links with its manufacturing past, that is, MRP and MRP II systems (2000, p. 141). Davenport advocates that these packages should be referred to as "business systems" and not manufacturing or technical systems; hence he coins the term "enterprise system" (ES) (Davenport, 1998, 2000a). This term is also supported by Markus (2000c) and Robey et al. (2001), who believe that the area has moved away from the original manufacturing concepts of the 1970s, 1980s and early 1990s, and now embraces enterprise-wide integration ideologies.

However, the definition dilemma does not stop here. Instead, with the arrival of new technologies[7], and the need for greater business process alignment, new definitions are continually presented, namely Internet-oriented ES packages (Callaway, 2000), Extended ES packages (Norris et al., 2000), and Enterprise-Wide Information Management Systems (Sumner, 1999, 2000). It, therefore, appears that a plethora of definitions abound within the field. These definitions are likely to continue as greater enterprise integration, and indeed inter-enterprise[8] integration is sought by organisations.

Yet, in order for us to study the field it is imperative that we define the topic. This chapter agrees with statements that negate ERP's links to its manufacturing past. In fact, some argue that ES packages never had anything in common with earlier systems (MRP and MRPII) other than their common promise to integrate business processes under a single software system. Despite the ephemeral nature of definitions, the term *Enterprise System* is probably the most appropriate definition available to date. It rids the field of any connotations it may have had with its manufacturing past, while at the same time it conjures an image of a system that fully integrates the enterprises IS needs. ES is, therefore, used throughout this chapter.

As a cautionary note, however, while definitions are important, they appear to be transitory and therefore should not preoccupy the field. Instead, it is much more important, regardless of the terminologies used, to define what is meant by these definitions. Davenport purports, for example, that whether customer-centric[9] or supplier-centric[10], by themselves or in combination with other technologies, Enterprise Systems are distinguished by their information commonality and integration (2000a, p. 3). In other words, an ES should not necessarily be defined by the number or use of other technologies and tools along with the central vendor package; instead the package should be defined by its ability to seamlessly integrate business processes and information flows up and down, and perhaps more importantly from now on, across value chains.

From the late 1990s onwards enterprise systems experienced massive growth in organisational uptake. By 1998, for example, approximately 40% of companies with annual revenues greater than $1 billion had already implemented an ES (Caldwell & Stein, 1998). In a survey by AMR Research, results showed that from 800 U.S companies queried, 43% of the companies' application budgets were spent on ES packages, while over half of these companies had installed an ES (1999a). Market predictions were made, which estimated that the ES industry would be worth over $66 billion by 2003 (AMR Research, 1999a). Unlike their prehistoric ancestors, enterprise systems were fast becoming a core part of everyday IT investments. These systems were breaking traditional manufacturing links, and soon represented a new "IS integration" alternative for all organisations[11].

Reasons for such organisational interest and ES growth have ranged from helping to replace legacy systems, coping with Y2K[12] issues, affording the firm greater competitive advantages and the ability to allow firms compete globally. According to Stefanou, global-wide phenomena such as outsourcing, joint ventures and alliances, and partnerships across value chains have created a new form of organisation known as the "virtual enterprise". Monolithic and stand-alone business information systems are giving way to more flexible, integrated and modular systems that support business operations across the value-chain from the supplier to the customer end (1999, p. 800). The Year 2000 problem also acted as a reason for ES implementation, allowing organisations to use the Y2K challenge to endorse enterprise integration and ES implementations (Hirt & Swanson, 1999). According to Sasovova et al. (2001), rapid technological changes, pressure from shareholders, fierce competition, deregulation, and globalisation have all contributed to the emergence of ES packages. Davenport believes that overcapacity and reengineering and dealing with constant change are prime reasons many organisations are implementing enterprise systems (2000a, pp. 20-22).

With the promise of seamless integration (Davenport, 1998), organisations were able to justify ES investments, believing that these systems were the answer to their IT integration problems. In response, software companies provided a myriad of application tools[13] that promised enterprise integration of all kinds and for every company. Comprehending the nature of these vendor packages and their promises requires consideration of the generic characteristics that make ES packages distinct from other IT investments.

Characteristics of Enterprise Systems

From a study conducted by Markus and Tanis (2000c), the authors found that there were five characteristics specific to enterprise systems, which help us to understand what they are, what they can do, and how they differ from other large IT packages. These distinct characteristics include integration, the nature of the ES package, best practices, assembly requirements, and the evolutionary nature of these systems. A brief review of each of these characteristics is now offered.

From an *integration* perspective, one of the core functions of an ES, in comparison to all previous integration technologies, is its promise to "seamlessly integrate" all information flowing throughout the organisation (Davenport, 1998). This characteristic is further adhered to by the ES literature. Enterprise systems are commercial software *packages* bought from market vendors. They differ from previous integration tools in the sense that they are not developed in-house by organisations, but instead can be customised to the enterprise's own specific needs. Another characteristic unique to ES is the suite of *best practices* afforded to implementing organisations. Enterprise systems are built to support generic business processes that may differ substantially from the way the implementing organisation does business. They are built to "fit" the generic needs of many organisations. *Some assembly requirements* may be necessary during implementation. From a technical perspective the term "seamless integration" seems slightly flawed when considering enterprise systems. Markus and Tanis believe that the software is "integrated," but the organisation's intentions for the package may not be (2000c). For example, some firms use bolt-on tools, or an amalgamation of ES vendors in order to achieve their version of seamless integration. Finally, like all IT systems, enterprise systems are constantly *evolving* and changing. During the 1980s, the MRP systems were developed to run on mainframe architectures, while current ES packages are running on client/server architectures (Nezlek et al., 1999). Future ES will need to focus on inter-enterprise integration features.

While these characteristics are generic, they do provide us with an understanding of the nature of enterprise systems. These characteristics also allow us to identify ES packages available in the market. Before moving on to review the benefits and limitations associated with implementations, this chapter will consider some of the possible future directions for these systems.

Future of Enterprise Systems

According to AMR Research, in 1998 the ES market was worth $16 billion, while by the end of 2003 the industry will exceed over $60 billion (1999a). The real driver behind such growth, however, comes from the ES "extensions" sector (Callaway, 2000), that is, applications that increase the functionality of the package and diversity of the business. AMR Research has estimated that yearly sales of ES extension tools will grow by 70% by the end of 2003, or to nearly $14 billion of the ES industry (1999a). As these technologies will form, and indeed many are currently forming, such an important part of future ES packages, this chapter provides a review of the type of extensions required.

The primary reason for ES extensions relates to the archaic nature of traditional ES packages. With constant change a norm in business, ES packages continue to grow in diversity and functionality to suit emerging organisational needs. These extensions need to occur organically[14], ensuring that the integration integrity of the ES package is maintained. Four main extension types have been identified; including (1) customer relationship management (CRM), (2) supply chain management (SCM), (3) e-business, and (4) business intelligence (BI) tools (Callaway, 2000).

According to Greenberg, *customer relationship management* (CRM) is "a comprehensive set of processes and technologies for managing the relationships with potential and current customers and business partners across marketing, sales, and service regardless of the communication channel. The goal of CRM is to optimise customer and partner satisfaction by building the strongest possible relationships at an organisational level" (2001, p. 16). Many ES package vendors are beginning to realise that satisfying the customer should be a core element or function of the entire package. Davenport reports that leading ES vendors are adding functions such as sales force automation[15] and customer service software[16] (2000b, p. 173) to their packages. According to AMR Research, the CRM market, which reached $1.4 billion in 1997, will reach $16.8 billion by 2003, clearly illustrating the importance for ES vendors to continue integrating CRM capabilities into their software packages (1999b).

The objective of supply chain management (SCM) is to "cut costs by taking excess time, redundant effort, and buffer inventory out of the system, and to improve service by giving customers more options, faster delivery, and better visibility into order status" (Davenport, 2000a, p. 238). ES packages with added SCM tools can extend the internal system out to the supply end of the organisation. According to Norris et al. (2000), ES packages with SCM functionality afford greater extensions to the enterprise (2000, pp. 85-88). These components include: (1) supply chain replenishment, which integrates production and distribution processes using real time to improve customer responsiveness, (2) e-procurement, which is the use of Web-enabled technologies to support key procurement processes such as requisitioning, sourcing, contracting, ordering, and payment, (3) collaborative planning—this is a B2B[17] workflow across multiple enterprises to synchronise production plans, product flows, and optimise resources, (4) collaborative product development, which involves the use of e-business to improve product launch success and time to market, (5) e-logistics, where Web-based technologies are used to support warehouse and transportation management processes, and finally (6) supply Webs—these are a futuristic function of current supply chain components, but their objective is to integrate supply chains of various buyers and sellers to create a virtual trading community throughout the supply chain. Many ES packages and SCM vendors[18] today already have incorporated, or are incorporating, many of these SCM functions and business processes.

The most prevalent tool to allow ES package extensions has been the Internet, in particular the practice of *e-business.* Not only have Web-enabled technologies allowed ES packages to integrate with supply chain management and customer relationship management technologies up and down the supply chain, but also these packages have enabled inter-enterprise collaboration for greater value chain integration. Web-enabled ES packages allow organisations to have an e-business[19] presence. Two other technologies, which offer greater functionality and diversity to ES packages, have also emerged as a result of Web-enablement. These include (1) componentisation and (2) bolt-on tools. In an effort to offer greater flexibility with ES packages, many organisations are using *componentisation* tools, that is, the redevelopment of the package using object development tools, component interface protocols such as CORBA, integration standards such as extensible mark-up language (XML), and semantic agreements such as those provided by CommerceOne (Sprott, 2000). The key to componentisation is that enterprises are able to customise the package to suit their needs, rather than having to accept the standard package and its proposed set of best practices. Therefore, the organisation might not have to buy the entire package, but bits of it, and match these to other vendor packages, and the companies own legacy systems to achieve their own version of organisational integration. Another approach to assist ES integration is through *bolt-on tools*. These are tools, such as middleware or third party vendor tools, which allow organisations to massage their ES packages with other technologies in order to achieve greater integration. Bolt-on tools can be referred to as *best of breed technologies* (Davenport, 2000a, p. 87), which can partner with other leading edge software vendors to offer a suite of applications.

One of the cited problems with ES packages is their inability to provide managers with sets of data that can assist decision-making and analytical diagnosis. For the cost and length of time it takes to successfully implement such systems, the lack of decision support tools available means that traditional ES packages are nothing more than large central databases. According to Davenport, due to the "insufficient capabilities within ES packages, most firms today try to extract data from their ES packages, and then massage it with third-party query and reporting tools, third-party data warehouse management tools, or third party statistical analysis tools" (2000b, p. 174). In an effort to remedy this problem, efforts are being made to include these functionalities in future ES packages. Callaway talks about how some ES packages are using *business intelligence* tools, such as the former online analytical processing (OLAP) or decision support systems (DSS) tools to turn data into knowledge and allow executives make better decisions (Callaway, 2000, pp. 113-115). According to AMR Research, the business intelligence (BI) industry will be worth millions by the end of 2003, and will assist in generating massive revenue for ES vendors through new software licenses (cited in Stackpole, 1999). Davenport (2000a, 2000b) expects the knowledge management field to become part of ES packages. Knowledge repositories, in the form of data warehousing and data mining, will become part of the ES package to assist with better strategy making and competitive advantages.

Future ES packages need to pay constant attention to technological advances and organisational needs. Such attention will increase package functionality and continued ES growth. Vendors have also identified expansion into new market sectors as an imperative for assuring continued ES growth and prosperity.

The Small to Medium Sized Enterprises (SMEs) are being targeted as such a market sector. Up until a few years ago, organisations that implemented ES packages were predominantly large conglomerate type companies[20], often with a manufacturing base, for example, pharmaceuticals, oil companies, and other industrial manufacturing companies. However, with the emergence of Internet technologies, implementation upgrade difficulties and cost of ownership have been dramatically reduced. According to Markus et al., Web-enablement means that individual users almost anywhere in the world can now access ES data and processes without requiring a local ES client or the technical support this entails (2000b, p. 185). Portals have also helped to reduce the total cost of package ownership, by allowing users to set up "hubs" where they can communicate online, for example, mySAP.com (Hayman, 2000, p. 138). Another fundamental solution for implementation upgrade difficulties and high cost of ownership is application hosting. Enabled by the Internet, in which the ES vendor (or another service provider) runs the software for an adopter, pricing this service is on a per transaction basis (Markus et al., 2000b, p. 185).

SMEs, with small budgets, are therefore in an ideal position to now embrace ES implementations. With this knowledge in mind, ES vendors have been quick to target this market sector, particularly European midsize companies where research has shown that the market here for IT products and services surpasses US$50 billion per year (Van Everdingen et al., 2000). With the larger company sector[21] almost saturated, small to midsize companies provide a huge opportunity for current ES vendors and future market growth (Callaway, 2000).

The future of ES packages will therefore involve constant technological configuration in order to meet changing organisational demands. Greater emphasis will be placed on total supply chain integration, with various new technologies offering such extensions, and inter-enterprise integration promising to be the penultimate prize. ES packages will also be expected to act as knowledge warehouses and support decision-making and corporate intelligence. ES packages will no longer be exclusive to large corporations; instead the SME market promises to be the most lucrative from a vendor perspective over the forthcoming years.

Enterprise System Benefits

In addressing the principles and foundations of ES packages it is necessary to review the benefits and limitations these packages bestow upon implementing organisations. A review of ES literature reveals some of these issues. ES benefits will be dealt with first, followed by ES package limitations.

ES benefits can be divided into five categories: (1) operational, (2) managerial, (3) strategic, (4) IT infrastructure, and (5) organisational benefits (Shang & Seddon, 2000)[22]. One of the main benefits for introducing an ES package is to achieve greater *operational benefits*. Such benefits can assist in reducing general labour and inventory costs. With a single central database there is also less duplication of tasks. From a *managerial perspective* an ES package is an integrative system that gathers all information flowing through the organisation (Davenport, 2000a). Top management are therefore able to make plans and better decisions with the aid of this enterprise-wide information. New advances in technology, and ES packages[23], will make decision making a core part of the ES package.

Such benefits in management will invariably allow for greater *strategic benefits*. ES packages can assist in building strategic partnerships, supporting alliances, creating new business opportunities and markets and developing a competitive advantage for the firm. The tight links along the supply chain allow ES users to have a greater understanding of customers' needs. This in turn allows companies to develop customised products for clients at lower prices. ES packages can assist in developing a greater competitive advantage for the implementing organisation.

ES packages afford organisations with an opportunity to implement an integrated IT plan, that is, greater *IT infrastructure benefits*. The introduction of an ES package assists in integrating a firm's business processes and removing disjointed legacy systems, unstable IT architectures, and IT expenditure related to maintenance of these systems. ES packages assist in preventing redundant data entry, duplication of data, and provide a single database for organisational-wide data. ES packages also support organisational change and business process reengineering, therefore providing the firm with new *organisational benefits*. An ES package facilitates organisational cultural change by allowing the ES package to give the enterprise a specific vision.

Enterprise System Limitations

Like all IT systems, there are as many limitations as there are benefits for enterprise systems. These issues will now be discussed. Excessive *focus on technical* aspects to the detriment of business aspects has been identified as a leading factor for many ES failures (Kreammergaard & Moller, 2000, Sedera et al., 2001). Sarker believes that a significant amount of ES projects fail because human aspects are often "overlooked" or "remain to be resolved"; hence the focus is on technology and not the organisation (2000, p. 414). Esteves and Pastor also believe that failure occurs because "too often, project managers focus on the technical and financial aspects of a project and neglect to take into account the non technical issues" (2001, p. 1019). *Financial costs* of ES packages can be enormous. According to Scheer and Habermann, "Baan, Peoplesoft as well as SAP calculate that customers spend between three and seven times more money on ES implementation and associated services compared to the purchase of the software license" (2000, p. 57). The authors believe that the ratio ranges between 5:1 for ES implementation efforts and the cost of software licenses. The reasons they give for such costs are due to the scale of business process reengineering (BPR) and change management issues involved in the implementation of the software. Stewart reinforces this point suggesting that ES implementations fail because of poor organisational attention in dealing with the issues of risk orientation and user involvement. They maintain that ES implementations are fundamentally agents for organisational change and such change requires effective leadership practices (2000, p. 966).

Sor believes that using an ES package can rob an organisation of its *competitive advantage* (1999, p. 229). This point is further supported by Porter, who states that if everyone in a particular industry sector or niche market is to adopt ES packages, then everyone will have the same set of best practices as determined by the software vendor and ES package (2001). ES packages can be structured, systematic packages that make the organisation "fit" the software rather than the software fit to the needs of the enterprise, that is, *inhibiting organisational flexibility.* This level of inflexibility can prohibit organisational change and business process growth (Sor, 1999, pp. 229-230).

Dong believes that the challenge to ES implementation lies in the nature of the system; that is, they are generic solutions reflecting a vendor's rather than a customer's assumptions of what organisational best practices are. It pushes companies toward full *integration,* and changes various business processes into generic ones even if the company wants to customise some of these business processes. Therefore, the real paradox facing organisations implementing ES projects is rooted in their ability to seamlessly integrate all business processes across the enterprise. The fewer changes made to an ES, the greater the level of integration and realised benefits for the implementing organisation (2001, p. 243). However, accepting the generic nature of an ES package means companies are accepting vendor integration, not company-specific integration; this in turn may not achieve the desired integration sought by adopting companies. Soh et al. talk about the problem of *"cultural misfits"* with ES packages, that is, the gaps between the functionality offered by the package and that required by the adopting organisation (2000, p. 47). Due to the fact that ES implementations are more complex and larger than other packaged software implementations, the "misfit" problem is exacerbated when implemented in a non-generic type organisation (2000). In other words, ES packages are designed by western vendors for western type organisations. Countries such as Japan often find the implementation of ES packages particularly difficult, as there is a problem with cultural identity. In short, Soh et al. point to "cultural misfits" with ES software, particularly when it is implemented outside of North America and Europe (2000).

Smyth believes that ES implementation disappointments can be largely attributed to the *size and complexity* of the packages and the associated problems in customisation and organisational change (2001, p. 1228). Another problem for ES packages is the cost of workarounds and upgrades in specific modules, particularly when an organisation is customising the package to suit organisational business needs. With add-ons or bolt-on technologies the cost and maintenance of the project increases dramatically (2001, p. 1228). Sasovova et al. believe that limitations to ES packages arise when *external assimilations,* such as mergers, acquisitions, and divestitures take place. Such occurrences cause huge external and internal changes, and make the process of both system and business process integration all the more difficult, particularly if new business processes and old legacy systems have to be integrated from the new companies into the central ES package (2001, p. 1143). Markus and Tanis (2000c) talk about the over-reliance or dependence on *ES software vendors.* Reliance on a single-vendor can weaken the organisation's ability to be technologically independent, forcing the enterprise to go into an appeasement mode with the software vendor.

Approaches to Implementation

With ES benefits and limitations in mind, the chapter now examines the approaches to implementation. According to current ES literature, there are two popular approaches, often used simultaneously, for assisting with the delivery of ES projects. These include the use of an implementation process model with supporting critical success factors (CSFs) for prioritising model phases.

Much of the current academic literature has contributed to assembling lists of perceived CSFs necessary for ES project implementation (Al-Mashari, 2000a, 2000b; Bingi et al., 1999; Brown & Vessey, 1999; Nah, 2001; Rosemann et al., 2000; Somers & Nelson, 2001). Parr and Shanks see CSFs as "those few critical areas where things must go right for the business to flourish" (2000b, p. 292). In order to further assist implementers understand the role of CSFs within the implementation process, several academic studies have developed implementation process models. Parr and Shanks believe that these process models help to "extend previous research that has simply enumerated CSFs for the entire implementation process" (2000b, p. 290).

Examples of process models include Ross' five-phase model based on case study research of ES implementation (2000). These phases included the stages of design, implementation, stabilisation, continuous improvement, and transformation. Somers and Nelson (2001) divide their CSFs into six phases, which include project initiation, adoption, adaptation, acceptance, routinisation, and infusion. Esteves and Pastor (2000) divided CSFs into an organisational and technological grid, both being once again sub-divided into strategic and tactical domains. Similarly, Kraemmergaard separates his analysis of ES CSFs into organisational, business, and technological areas.

Placing CSFs into process models allows practitioners and researchers to maximise the potential impact CSFs have throughout the implementation process. The basic tenets from all these different models include a planning phase, an implementation phase, and an evaluation phase, supported by CSFs. Process models allow organisations to move through the implementation process in a systematic manner. Prioritising CSFs allows firms to identify the most important elements necessary for project success and at the stages they should be conducted during the process model.

Understanding Outcomes

Understanding approaches to ES implementations leads to questioning the success rate of such projects. On the whole, studies have revealed a less than satisfactory performance rate from ES implementations. According to a survey conducted in December 2000[24], for example, only 34% of the organisations were "very satisfied" with their ES investments (McNurlin, 2001). Sammon et al. believe that over 90% of ES implementations are late or more costly than first anticipated (2001b, p. 1131). Research conducted by the Standish Group International shows that 40% of all ES installations achieved only partial implementation; nearly 28% were scrapped as total failures or never implemented, while only 25% were completed on time and within budget (cited in Crowe et al., 2002, p. 3). Further surveys also support these findings, even among ES "extensions"; for example, where in a study among 145 European companies carried out by Cap Gemini Ernst & Young, they found that 68% of companies surveyed could not provide any evidence of expected payoffs from their CRM investments (Financial Times, 2001). Similarly, in SCM the number of poor performances has been up to 60%, where supply chains are also slow to return any investments for implementing organisations (Larsen, 1999).

Addressing Challenges

With outcomes such as these there are clearly obvious challenges facing organisations implementing ES packages. The question, ominously enough, to ask is "why" do such poor performances exist? This chapter suggests that the answer to this question lies in two parts. The first part is as a result of the *approaches* taken when implementing ES packages, while the second part deals with the *nature* of the ES package.

ES literature, and indeed practice, assumes a systematic *approach* to implementation. This means that a process-oriented approach to implementation is adopted, with prioritisation of CSFs throughout the project. However, according to Robey et al., studies of critical success factors offer few surprises (2001). The authors believe that findings that point to the necessity of CSFs, such as top management commitment, are not substantially different from factors that are critical to the success of most IT projects and to organisational change of other kinds. This belief is also held for the development of implementation process models, which according to Robey et al. act as more of a description than an explanation of ES outcomes (2001). They believe that by adopting such a stage approach to ES project implementation, research is not carefully examining the events that occur during ES implementation. The process models to date tend to "assume that organisational changes follow ES implementation" (Robey et al., 2001, p. 10).

When we review reasons for poor ES performance, we find that "the main implementation risks associated with ES projects are related to change management and the business reengineering that results from integrating an organisation" (Sammon et al., 2000a). In a study by Deloitte and Touche (1998), the main reasons cited for poor ES performance range from people obstacles (which according to the study contributed to 68% of the problem), business processes (which were at 16%), and information technology issues (which were at 12%) (cited in Crowe et al., 2002). Many process models tend to move through the implementation process using CSFs as benchmarks, without paying adequate attention to the organisational and human elements of the project. This chapter suggests that, while process models and CSFs are excellent for illustrating the implementation challenges involved in a typical ES project, greater attention needs to be given to organisational and human issues.

The second part of the suggested answer cuts to the very core of an ES's existence, that is, questioning their *nature* to promise "seamless integration". When ES packages first emerged in the late 1990s, this was the battle cry of many vendors and service providers alike, for example, consultants and trainers. Over half a decade later this question still remains to be answered; that is, do ES packages provide for seamless integration of all information flowing throughout the company? In order to answer this question we need to examine the characteristics of integration. ES packages are comprised of two types of integration: these are technological and organisational integration.

In many ways the most obvious integration need comes from the technological sphere, where due to outdated legacy systems and dysfunctional information flows, ES packages are implemented in an effort to rid companies of these problems. Perhaps the greatest area of concern for ES packages in terms of *technological integration* comes from questioning whether these systems are achieving their initial objective, ridding the organisation of its old legacy systems and creating seamless integration throughout the enterprise. There is evidence to suggest that this process may be experiencing some difficulty. According to Themistocleous (2000), for example, ES packages are often incorporated with old legacy systems in order to improve technological integration. This point is also supported by Markus et al., who found that many companies needed to retain some form of their old legacy system, preferring not to customise the ES package for fear of the old adage of "thou shalt not change SAP" (2000a, p. 260).

The challenge of technological integration is further reinforced by organisational reactions. While seamless integration receives much anecdotal attention, the reality is, unfortunately, quite different. Glick, for example, tells us that many organisations today believe "integration to be a myth" (Glick, 2001). According to research conducted by Vanson Bourne, "real world integration is very different to the vendors' marketing hype" (cited in Glick, 2001, p. 19). So much so that many CIOs and project managers are preferring to put their integration issues on the long finger as much as possible, believing "integration issues to be of perennial importance, but simply too difficult and time consuming to achieve"; hence it is not a very appealing subject for most (Adshead, 2001, p. 8).

However, technological integration can ever only be successful if there is organisational alignment between the technology and business processes of the enterprise. ES literature reviewed talks about the absolute need for *organisational integration* as part of the success of ES packages. As Davenport purports, "computer systems alone don't change organisational behaviour"; it is the "companies that stressed the enterprise, not the system, that gained the greatest benefits" (1998, pp. 129-130). Organisational integration relates to how the business processes are aligned, or realigned, with the ES package, and how the elements of change are integrated into the overall ES strategy.

As stated already, the problem with many approaches to ES implementation is their inability, or often failure, to address the organisational and human issues. For many organisations the implementation of an ES package means massive reengineering of its business processes and the management of organisational change. Unfortunately however, this fact is seldom reflected in implementation models. Take, for example the contribution of critical success factors. While CSFs studies cite business process reengineering and change management as imperative to successful ES implementation, results show that many companies do not feel as fervent about these issues. One study, for example, from a list of 22 critical success factors, found that companies ranked business process reengineering 16th, while change management came in 19th (Somers & Nelson, 2001). The fact that these organisational integration imperatives ranked so lowly reflects the degree of satisfaction companies often experience with these processes. One could almost say that companies that rate organisational issues so low have a slim chance of succeeding with an ES implementation.

Overcoming Challenges

Suggestions will now be made for assisting organisations overcome some of these challenges. This chapter suggests that the implementation of ES software should be split into three stages: (1) pre-implementation, (2) implementation, and (3) post-implementation. The first stage, which is probably the most crucial, should be considered before project launch. It lists some of the critical success factors that can assist with the "why" and "what" questions, that is, why do we need an ES package and what needs to happen before launch. The second stage lists factors for consideration in dealing with the weaknesses of process models (and invariably the challenge of organisational integration), while the third stage deals with issues for consideration after project completion. While this appears to be a rather simple method for viewing ES implementations, it differs from previous approaches in its treatment of CSFs, process models, and attention to pre and post-implementation issues. It is also suggested that these stages are not viewed in a systematic manner, but instead as a systemic aid for comprehending some of the major issues with ES implementations.

The suggestion during the *pre-implementation* phase is for organisations to start with answering the "why" question. If the firm identifies ES as a method for achieving organisational gain, this will lead to the "what" question. Typical questions to be asked at this stage concern the relevance of ES packages. Does my organisation really need an ES package? Weigh up the pros and cons to such an implementation, considering the aforementioned benefits and limitations and indeed challenges. Ask yourself why you are implementing such a package; what does your organisation hope to gain from it? An ES package is an excellent system for achieving an envisioned level of organisational and technical integration; however it is a complex and long-term commitment. Justify your reasons from a long-term commitment perspective.

The pre-implementation stage is an ideal phase to conduct a review of critical success factors. CSFs are valuable in offering advise on "what" to do. If an ES package has been given the green light, the suggestion here is for organisations to identify their own critical success factors. This allows firms to compare and contrast their CSFs to prescribed CSFs emanating from empirical inquiry. It also gives organisations a perspective on their own critical success factors ratings. For example, if the firm placed little emphasis on organisational change, that is, it receives a low ranking on their CSFs, then the firm immediately knows that greater attention is required in this area for ES project success.

This chapter will now review *some* of the typical critical success factors[25] mentioned in the ES literature. *Top management support* is often cited as the most important CSF. Their task is to provide commitment, vision, and leadership, allocate resources, and develop a strategy that is inclusive of the new project. Similarly, every project needs an individual that is personally committed to its success, that is, a project champion. The champion represents the project at every level in the organisation and continually seeks support for it.

Another often cited critical success factor is that of *change management*. ES packages introduce large-scale change that can cause resistance, confusion, redundancies, and errors. A project of this magnitude involves massive cultural, human, and organisational change. It is vital that these issues are dealt with in tandem with ES implementation, not after the project is completed. *Business process reengineering* (BPR) allows organisations to align their business processes with the ES package. The objective of BPR is to bring greater performance to the organisation through better quality, speed, cost, and service of product.

A final example of some of the leading CSFs is that of the role *vendors and consultants* play during project implementation. From the beginning the expectations of both of these groups needs to be clearly identified. A sound relationship with the vendor company is an imperative for success. Considering the amount of power the vendor has in the relationship, that is, due to the enterprise-wide nature of the ES package, it is not merely a selection of a software company; it is the selection of an organisational partner. This relationship needs to be built upon trust, open communication, and a strong emphasis on collaboration and mutual partnership. If the use of a consultant is decided upon, their selection is equally as important. However, care must be taken when hiring consultants; the organisation and top management must know why these consultants are required and where best to employ them throughout the implementation process; otherwise, "for every pound spent on ES software licences, companies could spend a further 5 to 7 pounds on related services, mainly consultancy" (Adam & O' Doherty, 2000). This point is further supported by Caldas and Wood, who found from their research that while 91% of the companies surveyed hired external consultants during the ES implementation process, only 47% of all respondents claimed that the consulting firm was influential during the implementation process, while only 23% cited that the consultants had the necessary skills and experience relevant for the project implementation (1999, p. 8).

The main objective of the *implementation* stage is to make suggestions for overcoming ES challenges, that is, the problems encountered with process models and organisational and technical integration. The first suggestion is for implementers to move beyond process models and critical success factors. While these instruments play a vital role in structuring the ES project (particularly CSFs role at the pre-implementation stage), they are however limited when dealing with actual implementation and the wider organisational issues. Such wider issues will now be dealt with.

One of the main challenges facing organisations implementing ES packages is their approach. Critical success factors assist in highlighting "what" the organisation *should* do; however, they tell us little about "how" we *actually* implement the system. The suggestion here is that for every critical success factor used, the question to ask is how this factor should be addressed during implementation. For example, top management support is cited, by many studies, as the most important critical success factor for ES implementation success. Yet, we appear to know little about what top management support really entails. How much support is required, when should top management support occur, that is, at what stages of the implementation process? Who should be involved in the top management team? How do we measure top management support? What do top management actually do during project implementation; that is, should they organise steering committees, psychologically or physically get involved in project implementation? Or how do we maintain top management support for the entire length of the project (particularly ES projects which can take a couple of years to fully implement). This approach should be adopted for all critical success factors; that is, the most important question to continually ask during ES project implementation is: How does this factor affect project implementation; that is, what is its role?

Similarly, for process models the same approach is required. Process models are excellent for outlining the stages involved in an ES project. However, once again they fail to tell us anything about how things *actually* occur. Several empirical studies talk about the processes or stages ES software goes through. However, the central, and most important element of any implementation process is missing, that is, the effects on the organisation. As academic and business press repeatedly iterate, ES packages are more about organisational issues than software issues. Process models, sometimes, tend to assume that the organisational and human issues will be subsumed during model progress. This is, unfortunately, very erroneous, and for many companies, a terribly expensive mistake to make. This chapter suggests that for the betterment of process models, because undoubtedly they provide a very clear and systematic structure for ES implementations, an organisational change model should be included during project implementation.

The challenge for process models is to concurrently address technological and organisational change issues. A model that depicts both the process and organisational change issues is therefore the ideal. This chapter calls for an "integrated model," which incorporates both technological and organisational issues, thus ensuring they are addressed simultaneously during project implementation. A typical process model deals with issues such as project design, implementation, stabilisation, continuous improvement, and transformation, or an example of another process model with terms such as project initiation, adoption, adaptation, acceptance, routinisation, and infusion. Most models, for some reason, tend to have five phases and use language that at the very least sounds technical, systematic, and structured. In other words, the softer systemic issues, such as organisational change and integration, appear to be ignored. Organisational change models would include features such as coalition building, vision sharing, strategy building, and communication of change issues, developing broad-based actions and generating short-term wins for the project within the enterprise. Without attention to these issues, a strong focus on technical integration will occur to the detriment of organisational integration. Using process models alone, therefore, limits the level of organisational integration, and invariably level of success for ES implementation.

Perhaps the most important thing to remember about an ES implementation is its cyclical nature. The implementation process, in effect, does not end; that is, the project should continue into a *post-implementation* stage. As organisations are faced with constant change, this change will also reflect upon the ES package. This is particularly true when we consider the changing nature of technology and organisational business processes. Today, firms with ES packages are faced with the challenge of "extending" their organisational and technical integrations further. These challenges are coming from inter-enterprise integration needs. In an effort to keep up with these changes, and more importantly to ensure the ES investment maintains its original promise, that is, offering the enterprise seamless integration of all information flowing through the organisation, firms need to pay constant attention to their ES packages.

This attention becomes part of the post-implementation phase. Companies should be on the lookout for new business developments (such as a new business process or a merger with a competitor). An analysis of how these changes may impact on the ES package should be conducted. Adding extensions to the ES package can be difficult and for some organisations this has ended up going full circle; that is, with constant bolt-on and add-ons the ES package can lose its single application uniqueness and become a web of dis-integration like former legacy systems. The solution to this problem is to lead with organisational changes first and deal with technical issues afterwards. Perhaps the best way to maintain ES integrity is to focus on business processes that are unlikely to receive radical changes over forthcoming years. For business processes that will receive a lot of change apply an a la carte[26] ES policy, that is, a pick and mix approach to integration.

Further Inquiry

While the field of ES literature has received much attention over the past five years, the area remains prescriptive at best and empirically vacuous. The studies that do attest to empirical investigation focus upon building critical success factor taxonomies or the development of process models. While such inquiry offers the field valuable knowledge about factors necessary for ES implementation and methods for conducting such a process, empirical gaps relating to deeper organisation-wide issues exist. For the purposes of clarity, suggestions for further inquiry will be dealt with from a pre-implementation, implementation, and post-implementation perspective.

From a *pre-implementation* perspective, further inquiry is needed when reviewing the following areas.

- *Market Sector:* How can a SME know whether an ES solution is right for their organisation? What are the differences in terms of ES implementations for large companies and small to midsize companies?

- *Organisational Readiness:* How can the organisation tell if it is ready for an ES implementation? What are the factors that need to be in line before project begins? How can the organisation tell if consultants are required, and how can the firm make the best of their hire?

- *Vendors:* What affects do vendors have on the organisation? What is the relationship between the vendor company and the implementing organisation? What are the organisational consequences and costs of choosing an inappropriate ES vendor?

- *Integration:* What are the alternatives to ES implementation? What is the role of ES packages in inter-enterprise integration? Is there a need for new process models and CSFs for inter-enterprise integrations?

From *an implementation* perspective, further attention is required within the CSFs and process models arena.

- *Critical Success Factors:* How does a typical CSF (e.g., top management support) affect ES implementation? What stages should each CSF be implemented at during the project? How can CSF influence be measured? What are the costs for poor CSF implementation?

- *Process Models:* Greater attention to the "how" questions is required. Many process models tell us what we should be doing, but there is little empirical evidence suggesting how we can actually conduct such processes. There is also a need for a change management model with an inbuilt ES process model. Such a framework would assist organisations in aligning both vital models for project implementation.

Finally, *post-implementation* issues in need of further inquiry include the following areas.

- *Technology:* How has dependence on vendors affected the ES implementation? Is there a constant need for software upgrades and bolt-on/add-on extensions?

- *Organisation:* How has the ES implementation affected the organisation-cultural, social, hierarchical, and economic affects? Has the organisation experienced a growth in performance as a consequence of ES implementation? How can such advances be measured? What contributions has the

ES implementation made to organisational knowledge/organisational learning and intellectual capital?

- *Future:* What processes exist for ensuring the ES implementation remains cyclical by nature? How will new technology and business processes affect the current ES package?

Conclusion

ES packages offer organisations a huge opportunity for integrating their entire IT platform. Prior to these packages firms were constantly faced with difficulties in aligning technology to the business needs. As a result, the implementation of an ES package now alleviates a lot of the former integration problems. However, caution must be maintained with such implementations. Certain challenges exist, namely the poor attention organisational and human issues receive, resulting in poor overall performances. Greater focus on organisational change and reengineering of business processes is required. To date much lip service has been paid to these areas, yet the problems persist. Critical success factors, while valuable in determining what the firm requires for an ES implementation, needs to focus on the "how" question. Process models need to be more inclusive of organisational change issues, with this chapter calling for the development of an integrated model to deal with such organisational change and technological issues. Future ES packages will extend the integration challenge to embrace inter-enterprise integration. However, before we engage on this route we firstly need to resolve enterprise integration challenges. Understanding today's issues will make tomorrow so much easier.

Endnotes

[1] The first era is Data Processing (DP). This era allowed organisations to improve operational effectiveness by automating information based processes (Ward & Griffiths, 1996, p. 11). The second era is Management Information Systems (MIS). During the 1970s, this era allowed firms to increase management effectiveness by satisfying their information requirements. Finally, with the development of end-user computing, the 1980s

witnessed the emergence of the third phase, that is, the strategic information systems (SIS) era. The objective of this phase, according to Ward and Griffiths, was to improve competitiveness by changing the nature and conduct of business (1996, p. 11).

[2]   BPR is the fundamental rethinking and radical redesign of business processes to achieve dramatic improvements in critical, contemporary measures of performance, such as cost, quality, service and speed.

[3]   According to the authors typical business applications grew by 5,400%.

[4]   From both a human and financial perspective.

[5]   Within academic press. Lopes (1992) appears to be the first cited reference to coin the term ERP. The term ERP was used by many studies until recently, but due to its definitional similarity to MRP systems the term has been dropped within this study, in favour of just Enterprise Systems, that is, systems that incorporate the entire enterprise.

[6]   Davenport (2000) refers to these large systems as integrating all business processes of the company seamlessly under a single package.

[7]   New ES packages are including supply chain management (SCM), customer relationship management (CRM), bolt-on technologies from third party vendors, and e-business solutions.

[8]   Inter-enterprise integration is where companies connect to other companies along the value chain. It is often referred to as *value chain integration* and will become a valuable functionality of future ES packages.

[9]   For example, customer relationship management (CRM) software.

[10]   Supply chain management (SCM) software.

[11]   Even for Small-to-Medium sized organisations.

[12]   Year 2000 (Y2K).

[13]   Examples of typical ES vendors include SAP-R/3 (www.sap.com), Oracle Applications (www.oracle.com), Peoplesoft (www.peoplesoft.com), One World-JD Edwards (www.jde.com), and BaanERP, (www.baan.com). There are dozens of packages on the market today, each competing in terms of new functionality and the ability to integrate ever-changing business best practices into the organisation. However, of all the packages, the German produced SAP system has the largest share of the ES market, followed closely by Peoplesoft, Baan, J.D Edwards, and Oracle packages (Callaway, 2000).

14   In other words extensions should become part of the ES central system as opposed to remaining separate tools to the package.

15   Includes applications such as sales call planning, call reporting, contact management, sales team communication, product configuration, time and expense reporting, and sales collateral databases.

16   Includes call centre automation, field service tracking and dispatch, customer problem tracking and resolution, and product problem analysis and reporting.

17   Business-to-Business relationship.

18   Such as Manugistics and i2 Technologies.

19   Where companies can conduct B2B (business-to-business) or B2C (business-to-consumer) business.

20   One of the main reasons for this is due to the high price of system upgrades and costs of implementation.

21   Larger companies comprise firms that have earnings greater than $250 million. SME have earnings of anything less (Callaway, 2000, p. 29).

22   This study looks at ES benefits from senior management's perspective. The authors developed their own classification of ES package benefits because the ES literature did not appear to provide any rigorous methods for comparing ES benefits; hence the five types of benefits listed above.

23   Incorporating decision-making tools such as OLAP into ES packages and the development of knowledge-enabled ES packages.

24   Study was called "ES post implementation issues and best practices". One hundred and seventeen firms across 17 countries were surveyed on their satisfaction with ES implementation projects.

25   The list in this chapter is not definitive and is used as an explanatory tool only. For a detailed view of CSFs, the IS and ES literature is replete with studies detailing taxonomies and lists.

26   This term is used to denote a pick and choose approach to implementation.

References

Adam, F., & Doherty, P.O. (2000). Lessons from enterprise resource planning implementation in Ireland - Towards smaller and shorter ERP projects. *Journal of Information Technology, 15*(4), 305-316.

Adshead, A. (2001, December 13). IT chiefs do not plan integration. *Computer Weekly.*

Al-Mashari, M. (2000a). Constructs of process change management in ERP context: A focus on SAP R/3. *Americas Conference on Information Systems,* Long Beach, California.

Al-Mashari, M., & Zairi, M. (2000b). The effective application of SAP R/3: A proposed model of best practice. *Logistics Information Management, 13*(3).

AMR Research. (1999a, May 18). AMR research predicts ERP market will reach 66.6 billion euro by 2003. Press Release. www.amrresearch.com

AMR Research. (1999b, August). CRM 101: Building a great CRM strategy. www.amrresearch.com

AMR Research. (2002, December 20). The future of ERP: Extending today's ERP to build tomorrow's global infrastructure. www.amrresearch.com

Bingi, P., Sharma, M.K. et al. (1999). Critical issues affecting an ERP implementation. *Information Systems Management, 16*(3), 7-14.

Brown, C.V., & Vessey, I. (1999). ERP implementation approaches: toward a contingency framework. *International Conference on Information Systems (ICIS),* Charlotte, North Carolina.

Caldas, M.P., & Wood, T. (1999). How consultants can help organisations survive the ERP frenzy. Paper submitted to the *Managerial Consultation Division of the Academy of Management,* Chicago.

Caldwell, B., & Stein, T. (1998, November 30). New IT agenda. *Information Week,* 30-38.

Callaway, E. (2000). *ERP - the next generation.* CTRC Computer Technology Research Corporation.

Davenport, T.H. (1998). Putting the enterprise into the enterprise system. *Harvard Business Review, 76*(4), 121-131.

Davenport, T.H. (2000a). *Mission critical: Realizing the promise of enterprise systems.* Boston: Harvard Business School Press.

Davenport, T.H. (2000b). The future of enterprise system-enabled organizations. *Information Systems Frontiers* (special issue of *The Future of
Enterprise Resource Planning Systems Frontiers*), 2(2), 163-180.

Dong, L. (2001). Modeling top management influence on ES implementation.
Business Process Management Journal, 7(3), 243- 250.

Ein-Dor, P., & Segev, E. (1978). Strategic planning for MIS. *Management
Science, 24*(15), 1631-1641.

Esteves, J., & Pastor, J. (2000). Towards the unification of critical success
factors for ERP implementations. *10th Annual BIT Conference,* Manchester, UK.

Everdingen, V., Hillergersberg, J.V. et al. (2000). ERP adoption by European
midsize companies. *Communications of the ACM, 43*(4), 27-31.

FinancialTimes. (2001). Precision marketing: Back to the bottom line. *European Intelligence Wire.*

Glick, B. (2001, November 1). Integration is a myth, say managers. *Computing.* Greenburg, P. (2001). *CRM at the speed of light.* Osborne
McGraw-Hill.

Hayman, L. (2000). ERP in the Internet economy. *Information Systems
Frontiers* (special issue of *The Future of Enterprise Resource Planning Systems Frontiers), 2*(2), 137-139.

Hirt, S.G. & Swanson, E.B. (1999). Adopting SAP at Siemens Power
Corporation. *Journal of Information Technology, 14,* 243-251.

Klaus, H., Roseman, M. et al. (2000). What is enterprise resource planning?
Information Systems Frontiers (special issue of *The Future of Enterprise Resource Planning Systems*), 2(2), 141-162.

Kraemmergaard, P., & Moller, C. (2000). *A research framework for
studying the implementation of enterprise resource planning (ERP)
systems.* IRIS 23. Laboratorium for Interaction Technology, University
of Trollhattan Uddevalla.

Larsen, T.S. (1999). Supply chain management: A new challenge for researchers and managers in logistics. *Journal of Logistics Management, 10*(2).

Lopes, P.F. (1992). CIM II: The integrated manufacturing enterprise. *Industrial Engineering, 24*(11), 43-45.

Markus, M.L., & Tanis, C. (2000c). The enterprise systems experience-From
adoption to success. In R.W. Zmud (Ed.), *Framing the domains of IT*

research: Glimpsing the future through the past (pp. 173-207) Cincinnati, OH: Pinnaflex Educational Resources, Inc.

Markus, M.L., Axline, S. et al. (2000a). Learning from adopters' experiences with ERP-successes and problems. *Journal of Information Technology, 15*(4), 245-265.

Markus, M.L., Petrie, D. et al. (2000b). Bucking the trends: What the future may hold for ERP packages. *Information Systems Frontier; special issue of on The Future of Enterprise Resource Planning Systems, 2*(2), 181-193.

McFarlan, F.W. (1984). Information technology changes the way you compete. *Harvard Business Review, 62*(3), 98-103.

McKenney, J.L., & McFarlan, F.W. (1982, September/October). Information archipelago-maps and bridges. *Harvard Business Review.*

McNurlin, B. (2001). Will users of ERP stay satisfied? *MIT Sloan Management Review, 42*(2).

Nah, F.H., Lee-Shang Lau, J. et al. (2001). Critical factors for successful implementation of enterprise systems. *Business Process Management Journal, 7*(3), 285-296.

Nezlek, G.S., Jain, H.K. et al. (1999). An integrated approach to enterprise computing architectures. *Association for Computing Machinery. Communications of the ACM, 42*(11), 82-90.

Norris, G., Hurley, J.R. et al. (2000). *E-business and ERP - Transforming the enterprise.* Chichester, England: John Wiley & Sons.

Parr, A., & Shanks, G. (2000b). A model of ERP project implementation. *Journal of Information Technology, 15,* 289-303.

Porter, M.E. (2001). Strategy and the Internet. *Harvard Business Review, 79*(3), 63-78.

Robey, D., Ross, J.W. et al. (2001). Learning to implement enterprise systems: An exploratory study of the dialectics of change (pp. 1-45). Georgia State University and MIT Center for Information Systems Research.

Rosemann, M., Sedera, W. et al. (2001). Critical success factors of process modeling for enterprise systems. *Seventh Americas Conference on Information Systems.*

Ross, J.W., & Vitale, M.R. (2000). The ERP revolution, Surviving vs. thriving. *Information Systems Frontiers* (special issue of *The Future of Enterprise Resource Planning Systems*), *2*(2), 233-241.

Sammon, D., Adam, F. et al. (2001a). *Preparing for ERP-Generic recipes will not be enough.* BIT 2001, Executive Systems Research Centre, UCC, Cork.

Sammon, D., Adam, F. et al. (2001b). ERP dreams and sound business rationale. *Seventh Americas Conference on Information Systems.*

Sarker, S., & Lee, A. (2000). Using a case study to test the role of three key social enablers in ERP implementations. *International Conference on Information Systems ICIS*, Brisbane, Australia.

Sasovova, Z., Heng, M.S. et al. (2001). Limits to using ERP systems. *Seventh Americas Conference on Information Systems.*

Scheer, A.-W., & Habermann, F. (2000). Making ERP a success. *Communications of the ACM 43*(4), 57-61. Association for Computing Machinery.

Sedera, W., Rosemann, M. et al. (2001). Process modelling for enterprise systems: Factors critical to success. *Twelfth Australasian Conference on Information Systems.*

Shang, S., & Seddon, P.B. (2000). A comprehensive framework for classifying the benefits of ERP systems. *Americas Conference on Information Systems.*

Slee, C., & Slovin, C. (1997). Legacy asset management. *Information Systems Management, 14*(1), 12-21.

Smyth, R.W. (2001). Challenges to successful ERP use: Research in progress. *European Conference on Information Systems*, Bled, Slovenia.

Soh, C., Kien, S.S. et al. (2000). Cultural fits and misfits: Is ERP a universal solution? *Communications of the ACM, 43*(4), 47-51. Association for Computing Machinery.

Somers, T., & Nelson, K. (2001a). The impact of critical success factors across the stages of enterprise resource planning implementations. *Hawaii International Conference on Systems Sciences.*

Sor, R. (1999). Management reflections in relation to enterprise wide systems projects. *Americas Conference on Information Systems AMCIS*, Milwaukee, USA.

Sprott, D. (2000). Componentizing the enterprise application packages. *Communications of the ACM, 43*(4), 22-26. Association for Computing Machinery.

Stackpole, B. (1999). Business intelligence tools make ERP smarter. *Managing Automation, 63*(2).

Stefanou, C. (1999). Supply chain management SCM and organizational key factors for successful implementation of enterprise resource planning ERP systems. *Americas Conference on Information Systems AMCIS*, Milwaukee, USA.

Stewart, G., Milford, M. et al. (2000). Organisational readiness for ERP implementation. *Americas Conference on Information Systems*, Long Beach, California.

Sumner, M. (1999). Critical success factors in enterprise wide information management systems projects. *Americas Conference on Information Systems AMCIS*, Milwaukee, USA.

Sumner, M. (2000). Risk factors in enterprise-wide/ERP projects. *Journal of Information Technology, 15*(4), 317-328.

Themistocleous, M., & Irani, Z. (2000). Taxonomy of factors for information system application integration. *Americas Conference on Information Systems*, Long Beach, California.

Ward, J., & Griffiths, P. (1996). *Strategic planning for information systems.* John Wiley & Sons Ltd.

Yusuf, Y., & Little, D. (1998). An empirical investigation of enterprise-wide integration of MRPII. *International Journal of Operations & Production Management, 18*(1), 66-86.

Chapter II

An Overview of SAP Technology

Linda K. Lau
Longwood University, USA

Abstract

This chapter commences with a brief description of Enterprise Resource Planning (ERP), follows by a description of SAP, the largest enterprise software provider in the world. The timeline of activities since its inception in 1972 are summarized in a table. SAP's flagship software program, the R/3 system, is portrayed in more detail. The capabilities of the R/3 system, the three-tier client/server technology it employs, its hardware and software, and several problems associated with its implementation and use are discussed. The two R/3 implementation tools – namely, the Accelerated SAP and the Ready to Run systems – are also described.

Introduction

Since first envisioned in the 1960s, integrated information systems have expanded tremendously in scope, evolving from inventory tracking systems, to

Materials Requirements Planning (MRP), and finally to Enterprise Resource Planning (ERP) (Brady, Monk & Wagner, 2001). Today, almost every organization integrates part or all of its business functions to achieve higher efficiency and productivity. Since its conception in 1972, SAP has become the largest developer of enterprise software applications in the world.

The purpose of this chapter is to provide readers with a general understanding of ERP and a more detailed description of SAP and its flagship product, the R/3 system. After describing the major activities undertaken by SAP over the past 30 years, the bulk of the chapter is devoted to describing SAP R/3's capabilities, its three-tier client/server technology, the hardware and software needed, and some problems with the R/3 system. Two implementation tools – namely, the Accelerated SAP and the Ready to Run systems – have been developed by SAP to expedite the lengthy system implementation process, and both are described in the next section.

Enterprise Resource Planning (ERP)

Enterprise Resource Planning (ERP) is the process of integrating all the business functions and processes in an organization. It achieves numerous benefits. First, a single point of data entry helps to reduce data redundancy while saving employees time in entering data, thereby reducing labor and overhead costs as well (Jacobs & Whybark, 2000). Second, the centralization of information, decision-making, and control leads to increases in efficiencies of operations and productivity, as well as coordination between departments, divisions, regions, and even overseas operations. This is especially true for multinational corporations, for which global integration could result in better communications and coordination around the world and the global sourcing and distribution of parts and services could provide appropriate benchmarks for worldwide operations. Third, the sharing of a centralized database provides business managers with accurate and up-to-date information with which to make well-informed business decisions. Further, it reduces data redundancy while improving data integrity. Fourth, functional integration consolidates all sorts of data, such as financial, manufacturing, and sales, to take advantage of bulk discounts. ERP is especially important for companies that are "intimately connected" to their vendors and customers, and that use electronic data interchange to process sales transactions electronically. Therefore, the implementation of ERP is exceptionally beneficial to businesses such as manufacturing plants that mass-produce products with few changes (Brady, Monk & Wagner, 2001). ERP provides companies with a competitive advantage.

With the rapid growth of e-commerce and e-business in recent years, coupled with the growing popularity of concepts such as supply-chain management, customer relationship management, e-procurement, and e-marketplace, more and more organizations are integrating their ERP systems with the latest business-to-business applications. This new challenge is often referred to as Enterprise Commerce Management (ECM). The major enterprise software providers are Oracle, PeopleSoft, J.D. Edwards, and SAP.

SAP AG

Systemanalyse und Programmentwicklung (SAP) was founded in 1972 in Mannheim, Germany, by five former IBM systems engineers. In 1977, the company was renamed Systems, Applications, and Productions in Data Processing (SAP), and the corporate headquarters was moved to Walldorf, Germany. The primary goal of SAP is to integrate all the business functions in an organization, so that changes in one business process will be immediately and spontaneously reflected by updates in other related business processes. Designing revolutionary and innovative software packages implemented on a multi-lingual (in more than 20 languages by 2003), multi-currency, and multi-national platform, SAP is the world's largest enterprise software provider of collaborative e-business solutions (Buck-Emden, 2000).

Initially, the R/1 system (abbreviated for "runtime system one," indicating real-time operations) was developed in 1973 to solve manufacturing and logistics problems. Over time, it expanded into other contemporary markets such as services, finances, and banking, and added more business functions; for instance, the Asset Accounting module was added in 1977. The more integrated, mainframe-based R/2 system was launched in 1979. The first version of the R/3 system was released in 1992, while the Internet-enabled Release 3.1 was completed in 1996. By 2002, SAP had annual sales of $8.4 billion, making it the third largest software vendor in the world (behind Microsoft and Oracle). Currently, SAP employs over 29,000 people in more than 50 countries, has 1,000 partners around the world who have installed 64,500 systems, serves more than 10 million users at 20,000 organizations in over 120 countries, and

Table 1. Timeline of SAP, Inc.

Year	Activities
1972	• Founded by five former IBM employees in Mannheim, Germany.
1973	• Developed a standard, real-time financial accounting software package, which formed the basis for other software applications that was later known as the R/1 system.
1975	• Developed second standard product, a Materials Management Program with modules for Purchasing, Inventory Management, and Invoice Verification (Brady, Monk & Wagner, 2001).
1977	• SAP became a closely held corporation (GmbH). • The company was renamed Systems, Applications, and Productions in Data Processing (SAP). • The corporate headquarters was moved to Walldorf, Germany. • Added another central module, Asset Accounting. • Developed a French version of the Financial Accounting Module.
1978	• Began developing the R/2 system, a more integrated version of its software products.
1979	• SAP R/2 was launched.
1980s	• Developed additional modules for Cost Accounting, Production Planning and Control, Personnel Management, and Plant Maintenance. • Expanded into international markets.
1981	• Completed the development of the R/2 system, which can handle different languages and currencies.
1987	• Began developing the R/3 system, which incorporated the following concepts: o relational database management systems o graphic user interfaces o a runtime environment developed using C programming language o implementing applications in ABAP/4
1988	• Became SAP AG, a publicly traded company. • Established subsidiaries in numerous foreign countries. • Established SAP Consulting GmbH as a joint venture with Arthur Andersen. • Sold its 1,000th system to Dow Chemical. • Unix became the preferred development platform for R/3. • Launched the SAP University Alliances (UA) program in Germany.
1992	• Released R/3 Release 1.0 in October.
1993	• Cooperated with Microsoft to integrate PC applications with the business applications and to include Windows NT platform.
1994	• Opened a new U.S. development center in Newtown Square, PA, to develop new software technology for the R/3 system. • With R/3 Release 2.1, a complete Kanji version was available for the Japanese market.
1995	• R/3 Release 3.0 was ready. • Included IBM's AS/400 platform.
1996	• R/3 Release 3.1 was Internet-enabled. • Developed Customer Relationship Management (CRM) and Supply Chain Management (SCM) software applications. • The Ready-to-Run R/3 (RRR) program was available in the United States in August 1996. • The R/3 system was broken down into five components as part of the SAP Business Framework. • Launched the SAP University Alliances (UA) program in United States.
1997	• R/3 Release 4.0 was released, which included developments in the area of Supply Chain Management (SCM). • The Ready-to-Run R/3 (RRR) program was available in Europe in June 1997.
1998	• SAP was listed on New York Stock Exchange. • Most of Fortune 500 companies are clients. • Refocused marketing efforts on midsize companies (less than 1,000 employees). • Developed industry-specific pre-configured versions of R/3 for 19 different industry sectors. • Allowed application hosting; that is, a third-party company is allowed to provide the hardware and support. • Focused on new dimension products such as Customer Relationship Management (CRM), Supply Chain Management (SCM), and Business Intelligence.
1999	• Delivered http://mySAP.com. • R/3 Release 4.6 was available for shipping. • Developed Accelerated SAP (ASAP) implementation methodology to ease the implementation process.
2000	• SAP formed SAPHosting, a subsidiary dedicated to the Internet application service provider and application hosting business. • SAP formed strategic alliance with Commerce One to create SAPMarkets, a subsidiary dedicated to creating and powering globally interconnected business-to-business marketplaces on the Internet. • Started the High School Alliance program, where 34 American schools participated to teach students accounting and entrepreneurship using SAP software.
2001	• SAP acquired Top Tier Software and signed an agreement with Commerce One, moving into the electronic business market and forming SAP Portals.
2002	• Established the 7th research center in Queensland University in Australia.
2003	• Five hundred universities in 36 countries participated in the SAP University Alliance program. • There were more than 2,200 SAP-proficient faculty members and 130,000 students enrolled in courses supported by SAP software.

specializes in 23 industries (SAP Innovation Report, 2003). SAP has established seven "bleeding edge technology" research centers around the world. The latest research center, located at Queensland University in Australia, conducts research on voice recognition and mobile computing. The other corporate research centers are located in Palo Alto, CA; Karlsruhe, Germany; Brisbane, Australia; Sophia Antipolis, France; Montreal, Canada; and Johannesburg, South Africa (SAP Innovation Report, 2003). These centers conduct research on e-learning, mobile computing, intelligent devices, e-collaboration, advanced customer interfaces, and technology for application integration. As illustrated in Table 1, SAP, Inc. has participated in many major activities over the past 30 years that helped to secure its current standing in today's software industry (Brady, Monk & Wagner, 2001; Buck-Emden, 2000; http://SAP.com).

To keep up with customers' demand for easier and quicker system integration, SAP now focuses on the concept of system reusability, reaping benefits such as shorter development time, lower development costs, and improved solution homogeneity for the organizations. Further, the reusability approach also results in shorter learning curve and less training for SAP users who are already familiar with the products. To increase the users' acceptance of the integrated system, SAP is now employing a new development paradigm of getting customers and users directly involved in the system development process.

THE R/3 System

The R/3 system is a powerful enterprise software package with several significant updates over the mainframe-based R/2 version. The R/3 system has three major function modules: SAP Financials, SAP Human Resources, and SAP Logistics (Larocca, 1999). The financials module is an integrated suite of financial applications containing submodules such as financial accounting, controlling, investment management, treasury cash management, enterprise controlling, and real estate. All issues regarding recruitment and training are managed using the human resources module, which contains personnel administration and personnel planning and development submodules. The logistics module manages issues related to sales and distribution, production planning, materials management, quality management, plant maintenance, logistics information systems, project systems, and product data management. The R/3

Reference Model is equipped with more than 8,000 configuration options (Jacobs & Whybark, 2000). The newest version of R/3 is the SAP R/3® Enterprise, which has new and continuously improved functions, provides flexibility and optimization, and utilizes innovative technology to manage collaborative e-business processes.

Capabilities of the R/3 System

While designing the R/3 system, SAP developers choose the best, most efficient ways in which business processes *should* be handled, and incorporate these "best practices" into the system (Brady, Monk & Wagner, 2001). Therefore, clients of the R/3 system may need to redesign their ways of conducting business to follow the practices dictated by the R/3 developers. In some situations, organizations may need to reengineer their business processes in fundamental ways, revamping old ways of conducting business, redefining job responsibilities, and restructuring the organization. R/3 systems can, however, be customized to address global issues where different countries have different ways of doing business; country-specific business practices pertaining to accounting, tax requirements, environmental regulations, human resources, manufacturing, and currency conversion rules can be built into R/3 systems.

Unlike the R/2 system, the R/3 system requires only a single data entry, and it provides users with immediate access to and common usage of the data. This new system was designed around business processes and applications such as sales orders, material requirements planning, and recruitment. An important advantage of the R/3 system is its ability to run on any platform, including Unix and Windows NT. R/3 also utilizes an open architecture approach, so that third-party software companies are allowed to develop add-on software packages and integrate hardware equipment such as bar code scanners, PDAs, cell phones, and Global Information Systems with the R/3 system (Buck-Emden, 2000). Sophisticated and more advanced users can design customized graphical user interfaces (GUI) screens and menus and/or create ad hoc query reporting trees and customized reports using the ABAP (Advanced Business Application Program) Workbench developer's tools (Larocca, 1999). The object linking and embedding (OLE) technology allows files from other applications such as Microsoft Office and Corel Office to be easily integrated with the R/3 system. The SAP On-line Help Documentation, available in both standard and compressed HTML, is contained on a separate CD-ROM.

In 1996, the R/3 system was broken down into the following five categories of components as part of the SAP Business Framework to better streamline business operations: industry-neutral, industry-specific, Internet, complementary, and custom. SAP continues to develop software components such as the SAP Advanced Planner & Optimizer (SAP APO), SAP Customer Relationship Management (SAP CRM), and SAP Business Information Warehouse (SAP BW), to form the technical foundation for the http://www.mysap.com/e-business platform.

The Three-Tier Client/Server Technology

It was the advent of inexpensive hardware and the improvement of client/server technology in the 1990s that propelled SAP to develop the SAP R/3 system, which was designed for the client-server environment. The client/server distributed computing architecture allows users to access the system via any computer that is connected to the network, even working from home. The R/3 system utilizes the same three-tier hierarchy configuration as the Relational Database Management System (RDBMS). The user interface layer refers to the GUI of the client computer, which serves as a means for the end user to communicate with the applications and database servers. The business logic layer consists of the application server, which performs all the administrative functions of the system, including background processing, printing, and process request management. The innermost layer consists of a central computer that contains the database server, the data dictionary, and the Repository Information System, which is used to retrieve information on the objects in the data dictionary. An improved version of the three-tier architecture is the four-layer client/server configuration, with an additional layer for Internet service (Buck-Emden, 2000).

Hardware and Software Components

The hardware components of an SAP R/3 installation include the servers that house the databases and software programs, the client workstations for user interfaces, and the network communications system that connects servers and workstations. The software components of an SAP R/3 installation consist of the network infrastructure, the operating systems, the database engine, and the client desktop. Several application programs are installed onto the servers: the main function modules, the customized as well as the interface programs, and the ABAP/4 (Advanced Business Application Program) developer's work-bench programming tools. ABAP programmers use ABAP/4 to develop regular application programs that are included with the R/3 system as well as customized software programs for their clients (Buck-Emden, 2000). Some commonly used ABAP/4 tools are: the ABAP List Processing, used to list reports; the ABAP Query, used to develop queries; the Screen Painter, used to design screens; and the Menu Painter, used to create menus. Third-party vendors are permitted to develop customized add-on software programs to be linked with the R/3 system. The data repository for the RDBMS and the basis module (as a prerequisite for all application modules) are also installed onto the servers.

Problems with SAP R/3

Although SAP touts its R/3 system as a revolutionary, efficient, and innovative software program, the system does have a few drawbacks. Because of the complexity of the R/3 system, many assumptions must be made in order to confine the number of configuration options available. However, once the system is configured, all the options are fixed and cannot be changed. Further, users must enter all the fields before they are allowed to proceed to the next screen or activity (Jacobs & Whybark, 2000). Consequently, many people find the R/3 system to be relatively rigid. Nevertheless, the flexibility of the SAP system can be improved by installing specially designed customized applications developed by ABAP programmers.

A second potential problem with R/3 has been mentioned above. In order to increase the efficiency of doing business, SAP developers incorporated "best practices" into the R/3 system. Basically, they decided how clients *should* conduct their businesses. However, not all businesses agree with this philosophy, and this approach may not be acceptable or applicable to some organizations. In such instances, it may be extremely important for organizations to continue with their usual ways of doing business and hence for the system administrator to configure the system according to these established practices (Jacobs & Whybark, 2000). These simply may be incompatible with the R/3 system.

SAP attempts to incorporate all business practices, including environmental and other regulations into the R/3 system. However, three types of misfits (relating to data, process, and output) can occur due to incompatibilities between software functionality and organizational requirements (Soh et al., 2000). Major multinational corporations that installed similar R/3 systems in several different countries could experience any of these mismatches in the systems due to differences in cultural and regulatory environments. The unique context of each country in which an organization operates must be carefully enmeshed into the traditionally Western-biased business practices inherent in the R/3 systems. Further, there is the problem of migration between software versions, in which the newer version is sometimes not backward-compatible with the older version.

When using the SAP On-line Help Documentation, the version number listed on the Help CD-ROM must correspond with the version of the SAP GUI (Larocca, 1999). However, even when the two versions correspond, incompatibilities may be present, because changes and upgrades in a higher version of the software are not updated in the Help CD-ROM of the same version number. Further, the Help CD-ROM has limited searching capabilities on some concepts, rendering the help feature an inefficient support tool. In addition, not all materials are properly translated from the original German version, and not all the help documentation has been translated.

Two R/3 Implementation Tools

R/3 system implementation is both expensive and time-consuming; a complete implementation can cost between one and several million dollars and can take more than three years. Only Fortune 500 corporations can afford such extensive deployment of ERP as R/3 systems represent. In an attempt to target small and medium-sized companies as well as large organizations that are interested in only partial ERP integration, SAP developed two implementation alternatives: the Accelerated SAP and Ready to Run R/3 programs.

The Accelerated SAP (ASAP) program is a rapid implementation tool designed to install the full R/3 system quickly and efficiently by focusing on tools and training and utilizing a five-phase, process-oriented strategy for guiding successful implementation (Larocca, 1999). The five phases are project preparation, business blueprint, realization, final preparation, and go live and support.

Designed for small to medium-sized companies, the SAP Ready to Run R/3 (RRR) program complements the ASAP system by bundling the server and network hardware systems with a pre-installed, pre-configured base R/3 system, an operating system, and a database management system (Larocca, 1999). This approach yields significant cost and time savings by reducing the implementation schedule by as much as 30 days. The RRR solution includes a specially developed online tool called the System Administration Assistant, which allows a minimally trained system administrator to manage the system effectively. A RRR system can be purchased through any SAP hardware vendor partner such as Hewlett-Packard, Compaq, IBM, NCR, Siemens, or Sun Microsystems. It can be supported by operating systems such as Microsoft Windows NT, IBM AS/400, and Unix. The databases supported by the R/3 systems include Microsoft SQL server, DB2, Informix, Oracle, and Dynamic Server. All the options in the SAP system are configured using the SAP Implementation Guide (IMG).

Conclusion

This chapter provides readers with a general understanding of Enterprise Resource Planning (ERP); of SAP, the third largest software vendor in the world; major activities undertaken by SAP; and of SAP's R/3 system. The capabilities of the R/3 system include complete system integration, global accessibility, scalability, and open architecture. The three-tier client/server technology refers to the user interface layer, the business logic layer, and the database server layer. The hardware elements for an R/3 installation include the usual servers and client workstations, but the software requirements are more elaborate. Some of the problems associated with the R/3 system include the adopting organization's need to reengineer business processes, the misfits and mismatches between system functionality and organizational requirements, and inadequacies in the SAP On-line Help Documentation. The Accelerated SAP and Ready to Run systems are two implementation tools designed to expedite the implementation process.

References

Brady, J., Monk, E., & Wagner, B. (2001). *Concepts in enterprise resource planning.* Boston, MA: Course Technology.

Buck-Emden, R. (2000). *The SAP R/3 system: An introduction to ERP and business software technology.* Reading, MA: Addison-Wesley.

Jacobs, R., & Whybark, C. (2000). *Why ERP? A primer on SAP implementation.* New York, NY: Irwin McGraw-Hill.

Larocca, D. (1999). *SAMS teach yourself SAP R/3 in 24 hours.* Indianapolis, IN: SAMS.

Lau, L. (2003). Implementing ERP systems using SAP. In M. Khosrow-Pour (Ed.), *Information technology and organizations: Trends, issues, challenges, and solutions* (pp. 732-734). Hershey, PA: Idea Group Publishing.

SAP Innovation Report 2003: SAP makes innovation happen. Retrieved March 11, 2003, from http://www.sap.com/company/innovation/index.asp

Soh, C., Sia, S., & Tay-Yap, J. (2000). Cultural fits and misfits: Is ERP a universal solution? *Communications of the ACM, 43*(4), 47.

Chapter III

Integrating SAP Across the Business Curriculum

Jane Fedorowicz
Bentley College, USA

Ulric J. Gelinas, Jr.
Bentley College, USA

George Hachey
Bentley College, USA

Catherine Usoff
Bentley College, USA

Abstract

This chapter describes the integration of the SAP R/3 system into courses across the undergraduate and graduate business curriculum at Bentley College. It argues that the integration of the SAP R/3 system into existing business courses, rather than creating standalone courses covering enterprise systems concepts, is a preferable way to immerse students in information technology issues and help them understand how enterprise systems have significantly transformed the workplace. The authors describe the processes used to train faculty, develop and test curriculum materials, and coordinate the integration effort. Learning objectives and SAP R/3 curricular content are described for MBA, accounting, and finance courses.

Introduction

Business school faculty have always struggled with the sometimes antithetical demands of providing students with lifetime career knowledge while giving them enough practical skills to obtain a good entry level position upon graduation. A prime example of this dilemma relates to "hands-on" computer skills. Outside of the domain of information systems where learning programming languages and database management skills are key to the curriculum, business faculty face valid criticism when their hands-on exercises are nothing more than computerized versions of textbook problem solving. It is not adequate to acquaint students with simulated and simplified versions of real business computer system issues. To be truly useful, classroom computer applications must both reflect the theory of a subject area and expose the student to real, and therefore complex, software and data. Such exposure gives the students an increased appreciation of technology's role in their intended career paths while demonstrating the changes technology brings about in the business processes and workflow of the area under study. This, then, is the powerful lesson resulting from intensive immersion into the real world of information technology.

A primary mechanism for exposing students to the synergy of information technology and business theory is enterprise systems. Enterprise systems are used by companies and governmental organizations of all sizes to support and integrate internal business processes, and increasingly, to interact with their business partners. The results are simplified and automated data entry, more sophisticated analysis for decision-making, and coordination among previously isolated business functions. Thus, exposure to enterprise systems gives students a more accurate and sophisticated picture of the way business works today and will continue to evolve in the future.

Many colleges and universities have joined SAP's Educational Alliance (EA) program in the past few years and have used SAP's R/3 enterprise system in existing and new courses. However, some schools have been more successful than others in integrating SAP R/3 across disciplines within their business curriculum. One of the more successful efforts has been undertaken at Bentley College in Waltham, MA, USA. A critical success factor at Bentley has been the careful alignment of enterprise systems applications within the curriculum and with the mission and strengths of the College. In this chapter, we outline the Bentley perspective on technology integration in our classes, demonstrate how enterprise systems and SAP's R/3 system fit with the goals of the College, give examples of how SAP R/3 facilitates the teaching of a wide range of topics and courses, and provide guidance on the resources needed to successfully accomplish these goals.

Three Levels of Technology Integration

The President of Bentley College, Joseph Morone, promotes the integration of technology at colleges and universities on three levels (Hulik, 1998). In Level One, a school acquires the infrastructure necessary to support the use of information technology (IT) by students. This involves purchasing the hardware and software necessary to support a computer lab on campus, distance learning, and high-tech classrooms. This level of IT infrastructure has now become a practical necessity in higher education. Nevertheless, the resources necessary to support Level One integration are substantial.

In Level Two, a school seeks to include curriculum aimed at graduating information technology specialists. This level may involve the creation of new degree programs designed to produce candidates that will be demanded in the marketplace. Generally, this involves the recruitment of high-level IT-savvy faculty to nurture these specialists. In today's highly competitive market for IT faculty, this is likely to be an expensive, but nevertheless necessary, proposition for many schools.

In Level Three, the content of the curriculum changes. The integration is not limited to *how a course is being taught.* Rather, the integration entails a transformation of *what is being taught* in the classroom. Level Three is the most difficult level of integration to reach. It means that non-IT degree courses must be infused with IT applications and consideration of their organizational impacts. This integration usually necessitates a heavy time commitment from the faculty, especially those not adept at the use of IT or its application in non-IT courses. To successfully use technology as a teaching tool, instructors must be given the time and resources needed to provide a Level Three experience for their students.

A number of colleges and universities have chosen to integrate SAP's R/3 system or other enterprise system packages into their curriculum by creating standalone courses covering enterprise systems concepts (see, for example, Becerra-Fernandez, Murphy & Simon, 2000). This is an example of Level Two integration. At Bentley College we have chosen to integrate SAP's R/3 system into existing courses and to direct system usage toward program and course objectives, consistent with Level Three integration, through lectures, discussions, and exercises.

In this chapter we describe Bentley's SAP program objectives and the overall approach taken to implement SAP R/3 in our courses. For example, faculty were trained using a combination of external SAP R/3 training and in-house workshops. Assignments were piloted in one course and then adapted to others. After this background, we describe how R/3 was integrated into many courses and used to accomplish specific course objectives. Finally, we summarize the resources that were required to accomplish our R/3 integration objectives. Included here is a discussion of the importance of collaboration with organizations using SAP.

Getting Started (and Restarted)

The initial attempt to integrate SAP into the curriculum at Bentley revolved around the introduction of a new, full-time, cohort-based MBA program. The original concept was that R/3 exercises would be introduced in each of the introductory functional courses and in the Business Process course, to provide an underlying theme and integrating mechanism to the program. To accomplish this, Bentley became a member of SAP's Educational Alliance (EA) program. As a member of the EA, the college received the R/3 software, a quota of training days, and other types of support that would help faculty learn to adapt the system to their classes. This initial endeavor failed for a number of reasons, the principal one being that many of the faculty involved were not successful in integrating R/3 with course content in a meaningful way.[1] The vision of meaningful integration that we had was insufficient given the difficulty of determining what to do with the system once we got it. Meaningful integration of R/3 into courses requires a dedicated effort by individual faculty members and substantial support from a variety of sources. After this initial start, one or two faculty from the original full-time MBA group, plus others from the Finance and Accountancy Departments, formed a critical mass of faculty who were still determined to integrate R/3 into their classes.

In contrast to the slow start in the MBA program was the early success in the Advanced Accounting Information Systems (Advanced AIS) course, where enterprise systems were (and remain) an important topical area of study to those obtaining a degree in Accounting Information Systems. In the very first semester of SAP's availability on campus (spring semester, 1997), students were exposed to SAP in the Advanced AIS class and were offered attractive internship positions working in the then Big Five enterprise systems support areas. Nonetheless, this was an isolated offering, and its lack of integration with the rest of the AIS curriculum diluted its usefulness to students.

The discontinuity between the corporate style training in R/3 that was offered to faculty and their course objectives contributed to the frustration of the initial faculty group, as did the nature of the R/3 training database (called IDES), which is delivered with the system to all EA members. SAP's R/3 training courses are organized by levels in each SAP module[2]. Thus, level 2 courses, which provide the introduction to the system for most faculty, offers an overview of the functional activities that comprise that module. This training consists of lectures on the features of the module and exercises that demonstrate how the system should operate. Such an approach is very appropriate for corporate staffers who will work intently with a small portion of R/3, but does not match the needs of faculty who must tie system use into broader course and educational objectives rather than just presenting system options and details. Faculty needed to see more of the "big picture" of enterprise systems use in an organization to determine how the learning from the training class could be integrated with business courses in a meaningful way. Most faculty needed to take several R/3 training courses before they had enough knowledge to start building the bigger picture.

The temptation for many faculty beginning to use R/3 was to take the exercises taught in R/3 corporate training and use them directly in their classes. In this attempt, frequent problems surfaced due to the fact that most SAP training courses depend on the inclusion of additional data above and beyond what comes with the IDES database that EA members receive. To get these exercises to run at an EA school, one must add data to the system such as inventory items and customer records, and perform some customization and configuration such as closing and opening accounting periods and setting number ranges for transactions. Many of these actions are taken in what SAP refers to as the implementation guide (IMG). But instructions about how to access and use the IMG are given in level 3 SAP training courses, and are outside of the expertise of the typical faculty member. SAP trainers have the requisite expertise or support staff to accomplish such customizing for their training exercises to work. But similar resources were not available to support curriculum development and integration at an EA school.

Despite these difficulties, a number of faculty at Bentley recognized the value of R/3 integration in their classes and persisted in using the system, making incremental progress each semester. A jolt was given to the effort in its third year when a re-rollout of SAP was undertaken. The key difference between the first attempt and the second to integrate SAP exercises at Bentley was that one of the faculty involved in the effort had been granted a one-year sabbatical to figure out how to integrate the system into existing and new courses. He used his time to take a number of level 3 SAP training classes. This allowed him to help others make the necessary changes to facilitate the effective demonstration of the system's capabilities. In addition, some faculty in the group who attended SAP training would immediately attempt the exercises on the Bentley R/3 system and would consult with their training instructors to determine what adjustments needed to be made. This realization about the effort and knowledge required to translate the training available into business curriculum applications was very important in determining if a re-rollout of the effort was possible.[3] The core group of faculty interested in the re-rollout decided that the pedagogical benefits were worth the burden.

The first step in the re-rollout was the creation of an SAP User's Group of faculty and technical staff who would manage the resource, share exercises and insights into using the system, and plan for the gradual spread of SAP usage into courses outside an initial core. The initial group of courses with R/3 exercises was determined by the teaching interests of the faculty involved and included Accounting Information Systems (AIS), Advanced AIS, Cost Management, Treasury Management, IT Auditing, and Business Processes.

One lesson from the first experiences with R/3 is that both faculty and students need a great deal of support in order to have a successful encounter with the technology. Our initial efforts involved a single, part-time staff member who oversaw the running of the server and provided limited faculty support. There were no student assistants in the computer lab who could help students with SAP problems, leaving individual faculty to troubleshoot when they were available to do so. In the restart period, we found it took three part-time technical staff people to provide ongoing support of the system. In addition, one recent MBA graduate was hired half-time to provide faculty support and two graduate students provided assistance to students in a learning lab. This level of support is adequate for our present level of usage.

Coordination Across the Curriculum

As the group met over time, it was clear that they had two major pedagogical objectives for the integration of SAP into their classes. These two objectives correspond with the benefits that companies hope to attain with investments in information technology (IT) that Zuboff enunciated in her classic 1985 article entitled "Automate/Informate: The Two Faces of Intelligent Technology". Zuboff (1985, p. 8) asserted that when firms use IT to automate, they are looking to "replace human effort and skill with a technology that enables the same processes to be performed at less cost and with more control and continuity". At the same time, however, computerized business applications also generate "information about the underlying processes through which an organization accomplishes its work". Managers can use these data to "informate" the firm or find out more about the firm's underlying processes. At Bentley, SAP is integrated into courses to accomplish learning objectives in both areas, automating and informating.

Enterprise systems such as SAP's R/3 certainly embody both capabilities enunciated by Zuboff. These systems are customized to reflect the business processes of companies that implement them. They allow for the automatic transmission of information derived from the basic transactions of the company across the various modules of the system. For example, in the order-to-cash process, the shipping department will post a goods issue at the point when the items ordered by the customer are ready to be shipped. This action, initiated in the Sales and Distribution (SD) module, results in the automatic updating of the customer's account and the relevant general ledger accounts in the Financial

Accounting (FI) module, adjustment to the inventory levels maintained in the Materials Management (MM) module and even the reports in the Treasury (TR) module that forecast when the cash flow implications of the transaction will be realized. In addition, by automating all of these functions, the roles of the accountant, sales staff, inventory manager, and corporate treasurer must be redesigned to reflect a move from data entry activity to decision support.

Our exercises allow students to view how the system tracks every step of such processes. Students can experience how an enterprise system facilitates the functioning of the organization's business and provides records that business events have occurred. These are both "automate" type functions. Thus, we can illustrate how the information flows across modules in an integrated system and how the enterprise system provides IT support for a company's business processes.

As transactions such as those in the order-to-cash process occur, the R/3 system stores tremendous amounts of transaction data in more than 13,000 tables. System users can access these data directly by going to the tables themselves or by using any of the various reporting routines that come with each module. Consequently, enterprise systems end the fragmentation of information that occurred when companies were using individual "legacy" systems to keep track of activity in each functional area of the firm and which were poorly integrated (Davenport, 1998). The use of data for decision making begins to approximate the higher-level analytical process that Zuboff calls *informating*. Several exercises ask students to recognize the use of SAP R/3-generated data for informating.

The SAP users group at Bentley College has gradually expanded to include seven faculty who have adapted R/3 exercises into most of their classes at both the undergraduate and graduate levels. Others have also begun to adopt exercises in other sections of SAP-centric courses. The SAP modules and features that have been covered in various assignments include Materials Management (MM), Sales and Distribution (SD), Financial Accounting (FI), Treasury (TR), Controlling (CO), Audit Information System, and User Maintenance. Tables 1 and 2 summarize the present uses of SAP in our undergraduate and graduate courses. In the following sections, we expand on the objectives and activities within the courses summarized in the tables.

PDP CENTER
(CDS=PDPCNTR)

Table 1. Uses of SAP R/3 in the Bentley College undergraduate curriculum.

SAP Functionality	Finance	Accountancy and Accounting Information Systems	Corporate Finance and Accounting
Business Processes (SD and MM)		Accounting Information Systems	
Accounting		Financial Accounting and Reporting I	
Controls		Accounting Information Systems IT Auditing	
Audit		IT Auditing	
Treasury	Corporate Treasury Management		Corporate Treasury Management
Reporting	Corporate Treasury Management	Cost Management Advanced AIS	
Cost Management and Decision Support		Cost management Advanced Topics in Cost Management	

Table 2. Uses of SAP R/3 in the Bentley College graduate curriculum.

SAP Functionality	Finance	Accountancy and Accounting Information Systems	Information Age MBA
Business Processes (SD and MM)		Business Process and Systems Assessment	Business Processes
Accounting		Financial Accounting Problems I	
Controls		Business Process and Systems Assessment IT Auditing	
Audit		IT Auditing	
Treasury	Short-Term Financial Management		Financial Statement Analysis for Decision-Making
Reporting	Short-Term Financial Management	Advanced AIS	

Course-by-Course Descriptions

This section outlines the courses into which R/3 has been successfully integrated at Bentley College. Each course is briefly described, and a set of learning objectives is provided that explains how the SAP R/3 system is used to enhance the theoretical material presented in the course.

Accounting Information Systems

The Accounting Information Systems (AIS) course is required of all undergraduate and graduate Accountancy and AIS majors. The main themes of the course are to expose students to the major business processes in companies, understand the operational and informational components of those processes, identify appropriate internal controls to assure process quality, and introduce the students to the information technology used within typical business processes. Enterprise systems are a major theme within the course, and two extensive assignments based on SAP are integral in achieving the following objectives:

- Illustrate basic business processes, focusing on how SAP integrates business events within the order-to-cash and purchase-to-pay processes.
- Create customer, trading good, and vendor master records, and show how sales and purchase activities are completed and linked through their document flow.
- Identify how internal control is supported by integrated enterprise systems.
- Demonstrate how integrated systems are used to accomplish business objectives.
- Familiarize students with the complexity of a leading enterprise system product.
- Contrast the theoretical examples of the textbook with their complements in a live system environment, including information technology options and documentation of real system activity.

Advanced Accounting Information Systems

The Advanced Accounting Information Systems course is required for all undergraduate and graduate AIS majors, and is a popular elective for Accountancy students. This course covers a range of current IT topics related to data and software quality and the creation and use of nontraditional management reports, using a range of information technology products and resources. A major topic within the course entails selecting and implementing enterprise systems. In support of this activity, the course includes as one of its texts a book on enterprise system selection. The students also are given the option of sitting for an SAP certification exam. The objectives of SAP activities in this course are to:

- Introduce students to the reporting in SAP R/3 and have them execute some reports within each functional module to illustrate business reporting functionality.
- Link the theory of system selection options to a real and complex system.

Intermediate Accounting

The Intermediate Accounting course is required for undergraduate Accountancy and Corporate Finance and Accounting majors. A similar course, with a similar R/3 assignment, is required of students in the MS Accounting (MSA) program. The assignment is related to the valuation of accounts receivable and recognition of bad debt in SAP and is assigned after those topics have been covered in class. The objectives for this assignment are:

- Locate a customer master record and determine the payment terms for credit sales.
- Locate and analyze customer open invoices.
- Execute an R/3 program to value accounts receivable for periodic reporting.
- Execute R/3 programs to age accounts receivable and record the allowance for doubtful accounts and bad debt expense.
- Explain how the configuration of the R/3 system at Bentley College controls the valuation, recording, and reporting of accounts receivable, allowance for doubtful accounts, and bad debt expense.

Cost Management

The Cost Management course is a required course for undergraduate Accountancy and Corporate Finance and Accounting majors. This course "emphasizes analysis, interpretation, and presentation of information for management decision making purposes". Therefore the objectives of this course are very much aligned with the capabilities of an enterprise system and how it might support the analysis, interpretation, and presentation of information. The R/3 assignment requires that the students navigate through data that are already entered into a particular company's database to think about how the information might specifically support management decision-making. Through the learning objectives of this assignment, the students obtain a sense of what types of systems they may be interacting with in their future careers and how such a system may be used to access, analyze, and format information to support management decision making. The learning objectives for using SAP R/3 in the Cost Management course are:

- Recognize the breadth and depth of data in the enterprise system database that supports the revenue cycle of the organization.
- Understand the nature of the data and how they specifically support the execution of the business process (here, sales and distribution).
- Understand how the information in customer master records might be combined with transactional data to present information in the most effective way to support specific decisions.
- Understand the integration of the enterprise system by tracing the document flow initiated by the sales transaction.
- Execute simple reports from the sales information system.
- Understand how the specific report generated would support management decision-making.

Advanced Topics in Cost Management

The Advanced Topics in Cost Management course is an elective course that has the Cost Management course as a pre-requisite. Students in the advanced course should have done the SAP R/3 assignment in the previous course and therefore have met certain learning objectives already related to using R/3 generated information to support decision-making. The advanced course then builds on these objectives to explore other aspects of an enterprise system. In keeping with the objectives of the course to cover advanced topics related to costing systems, the use of R/3 in this class focuses on the activity based costing (ABC) module in R/3. The learning objectives for using R/3 in the advanced cost management course are:

- Experience the basic functionality of the activity based costing module in an enterprise system.

- Understand the use of and the relationship between cost centers, secondary cost elements, activity types and prices, business processes, and cost objects in the execution of an activity based costing system.

- Document the underlying ABC model that is implied by the enterprise system's representation.

- Evaluate the use of an enterprise system for activity based costing along the dimensions of: the ease of use of the software, the ease of understanding the underlying ABC model through the system, and the usefulness of the application of the ABC model for decision making.

- Compare and contrast the ABC application in the enterprise system to a software product specifically designed for activity based costing.

- Understand the trade-offs between using an enterprise system for a specific application versus using a best of breed software designed specifically for that application.

IT Auditing

The Information Technology (IT) Auditing course is required of all Accounting Information Systems (AIS) majors and may be elected by Accountancy majors. A similar course is offered at the graduate level, is required for MSAIS students, and may be elected by MSA (MS Accountancy) and IAMBA (Information Age MBA) students. Similar SAP-related assignments are required in the graduate and undergraduate courses. The IT Auditing course introduces three typical aspects of IT audits: the audits of computerized information systems, the computer facility, and the process of developing and implementing information systems. Through readings, case studies, exercises, and discussion, students learn to plan, conduct, and report on these three types of audits, and to apply IT auditing techniques and advanced audit software. The learning objectives for using SAP R/3 in the IT Auditing course are:

- Be able to plan, conduct, and report on an application audit and an audit of the IT environment.
- Understand the audit challenges posed by emerging technologies.
- Appreciate the role of the IT auditor as a business and management advisor.
- Identify ways in which advanced IT auditing techniques and audit software can be used.
- Be able to extract, download, and analyze, using audit and other software packages, data from the R/3 system.
- Create user accounts and user roles and audit those to determine that desirable levels of security have been achieved.

Treasury Management

Corporate Treasury Management (CTM) is an elective in the undergraduate programs in Finance and Corporate Finance and Accounting. CTM is an applied course that builds on the financial theory developed in other courses. Given its practical orientation and because SAP's R/3 system has a Treasury Module with most of the typical features used by treasury personnel in major companies, this course is a logical candidate for R/3 exercises. And, this orientation also helps to set the course objectives for the R/3 exercises that have been developed for it; namely:

- Illustrate some of the basic functions and processes of cash management, including how a transaction is posted, how the system disseminates information across the FI and TR modules and updates customer and general ledger accounts, and how it impacts the cash management reports.
- Understand why the Liquidity Forecast and the Cash Position reports are important tools for treasury management decision-making.

- Help students understand the structure of the banking subledger accounts used to clear transactions.

- Develop an understanding of the check clearing and manual bank statement clearing processes, develop an understanding of how the Liquidity Forecast and Cash Position reports change as a check and/or bank statement is cleared through the system and see how the customer subledger and general ledger accounts are updated in the check and statement clearing processes.

Business Processes

The Business Process course is a required course for all MBA students. This course "provides a conceptual framework for understanding the fundamentals and characteristics of business processes". To complement this framework, SAP R/3 is used to demonstrate how information technology facilitates the execution and analysis of business processes. Two candidate business processes are the focus of the R/3 assignments, the sales and distribution process and the procurement process for materials. For each of these processes, students create master records and execute transactions in R/3. In addition, they are asked to consider the use of the resulting data in decisions that could be made to execute the business process or to improve the process. Students in this class also study and prepare a case analysis on the non-production purchasing process in a company that is converting this process from a legacy system to R/3. Therefore, learning objectives related to R/3 are achieved through both the traditional R/3 assignments and as part of a case that focuses on a specific business process. The learning objectives for the use of SAP R/3 in the Business Process course are:

- Understand the integration of an enterprise system by entering transactions and tracing the document flow across functions.

- Recognize the breadth and depth of data in the enterprise system database that supports the organization's business processes.

- Explain how efficiency and control objectives are met by an integrated system.

- Understand how specific reports would support management decision-making.

Resource Requirements

There are three main categories of resources required for effective SAP R/3 curriculum integration: adequate funding, faculty time, and administrative support. Funding is required for membership in the EA, for hardware if the school hosts its own instance of R/3, for support staff, subsidized training fees (when fees apply), and for airfare and lodging when faculty attend training. The EA provides the software for a fee either through having an instance of R/3 on the school's own servers or by allowing connection to a UCC (University Competency Center). Support staff should be knowledgeable about the underlying database system chosen for the R/3 instance, and with systems maintenance (for creating users, allocating table space, and copying clients). We have three staff dedicated on a part-time basis to SAP-related activities.

In addition to funding, the largest resource required is faculty commitment and time. The faculty at Bentley have spent time attending workshops; developing, testing and revising exercises; meeting with corporate representatives of companies that use SAP software; meeting with administrators to keep the SAP effort in the forefront; presenting workshops to educate other faculty; and making presentations to outside groups to spread the knowledge outside of the school.

Targeted support for faculty members has also helped to sustain the SAP effort at Bentley. As was previously mentioned, one of the SAP teaching team was funded for a full year sabbatical to immerse himself in SAP and to gain higher-level knowledge that would allow him to make the necessary changes to exercises or to the R/3 system to get the exercises to run smoothly. This faculty member also received a grant from SAP to continue his efforts after the sabbatical. Because of the concentrated amount of time this faculty member was able to devote to learning and thinking about R/3, he has become a champion on campus for curriculum integration.

In addition to the technical support required to maintain the software, Bentley has found it essential to have two other types of support staff. One is a person who works directly with faculty to develop and test exercises and the other type consists of tutors who directly support students working on assignments. The faculty support person also regularly offers introductory workshops to students so each faculty member does not have to provide those in class. This person should have technical R/3 skills as well as business knowledge, so he or she understands the objectives of the business assignment as well as how to accomplish those objectives in R/3. Having the tutors to work directly with students with specified hours in a lab has helped to reduce student anxiety levels and freed up instructors' time that would otherwise be taken up with extensive student questions.

As with any major endeavor in an organization it is important to have top administrators' support for the project. The administration has provided travel funds for faculty and staff to attend training. Hardware has been purchased to host the system and upgraded to increase performance of the system when necessary as more users are involved. The school did not hire any new technical staff specifically because of their SAP skills but they have made technical staff time available to support the effort and hired an SAP consultant on an hourly basis when necessary to supplement the more general technical staff. The administration has also demonstrated flexibility in targeting other existing resources (e.g., graduate tutors in the lab) for SAP R/3 support.

In addition to funding, faculty time, and support staff, cooperation from local corporations that use SAP software has been a useful resource. The faculty and local company representatives have interacted in several ways to bolster faculty efforts. Corporate professionals have participated in making a video that demonstrates the link between SAP R/3 and a key business process, helped faculty to design realistic assignments, spoken in classes about implementation and use of SAP R/3, provided relevant sabbatical projects, and shared experiences with faculty in interviews. These corporate relationships have provided invaluable insight to the faculty that they can use to make the learning experience much richer for the students.

Collectively, these efforts make the introduction to SAP in the business curriculum a broader experience than what the students would get in a corporate training setting. Although the students will not come out of our degree programs with detailed hands-on SAP expertise, they will leave with an appreciation of how enterprise systems support business processes and business decisions. They start their professional careers with a framework for integrating IT and business that can be easily supplemented by the specific training the company requires for their particular position. Our experience to date is that these students are highly regarded by recruiters for positions in IT consulting, business process analysis, and IT auditing in enterprise systems environments.

Going Forward

As we move forward with our efforts to integrate SAP R/3 exercises in our classes, the SAP Users' Group is looking to both deepen its own use of the system and broaden the extent of participation by faculty at the College. Our guiding principle in requesting additional resources is the recognition that these resources must show a direct link to curriculum development. There are two areas in which we intend to focus additional development efforts, controlling/profitability analysis and reporting.

Additional development efforts in the controlling/profitability analysis (CO/PA) area will initially be focused in a new course on Performance Management and Evaluation, which is the capstone for a major in Corporate Finance and Accounting. The course has a section on IT for managers and we are planning to include exercises to demonstrate some of the reporting capability of the system in the CO/PA area.

We have found it to be a more daunting task to effectively use R/3's reporting capabilities in a way that deepens students' understanding of the system. In particular, we plan to develop exercises that better simulate the way students will use an enterprise system in their professional careers, as a decision support technology, to enrich their experience with R/3, and deepen their understanding of how information technology shapes decision making.

An example drawn from Kaplan and Norton (1992, p. 75) illustrates the type of exercise we would like to develop. They make the point that an efficient information system is critical to helping managers solve business problems. They pinpoint the system's drill-down capability as helping managers discover the source of problems that show up in aggregate data. "If the aggregate measure for on-time delivery is poor, for example, executives with a good information system can quickly look behind the aggregate measure until they can identify late deliveries, day by day, by a particular plant to a particular customer." Given the capability of enterprise systems to accumulate information and to display it from many different perspectives (by plant, product line, geographic region, marketing region, etc.), this seems to be an appropriate focus of our attention. In this way we will have more fully achieved learning objectives in Zuboff's two faces of IT. We will have helped students understand how IT can automate AND informate.

Enterprise systems-based curriculum is an important component of Bentley College's goals to provide a level 3 educational experience for our students.

Our efforts to date have met with success as measured by student enthusiasm and recruiter interest. Our plans for extending R/3 integration across the curriculum will only improve the quality of the educational experience at the College.

Endnotes

[1]   Four years after its launch, the cohort-based MBA program currently incorporates SAP in the Business Processes and Finance classes.

[2]   Note that SAP course levels have no relationship to the Bentley College levels of IT integration.

[3]   In the past two years, SAP has been offering training workshops specifically for faculty. This has made the transition from learning to implementing much easier than it was under the old model of having corporate-centered training available.

References

Becerra-Fernandez, I., Murphy, K.E., & Simon, S.J. (2000, April). Integrating ERP in the business school curriculum. *Communications of the ACM, 43*(4), 39-41.

Davenport, T.H. (1998, July/August). Putting the enterprise into the enterprise system. *Harvard Business Review,* 121-131.

Hulik, K. (1998, April). Morone, Bentley president, foresees radical change overtaking MBA curricula. *MBA Newsletter.*

Kaplan, R.S., & Norton, D.P. (1992, January/February). The balanced scorecard – Measures that drive performance. *Harvard Business Review,* 71-79.

Zuboff, S. (1985). Automate/informate: The two faces of intelligent technology. *Organizational Dynamics, 14*(2), 5-18.

Section II

Impacts and Challenges of ERP/SAP Systems

Chapter IV

The Impact of Agile SAP on the Supply Chain

Sue Conger
University of Dallas, USA

Abstract

Enterprise Resource Planning (ERP) packages, such as SAP, present different competitive challenges to vendors and users. Vendor competitiveness demands an agile deployment process for ERP software while offering increased functionality. User competitiveness depends on obtaining optimal benefits from ERP while not sacrificing competitive agility. This research shows that as deployability of SAP software becomes more agile, using organizations experience increased business agility. In addition to agile ERP deployment, the importance of process understanding and targeted agility impacts are shown to influence user SAP outcomes.

Introduction

As technology advances and the rate of change accelerates, the typical organization has come to rely on Enterprise Resource Planning (ERP) as a tool for managing materials and information across functional silos. ERPs enable agile manufacturing operations, especially in the area of supply chain management. By making business processes and information visible, and therefore, capable of management, ERP provides a means for companies to improve their customer experience, time to market, order fulfillment, and, eventually, net income (Ross, 1999).

Several serious liabilities of ERP exist, however. ERP packages are not cheap and have long, idiosyncratic implementation cycles; business processes, once changed, become frozen in place, with business improvement either elusive or not seen until many months after complete organizational production has begun (Ross, 1999).

Most large business organizations now use one or more ERP software packages to integrate their supply chains and thus, improve their organization's agility. However, while the problems of ERP deployment have been discussed in many case studies, the concepts of agility as applied to ERP deployment have been ignored (cf. Biggs, 2001; Basu & Humar, 2002; Lee & Lee, 2000; McCormick & Kasper, 2002).

In this research, we sought to determine the impact on organizational agility provided by agile ERP software deployment. We apply agility concepts to SAP installations to demonstrate the applicability of agility theory to ERP implementation. We show that agile deployment has competitive benefits both for the software vendor and for the licensing business organization.

In the remainder of this report, software deployment and the extent of agility with which the software is deployed are discussed using a case study of an organization that deployed SAP's ERP system; then, we analyze survey results for several organizations. We develop the notion that the more self-aware the organization, the more their potential gain from deploying ERP software. We conclude with recommendations and trends for companies seeking to improve their business process operations through SAP software deployment, and recommendations and trends for SAP, Inc. to improve their product deployment agility and, thereby, improve their customers' agility.

Background

The Supply Chain

A manufacturing supply chain traditionally is comprised of sources of raw materials, manufacturing, inventory management, distribution to wholesalers, warehouses or retailers, and finally, consumers who purchase the product (see Figure 1).

Figure 1. Typical supply chain (adapted from Dove, 2001).

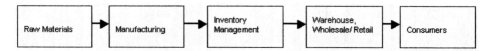

A supply chain can be loosely or tightly-coupled, and can accommodate any variety of networked relationships between manufacturers, logistics, service, internal, or external organizations. The participants in a supply chain require connectivity, the right information, in a useful format, and at the needed time, to inform decisions. Thus, an organization's supply chain is a network of organizations that must be able to assimilate change and have the ability to react to new requirements; ideally, the *supply network* is able to react as one (Hult et al., 2002; Lau & Hurley, 2001).

Agility

Agility is the term applied to an organization's ability to react to unanticipated market change, defining informed rapid transformation of organizational process and product (Goldman et al., 1995). Most work refers to agility as applying to supply chain activities, although it is not limited to them (cf. Dove, 2001; Hult et al., 2002; Lau & Hurley, 2001). Both manufacturing and service organizations' ability to change to take advantage of market changes directly affects their profitability (Power & Sohal, 2002; Weber, 2002).

Due to the pace at which business is conducted, the supply chain must be able to respond with agility. To be agile and able to respond to unanticipated change, the entities which comprise the agile supply chain must address four main agility characteristics: 1) *cooperate to enhance competitiveness*, 2) *enrich the customer*, 3) *master change and uncertainty,* and 4) *leverage the impact of people and information* (Goldman et al., 1995; Meade & Sarkis, 1999; Sarkis, 2001; van Hoek et al., 2001). In this chapter we focus on these agility principles for determining the impacts of deploying ERP software systems.

- *Cooperating to enhance competitiveness* requires that all partners work toward a common goal with clearly delineated processes and individuals identified to ensure information accuracy, responsibility, and to support decisions based upon the shared data. All parties involved need to have a stake in the collaboration's outcome to ensure long-term commitment and an understanding of what is expected of them and others in the relationship (Forger, 2001). The outcome is an ability to bring products to market faster and more cost effectively. The optimal strategy for doing this is using existing resources regardless of location and ownership.

- *Customer enrichment* occurs through the provision of solutions to customer problems in addition to the provision of products. Enrichment may be through, for instance, customization of a Web experience or increased visibility into a supplier's own supply chain and manufacturing process.

- *Mastering change and uncertainty* is the ability to rapidly reconfigure human and physical resources. An agile organization can support multiple, concurrent organizational configurations keyed to the requirements of different market opportunities, and can change process or product as needed.

- *Leveraging of people and information* implies longevity of employment, empowerment of ever more-highly skilled workers, and the use of technology to provide information support to all aspects of the business. Part of the ability to manage information is the ability to manage employee knowledge, leveraging it to provide a basis for swift, informed change management. Some examples of large-scale change initiatives, such as Baldrige Award improvements, TQM, and 6-Sigma, enhance organizational business execution and increase agility of change management efforts in the implementing organization. Small-scale change initiatives are equally valuable, for example, for increasing information access to expand a person's job.

As manufacturing companies move toward e-business, they seek to reduce inventory and logistics costs at the same time that the technology to manage agile e-relationships is still maturing (Biggs, 2001; Nellore & Motawani, 1999; Schwartz, 2001). Methods of cost reduction frequently require software applications to better manage information and business processes. The software must be as agile as the processes it supports.

Software development agility is a concept that has been applied recently to a further streamlining of development practices from rapid application development (RAD) and traditional project life cycle activities to include activities that directly lead to completion of some software or application need (Radding, 2002). This research extends the concept of software agility to software deployment.

Deployment

Deployment is the process of software implementation that includes activities relating to the release, installation, integration, adaptation, and activation of an initial product release (adapted from Hall et al., 1997) (see Figure 2). The ease or difficulty with which software is deployed has direct effects on its initial selection, the extent to which software can be integrated with existing legacy

Figure 2. Initial software deployment life cycle process (adapted from Hall et al., 1997).

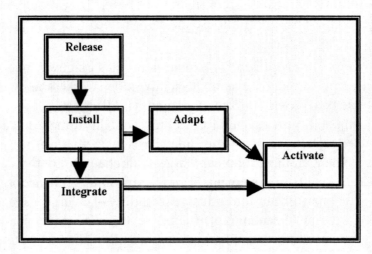

applications, the time from which software is selected until it is fully operational, and the extent of customization to the software, company structure, and business processes (Bermudez, 2002; Biggs, 2001; Durand & Barboun, 2002; Ross, 1999).

Figure 2 depicts the relationships between the five basic stages of software deployment, which are defined below.

- **Release.** With respect to software deployment, a *release* is a software package that includes new and/or upgraded software, platform requirements, instructions on customization and installation, and a description of changed functionality. From the release description and organizational needs analysis, customer organizations decide whether or not to invest in the change (Lee & Lee, 2000).

- **Install.** *Installation* is the establishment of operating platforms and connectivity, physical set up of software, and establishment of the initial settings for operation (Singh et al., 2002).

- **Adapt.** *Adaptation* is the customizing or altering of software, business process structure, or organization structure to fit the needs of the business environment (Hall et al., 1997). In some ERP implementations, organizations opt for little software customizing and, instead, change their structure to fit the software (Higgens, 2001; Price-White, 2001). In others, extensive software customizing is done to fit the organization (Brown, 2001; Higgins, 2001). ERP implementations provide an opportunity to optimize the business process and organization structure while customizing the ERP software to fit the optimized process (Ross, 1999).

- **Integrate.** In application development, *integration* is the connecting of one software or its transactions to another software, for instance, to legacy applications or data mining software packages (Hall et al., 1997). For example, an order developed in a browser-based Internet transaction may flow through an XML application to be processed and tracked through SAP. Integration can be to front-end, middle, or back-end software relative to the ERP package.

- **Activate.** *Activation* includes training, conversion, and phasing the product into production (Hall et al., 1997). For early SAP versions, the implementation process was the responsibility of the customer. Customers tended to use third party consultants and the consultant companies' implementation processes that may or may not have fit their organizations.

Activation of software is the most difficult activity because organizational change is usually a concomitant activity.

ERP software is viewed as difficult to deploy, a fact that has hampered its selection and implementation by all but the largest organizations (Meehan, 2001). Return on ERP investment is a long, uncertain process (Ross, 1999).

In the last five years, research by large vendors has led to many initiatives to provide "plug-and-play" software deployment (e.g., Microsoft, 1997; van Hoff et al., 1997). Hands-off deployment for PCs and other computer products has been a goal for several years, while SAP and other ERP vendors have worked both to improve their product deployment and to improve their customers' ability to react to market change through the use of their software (Johnson, 1999; Singh et al., 2002; Songini, 2002).

For instance, to address user concerns, MySAP, named to imply infinite customizability, and SAP Business One are expected to ease SAP deployment and are expected to be easier to use, cheaper to operate, and less complex to understand (Songini, 2002). Furthermore, SAP, in the continuing quest for agility, continues to work with business partners to deliver custom solutions.

The next section describes a case study conducted with the Celanese Corporation, a large SAP user, to determine the extent to which agile deployment characteristics are identifiable, and how they relate to customer deployment of the software.

Case Study

Celanese Background

Celanese, A.G., exemplifies deployment issues. In 1993, the chairman of Hoechst, A.G., a German multi-national corporation, announced that his company would deploy SAP's ERP software throughout the organization.

Part of the motivation for Hoechst's implementation of SAP was the looming Y2K problem and, at least in the U.S., its accompanying software tax consequences (Bockstedt, 2002). U.S. tax laws equate software maintenance to plant and equipment maintenance and, as such, it is a business expense in the year of the work. Conversely, purchased software is similar to building a new building and may be capitalized and written off over a period of the software's projected useful life, sometimes as much as 20 years. Facing multi-million dollar expenditures for Y2K fixes, and knowing that every problem might not be identifiable in advance, Hoechst, like hundreds of other large corporations, opted for enterprise resource planning (ERP) software with the hope that they could more efficiently manage their supply chain at the same time they finessed their Y2K problems, by simply replacing the software causing the problem, all with favorable tax consequences.

To soften the edict and also hopefully alleviate some ERP implementation problems, each Hoechst division was allowed to determine its own SAP fate by deciding its own needs for customization. By the time SAP was in full global production, there were 12 versions of SAP within Celanese, with dozens of versions in all of Hoechst.

Celanese, originally a U.S. corporation purchased by Hoechst in 1987, was divested as a German-run, Celanese, A.G., in 1999 (Aventis, 2002). Celanese currently is a $5 billion company with approximately 12,000 employees and three main product lines: chemicals, acetates, and polymers (see Figure 3, Celanese, 2002).

In 2002, Celanese had 12 active production versions of SAP throughout its organization (Bockstedt, 2002). Mr. Russell Bockstedt, Chief Information Architect, discussed the history of SAP in Celanese and the issues for the current initiatives. Unless otherwise cited, the Celanese information is from that discussion.

Figure 3. Celanese product mix.

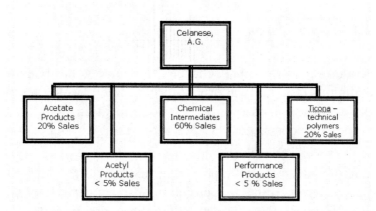

In 1993, when the first projects were initiated, SAP was at SAP Release 2.2. For the sites implementing that version, including Dallas, TX; Summit, NJ; Frankfurt, KY; Frankfurt, Germany; Tokyo, Japan, and others, customization varied from almost nothing (Kentucky) to a significant extent (Dallas) to add functionality Celanese needed. Over the last nine years, Celanese has installed five software upgrades to enhance the initial SAP versions. These, along with the current effort are the focus of this research.

Currently, Celanese has embarked on a new "1-SAP" project to integrate the 12 disparate SAPs into a single version of SAP (Berinto, 2003). The steering committee for the project is comprised of a corporate plant manager, CIO, chief architect/integration manager (Bockstedt), and a project director. The plant manager has overall budget and management responsibility for the project, the planner acts as the project office, and Bockstedt is charged with all implementation activities. The organizational strategy is to review shared services throughout the organization as the 1-SAP project begins production to determine how consolidation may provide more efficient and effective operation in each area. 1-SAP is scheduled to phase into production beginning in early 2004.

In the next section, we briefly describe SAP's changes since 1995. The changes to SAP's software deployability and the resulting agility gains are discussed with Celanese's initial and on-going implementation experiences and the impacts of SAP's changes on Celanese. We demonstrate that as SAP became more agile in its deployability and functionality, Celanese's own agility was further enabled. That is, an organization that commits to ERP software that is agile – easily, continuously, and intelligently changed – enables its own continuous agility.

ERP and the Supply Chain

In this section, SAP and the major changes it has undergone in Celanese since 1995 are summarized. SAP was originally conceived to integrate all departments and functions across a company with application modules that maintained internal data consistency and appeared as a single system serving varied organizational needs (Scheer, 1994).

The benefits of SAP are touted as providing business process and information visibility across an enterprise, thus providing an integrated single "view" of an organization (Scheer, 1994). The underlying structures were designed originally to support manufacturing operations. Subsequent releases included support for accounting, reporting, analysis, and planning.

Because initial SAP (c. 1994-1997) was infinitely flexible but extremely complex in its installation process (10,000+ switch settings), once installed it became inflexible without significant additional custom application development (Brown, 2001). Today ERP, in general, and SAP in particular, includes automated, integrated support for human resources, payroll, manufacturing, purchasing, and inventory (Koch, 2002). Each major release of SAP has simplified deployability in moving from switch settings to interactive template completion. Each release has also become more functionally flexible in terms of providing more options and simpler integration interfaces (SAP, 2003; Yankee Group, 2003). For example, mySAP.com Internet software suite allows an enterprise to integrate between selected "plug-and-play" software partners (i.e., with little or no required customization).

In short, for each aspect of software deployment, SAP has improved its methods, architecture, interfaces and/or software; in essence, SAP has become more agile.

SAP Agility and Celanese Agility

In this section, we describe the characteristics of agility and how they relate to both SAP and Celanese's implementation of SAP over the last seven years.

Release

The first Celanese decision to deploy SAP was by edict, motivated by Y2K issues and a desire to improve the organization. Subsequent changes and upgrades were done less because the release descriptions were attractive, than because a business need forced the upgrade (i.e., client "pull" rather than vendor "push"). In general, the SAP environment has been relatively unchanged and has proven to be a stable software product for about four years (1999-2003). Some changes did occur; for instance, the financial aspects of the software were upgraded to accommodate the change to Euro currency. For the acetate business, a move to SAP 4.6c was done because specific functionality was desired. In all other cases, the only reason for changing was an imminent withdrawal of support for the version currently in production.

SAP provided tools that maintained its competitiveness by offering new features such as Euro conversion (see Figure 4, 1.1). By remaining competitive,

SAP enabled Celanese customer enrichment (see Figure 4, 1.1a). In turn, the features in SAP 4.6c motivated a Celanese upgrade, thus enriching the customer by providing desired functionality (see Figure 4, 1.2). SAP product stability supported Celanese's capability to leverage its information assets while minimizing the on-going cost of that information (see Figure 4, 1.2a).

Install

In 1993, SAP customizing efforts were programmed in ABAP, the SAP-proprietary language. Integration with legacy applications was clumsy. In the current version of SAP, customizing uses Java and JavaScript. The thousands of switch settings that characterized early SAP have been replaced with programmed templates that hide the complexity of the underlying decision tree that supports six levels of detail. For each level, the client organization enters answers to questions that are increasingly detailed and moves from the organization description, to logical business rules, to physical requirements. If more than six levels of detail are required, further customizing of the software is possible.

Celanese has taken advantage of this greater simplicity and has been forced to have a deeper understanding of its business processes to correctly configure the software to fit each division's needs. This deeper understanding has evolved from the development of staff skills and knowledge. The initial implementation that was on-going from 1993 through 1996 was managed using a life cycle and conversion plan provided by the consultants who were brought in as experts in SAP to lead the implementation teams, install the switch settings of SAP, and perform custom programming. As with many consulting engagements, many of the consultants were true SAP experts, but few had the domain expertise necessary to customize the complexities of Celanese's core chemicals, fibers and engineering resins businesses. This lack of domain knowledge partially explains the extended installation phase.

Celanese recognized, by the 1996 implementation, that they needed to develop and maintain their own in-house SAP experts, develop their own installation process, and also keep in-house the domain expertise that allowed them to customize SAP.

While the people involved in the initial SAP implementations have all moved up the corporate ladder, many are still involved in on-going implementations and upgrades, and others have become the "users" for whom the changes are being made. Thus, Celanese has been able to leverage its staff knowledge, by continuously building their technical, product and domain skills. The company has smoother, faster implementations today than the initial implementations even though many are as organizationally complex and cover as much of the business. The on-going SAP upgrades use mostly in-house resources with few extra staff supplied by contractors; none of the teams are led by outside consultants.

The change to templates increases SAP agility in enhancing its competitiveness by making its product easier to install and set up than some of its competitors (Figure 4, 2.1). From Celanese's perspective, the change to templates has increased its leverage of people and information since they have continued to use a core staff of people who have worked on every SAP implementation (see Figure 4, 2.1a). Further, by hiding the complexity of the switch settings in the software, SAP increased Celanese's ability to master the change and uncertainty relating to product installation (see Figure 4, 2.1b). By faster, easier implementation, Celanese experienced enhanced competitiveness by allowing the company to focus on its core businesses rather than software implementation (see Figure 4, 2.1c).

Adapt

Celanese has done all variations of adaptation over the last seven years. While the extent of customization varied greatly by location, with little in the R&D plant in Kentucky, and substantive customization in the Ticona corporate office in Dallas. Several projects begun in 1993 were not actually phased into production until October 1996. For these systems, all hardware was new, allowing the company to move away from IBM mainframes to more generic client-server architectures with more generic equipment and software. Hardware leases have expired every third year, giving Celanese an opportunity to upgrade at less expense than purchase of hardware would have allowed. Bockstedt says this "technology refresh" cycle has become a recurring part of the IT organization plan and budgets.

Celanese customization of SAP software over the last seven years related to software immaturity. For instance, Celanese produces "Letters of Certification" for its products that certify engineered properties of a product, for instance, tensile strength. The SAP 2.2 version of certification letters did not accommodate the degree of complexity necessary for Celanese's letters of certification. In SAP 2.2 and other early versions of SAP, software for letters of certification was highly customized by Celanese.

According to Bockstedt, many of the customized functions were embodied in new releases of the software so that de-customizing was necessary when upgrading was done. For instance, the letters of certification function in the current software release does have all the functionality necessary for Celanese. Therefore, the need to customize this function has disappeared with time.

Contrary to much literature about enterprise resource planning implementations at the time (Brown, 2001), Celanese reorganizations were planned as needed to streamline a business process and were more coincident to SAP than they were dictated by it. For instance, North American Ticona reorganized at the same time the first SAP was installed; however, the region also experienced significant customizing of the software. So, the reorganization was to streamline the business processes along with the streamlined, customized software supporting those processes. Conversely, the European groups, and North American Chemicals group installed SAP, and then alternated enhancing the organization and the software over time.

Currently, Celanese is working on a joint development project with SAP to develop a transportation planning solution for North American Ticona. The plan is to eventually migrate the software to other Celanese sites. Because the solution is customized, no reorganizations are planned.

The original SAP implementation was increasingly less agile as the extent of customization increased. The Letters of Certification example (and the change to Euros cited above) demonstrates one instance of SAP's becoming more adaptable to their customers' needs to enrich their customers (see Figure 4, 3.1). Celanese, in turn, received enhanced competitiveness from SAP's provision of previously proprietary software. By providing generic, configurable Letter of Certification software, the Celanese fear of upgrade and customizing cost decreased and their consideration of upgrades shifted from externality-driven (e.g., SAP removal of software support) to business need-driven (see Figure 4, 3.1a).

The joint venture increases the agility of both parties to the venture. SAP increases its customer enrichment (see Figure 4, 3.2), leverages its customers' people and information expertise (see Figure 4, 3.3), and in the bargain enhances its own competitiveness (see Figure 4, 3.4). Celanese enhances its competitiveness in developing a "custom" solution (3.4a) and leverages its and SAP's people and information expertise (see Figure 4, 3.3a). Further, Celanese has mastered the uncertainty of this change by developing it for themselves (see Figure 4, 3.1a).

Integrate

ERP software exemplifies tactical software that was deployed with the expectation of providing flexibility and agility across organizational, functional silos. The ability to integrate information across functions and to raise the visibility of business processes throughout an organization are valued as necessary to maintaining competitiveness. However, early ERP, because of installation complexities and long lead time to production, reified business processes in its software at the same time that it raised their visibility. Thus ERPs in the late 1990s stifled the very creativity and agility for which their using organization strived (Brown, 2001).

Celanese offers some examples of this hope and reification. One hope in the original implementation was to develop a service called "One-call Commit," which allowed a customer, whether via telephone or Internet, to place an order, verify availability of inventory, and obtain a committed shipping date in a single contact. SAP R/2, the original software installed, checked only a single "primary" manufacturing plant's inventory. In addition to wanting other plants' inventories checked, Celanese desired searches of work-in-process and other inventory classifications as well. Therefore, the multi-plant, multi-source capability was customized for the 1996 implementation and it has not changed substantially since then. Thus, Celanese's hope to significantly improve customer service occurred at the expense of flexibility in what became a fixed process. The company did achieve 90% 1-Call Commit success. In this instance, Celanese's ability to act swiftly with informed intelligent business change was a goal which partially eluded them with its first ERP implementation.

The new version of SAP being installed has few of the limitations of the original software in checking product sources and all of the customized programming for 1-Call Commit is being dismantled and replaced as part of the upgrade. Thus, SAP's sensitivity to its own original limitations and removal of those limitations enhanced its competitiveness (see Figure 4, 4.1). Further, by removing those limitations, SAP enriches its customers' experience (see Figure 4, 4.2) and leverages its customers' and its own people and information by acting on requests for changes through its user groups (American SAP User Group (ASUG), Australian SAP User Group (AUSUG), SAPphire, etc.) (see Figure 4, 4.3). From the customer perspective, Celanese experiences enhanced competitiveness any time a limitation to change is removed from a monolithic product it uses, such as SAP. By providing the flexibility to do the product sourcing as needed by the company, Celanese's competitiveness is increased (see Figure 4, 4.1a); Celanese's ability to master uncertainty in terms of new requirements in their industries is enhanced because they are no longer tied to a single method of, in this case, product sourcing (see Figure 4, 4.2a).

Activate

The first implementations of SAP for North America Ticona went into production in 1996, as advised by the consulting partners who managed the implementation and recommended by SAP to gain the most favorable outcomes. Celanese used a "big bang" cut-over which proved to be a painful experience with numerous bugs and fixes required for the first six months of production. But, the company committed to making SAP successful and eventually it was.

Current versions of SAP are more modular and, therefore, deployable as either stand-alone processes or as processes integrating single aspects of a supply chain or business. SAP's architectural revisions have made it more amenable to partial, controlled, "small bang" implementations as a result of its re-architected software.

Since that first implementation, Celanese has phased implementations based on region, function, or product; planning and execution of phased implementations has become easier as SAP has evolved. Several examples of this include functional, regional order processing for Ticona North America that did not change manufacturing, finance or general ledger; regional product processing for Acetel™ only for Ticona Europe; and two staged-functional product implementations for procurement, followed by finance and plant management for the Acetate™ business.

SAPs modularity increased its competitiveness (5.1) and enriched its customers (see Figure 4, 5.2) by making it more easily deployed by providing stand-alone components and single-component update capabilities. In addition, by increasing the marketability of its products as stand-alone components, the effect is to decrease SAP's uncertainty about package attractiveness by allowing its marketing teams to target individual components (see Figure 4, 5.3). The ability to stage implementations based on its business needs has contributed to Celanese's ability to react to changes in its business more quickly than if an entire SAP implementation were required (see Figure 4, 5.2a). Thus, SAP's support of multiple methods of product conversion improves Celanese's competitiveness and change management agility.

Summary of SAP Agility Effects on Celanese Agility

The evolution of ERP at Celanese shows that as SAP has become more agile and functional, Celanese's agility has also improved. As Celanese installs ever more agile SAP, its ability to manage and compete effectively is also enhanced. Figure 4 summarizes the discussion and identifies the deployment agility

Figure 4. Summary of SAP agility impacts by deployment stage.

```
1.0 Release
1.1 SAP Euro Conversion Feature
    1.1a  Celanese enriches customer by providing invisible Euro conversion

1.2 SAP added functionality
    1.2a  Celanese leverages information assets while minimizing cost

2.0 Install
2.1 SAP uses installation templates
    2.1a  Celanese develops own in-house SAP support people
    2.1b  Celanese installs product faster and more custom
    2.1c  Celanese focuses on core business rather than software implementation

3.0 Adapt
3.1 SAP develops customizable "letters of certification"
    3.1a Celanese can upgrade at lower cost

3.2  SAP joint ventures enrich customer
    3.2a  Celanese leverages its staff's domain knowledge in the joint venture

3.3  SAP leverages its technical expertise
    3.3a Celanese leverages its staff's domain knowledge in the joint venture

3.4  SAP enhances its competitiveness with this new functionality
    3.4a  Celanese enhances its competitiveness through the custom solution

4.0 Integrate
4.1 SAP removes limitations on checking product sources and creates enhancement
    4.1a  Celanese now has product sourcing flexibility

4.2  SAP removes product limitations
    4.2a  Celanese increases its competitiveness by becoming more agile

4.3  SAP leverages its knowledge through user group interactions

5.0 Activate
5.1 SAP modularity increases its competitiveness

5.2  SAP modularity enriches its customers
    5.2a Celanese competitiveness is enhanced through ability to do selective modular
    upgrades

5.3 SAP uncertainty about product attractiveness decreases
```

Figure 5. Agile deployment of SAP and its benefits to Celanese system.

Agile Dimension	SAP					Celanese				
	Release	Install	Adapt	Integrate	Activate	Release	Install	Adapt	Integrate	Activate
Enhance Competitiveness	1.1	2.1	3.1, 3.4	4.1	5.1		2.1c	3.1a, 3.4a	4.1a, 4.2a	5.1a
Enrich Customer	1.2		3.1, 3.2	4.1, 4.2	5.2	1.1a				5.2a
Master Change and Uncertainty					5.3		2.1b	3.3a	4.1a	
Leverage Impact of People and Information			3.3	4.3		1.2a	2.1a	3.2a 3.3a		

improvements in SAP and the impact on Celanese and their business agility. Whether the effect is additive or multiplicative is unknown.

Figure 4 summarizes Deployment phases — Release, Install, Adapt, Integrate, and Activate — and the dimensions of agility impacted by the changes made by both SAP and Celanese in these phases.

Figure 5 shows that for many of the SAP increases in agile software deployment and increased functionality there are one or more increases in the business agility of Celanese. Celanese appears to have taken significant advantage of SAP's capabilities over the last six years given the constraints of the early software. If accurate for this particular organization type (MNC), the multiple secondary agility increases in Celanese highlight the notion that SAP (and all ERP vendors) should concentrate upgrades and changes in such a way that it maximizes not only their own agility but also those of its customers.

Organizational and Vendor Challenges

Three main challenges present themselves for ERP user organizations' consideration. First, ERP software is viewed as difficult to deploy, a fact that has hampered its selection and implementation by all but the largest organizations

(Ross, 1999). The problem to be solved by all ERP vendors is how to provide the diversity of services offered, while at the same time simplifying their software's deployment.

Second, not every SAP increase in agility leads to a specific Celanese agility benefit. For SAP, this finding poses a challenge to identify those changes that most facilitate and simplify customer deployment and use of their software, thereby enhancing the client organization's agility, and to prioritize those changes for early implementation in their software.

Last, Celanese did not have a good understanding of its business processes in its initial SAP implementation. They realized that their success with ERP relied in part on their ability to develop an intimate understanding of their business processes and how they could be leveraged to minimize SAP customization. Over time, Celanese documented their business processes, thus making them capable of management and integration in the 1-SAP project. This growing maturity of Celanese in its understanding of its business processes is a challenge for other companies that seek to deploy ERP software. Over the next decade, business process documentation and specific management will be one of the key problems facing organizational executives.

Survey

Survey Method

Based on the findings of the Celanese case study, a questionnaire survey was conducted to determine the relationship between ERP deployment and agility outcomes (Conger & Meade, 2002; a copy of the survey can be obtained by writing the author). Telephone and e-mail surveys were conducted between September 2002 through December 2002, with a total of 12 surveys relating specifically to SAP implementations. The number of completed surveys lacks sufficient power to conduct adequate statistical analysis; therefore, non-statistical analysis is conducted.

Results

The results for the three lowest and three highest organizations are shown as spider diagrams with a low-rated organization contrasted with a high-rated organization in Figures 6 through 8. The upper left quadrant of the spider diagrams depicts results for the implementation/deployment of the ERP software in terms of perceived quality of installation, adaptation, integration, and activation for selecting, planning, and actually implementing the ERP software. The right half of the diagram illustrates the perceived agility outcomes for leveraging people, enhancing customer experience, managing change, and increasing competitiveness of the organization. The lower left quadrant of the

Figure 6. SAP organizations A and B.

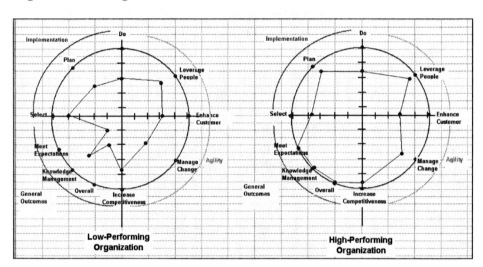

Figure 7. SAP organizations C and D.

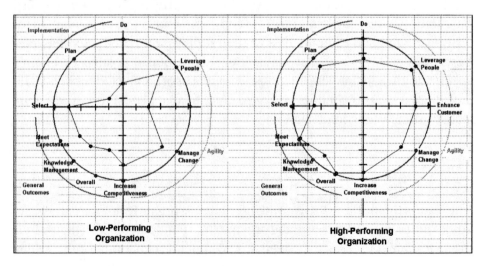

Figure 8. SAP organizations E and F.

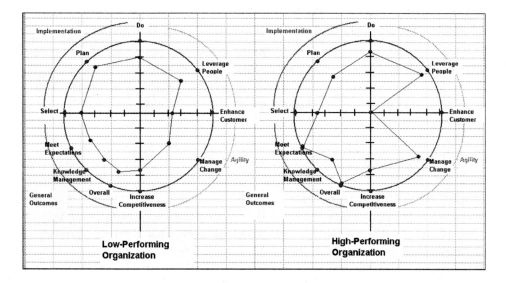

diagrams depicts the general outcomes, including how well the implementation met management expectations, increased knowledge management, and overall executive satisfaction with the ERP project results.

First, the low-rated organizations are discussed (Figures 6-8, left diagrams). Results of two of the three low-rated organizations (Figures 6 and 7) show that the lower the implementation/deployment ratings, the lower the agility outcomes. The results are inconclusive for the low-rated organization in Figure 8, which appears to have highly perceived implementation ratings coupled with poor agility outcomes.

For the high-performing organizations (right diagrams of each set), the results are also mixed. The high-performing organizations in Figures 6 and 7 exhibit expected results: the highly perceived implementation/deployment activities are coupled with highly perceived increases in agility outcomes. The high-performing organization in Figure 8 is inconsistent with a zero rating for the *Enhance Customer* outcome. The interviewee stated that no customer outcomes were planned; therefore it was not changed.

Some analysis of the anomalous organization results is required. Further discussion with the organizations uncovered different priorities for the low-rated organization in Figure 8 to *reduce headcount*. Thus, their *leverage people* resulted from having a reduced staff performing more work, coupled with the high-performing organization in Figure 8 not having *customer enhancement* as a priority. These results indicate that organizational priorities, at least to some extent, drive the expected ERP-deployment outcomes.

The results from the spider diagram analysis, coupled with interviewee comments, point to two conclusions: First, that poor ERP planning and deployment result in poor agility outcomes and second, that good planning and deployment result in positive agility outcomes.

Organizational and Vendor Challenges

Several issues result from the surveys: Agile deployment appears to be a measurable, important issue; the need for process understanding is key to ERP deployment success; and priorities are important to determining ERP deployment outcomes.

Agile deployment is an issue that will become a defining factor between ERP vendors who survive in that field and those who will not. At this writing, i2, which is known for its difficult deployment, is having corporate problems and several vendors have left the ERP business. In addition, companies that opt for self-deployment of new ERP software are most likely going to have significant deployment problems.

No software by itself can provide a competitive advantage; process management along with quality work is also necessary. Understanding by client organizations of their business processes will come to be understood as a key factor in determining success of ERP deployment.

Literature on problem analysis and resolution always admonishes to ensure that the *right* problem is being solved. ERP deployment demonstrates similar needs in that organizational priorities tend to drive the expected outcomes. Research on ERP deployment must attend to this organizational reality by attending to priorities and their impact on the outcomes. Organizations should specifically define their goals with *before* and *after* measures of goal achievement.

Solutions/Recommendations

ERP software is becoming commoditized as vendor offerings begin to resemble each other in the functions supported. Agile product deployment should become a priority of ERP vendors since it will be increasingly important in the ERP selection decisions of many companies (Yankee Group, 2003).

Business process understanding is still unknown in most business organizations. As managers become more aware that business process understanding is crucial to becoming or maintaining an industry leadership position, organizations will spend significant monies to map their business processes, seeking to actively manage their activities.

Future Trends

Two trends appear to underlie SAP and agility discussion. The trends relate to SAP software agility and client organizations agility needs. These are discussed below.

SAP will continue to become more functional. As SAP better understands the impact of their software's deployment and functional agility on their client organizations, they will begin to specifically identify agility impacts as targets for development.

Large organizations seeking to optimize their commitments to SAP will identify strategic areas for development partnerships with SAP to maximize their strategic goal attainment. As organizations better understand their agility needs, they will press SAP to develop software that meets those needs.

Conclusion

Manufacturing organizations use Enterprise Resource Planning (ERP) software, such as SAP, to make visible and manage their supply chains. ERP software, however, has a long payback period, costs millions to install across a supply chain, and requires *some* organizational change. The challenge to ERP vendors has been to determine how to simplify and smooth both initial and upgrade software installations.

Agility is the ability of an organization to react to unanticipated market change and to define informed rapid transformation of one or both of the organizational process and product. Deployment encompasses all activities required of the using organization to install, customize, integrate, and place into production purchased software. This research reported on the results of a case study at Celanese Corporation to identify the characteristics of agile software deployment in an SAP user organization and its impact of the organization. In addition, a subsequent survey evaluated the impact of increased agile deployment on SAP client organizations.

The results of these analyses showed that as SAP becomes more functional and more agile to deploy, ripple effects are seen in the agility of the SAP client organizations. In addition, while agile deployment appears important, the survey results show that prior planning and knowledge of business processes and specific goal definition appear crucial to gaining the desired organizational agility outcomes. Businesses that seek to maximize their return on their SAP investment should perform a business process analysis before they do any ERP implementation. Then, they should specifically analyze the tradeoffs on organization change versus software customization to inform the planning process. Organizations that have a successful deployment process, with excellent understanding of their business processes and attendant changes, appear best able to gain the agility results they sought from the installation of the software.

Endnote

*   Each instance of an agile characteristic is identified. These are summarized in Figures 4 and 5.

References

Aventis. (2002). Company history. Retrieved July 20, 2002, from http://www.aventis.com/main/page.asp?pageid=63322149025 14456564 &lang=en.

Basu, A., & Humar, A. (2002). Research commentary: Workflow management issues in e-business. *Information Systems Research, 13*(1), 1-14.

Berinto, S. (2003, January 15). A day in the life of Celanese's big ERP rollup. *CIO Magazine*. http://www.cio.com/archive/011503/erp_content.html.

Bermudez, J. (2002, March 1). Supply chain management: More than just technology. *Supply Chain Management Review.*

Biggs, M. (2001, January 29). The technologies that 2000 forgot. *InfoWorld,* 74.

Bockstedt, R. Chief Architect of Celanese Corporation. (2002, July 15). Personal interview.

Brown, J. (2001, February 9). Sobeys fires SAP over ERP debacle. *Computing Canada, 27*(3), 1-3.

Celanese. (2002). Company history. Retrieved July 20, 2002, from http:www.celanese.com.

Conger, S.,& Meade, L.M. (2002). Agile software deployment: A case study of ERP. Working paper, University of Dallas, Graduate School of Management, Irving, TX. Under review.

Dove, R. (2001). *Response ability: The language, structure, and culture of the agile enterprise.* NY: John Wiley and Sons.

Durand, B., & Barboun, T. (2002, May). *Aligning IT and business strategy.* Presentation to Annual SAP Saphire Users Group.

Forger, G. (2001, November/December). The problem with collaboration. *Supply Chain Management Review.* http://www.manufacturing.net.

Goldman, S.L., Nagel, R.N., & Preiss, K. (1995). *Agile competitors and virtual organizations.* New York: Van Nostrand.

Hall, R.S., Heimbigner, D., & Wolf, A.L. (1997, December 18). *Software deployment languages and schema.* University of Colorado Technical Report # CU-SERL-203-97.

Higgens, K. (2001, October 29). Purina Mills gets its network in shape for SAP. *Network Computing, 12*(22), 73-76.

Hult, G.T., Ketchen, D., Jr., & Nichols, E., Jr. (2002). An examination of cultural competitiveness and order fulfillment cycle time within supply chains. *Academy of Management Journal, 45*(3), 577-586.

Johnson, A.H. (1999, October 18). Hands-off PC deployment tools. *Computerworld.* Retrieved July 22, 2002, from www.computerworld. com/printthis/1999/0,4814,42789,00.html.

Koch, C. (2002, June 19). The ABC's of ERP. *CIO,* 11.

Lau, R.S.M. & Hurley, N.M. (2001, September). Creating supply chains for competitive advantage. *South Dakota Business Review.*

Lee, Z., & Lee, J. (2000). An ERP implementation case study from a knowledge transfer perspective. *Journal of Information Technology, 15,* 281-288.

McCormack, K., & Kasper, K. (2002). The extended supply chain: A statistical study. *Benchmarking, 9*(2), 133-145.

Meade, L., & Sarkis, J. (1999). Analyzing organizational project alternatives for the agile manufacturing process: An analytical network approach. *International Journal of Production Research, 37* (2), 241-261.

Meehan, M. (2001, December 17). Beyond paper clips. *Computerworld.* Retrieved July 22, 2002, from www.computerworld. com/printthis/2001/ 0,4814,66623,00.html.

Microsoft Corp. (1997). "The 'zero administration' initiative for Microsoft Windows. Retrieved March 1997, from http://msdn.microsoft.com/ library/default.asp?url=/library/en-us/dnentdevgen/html/msdn_ zerowin.asp.

Nellore, R., & Motwani, J. (1999). Procurement commodity structures: Issues, lessons and contributions. *European Journal of Purchasing and Supply Management, 5,*(3-4).

Power, D.J., & Sohal, A.S. (2002). Implementation and usage of electronic commerce in managing the supply chain: A comparative study of 10 Australian companies. *Benchmarking, 9*(2), 190-208.

Price-White, C. (2001, October). They're top of the pops. *Frontline Solutions Europe, 10*(8), 64-67.

Radding, A. (2002, February 4). Extremely agile programming. *Computerworld.* Retrieved July 22, 2002, from http://www.computer world.com/softwaretopics/software/appdev/story/0,10801,67950, 00.html.

Rombel, A. (2002, May). ERP rises from the scrap pile. *Global Finance, 16*(5), 58-60.

Ross, J. (1999, November 1). The ERP path to integration: Surviving vs. thriving. *EAI Journal.* Retrieved July 17, 2002, from http://www.eaijournal. com/ArticlePrint.asp?ArticleID=158.

SAP. (2003). http://www.sap.com.

Sarkis, J. (2001). Benchmarking for agility.; *Benchmarking: An International Journal, 8*(2), 88-107.

Scheer, A.-W. (1994). *Business process engineering: Reference models for industrial enterprises* (2nd ed.). Berlin: Springer-Verlag.

Schwartz, E. (2001, February 5). Skipping steps. *InfoWorld, 23* (6), 1, 29.

Singh, M.K., Nunn, D., & Zia, K. (2002, August). *Improving the software deployment process: Approaches and challenges.* Final Project for Mgmt 8390- IT Capstone, University of Dallas Graduate School of Management.

Songini, M.L. (2002, June 10). SAP to simplify, streamline apps. *Computerworld.* Retrieved July 22, 2002, from http://www.computer world.com/softwaretopics/crm/story/0,10801,71892,00.html.

Van Hoek, R., Harrison, A., & Christopher, M. (2001). Measuring agile capabilities in the supply chain. *International Journal of Operations and Production Management, 21*(½), 126-147.

Van Hoff, A., Partovi, H., & Thai, T. (1997, August 13). The Open Software Description Format (OSD). Submitted to W3C. http://www.w3.org/TR/NOTE-OSD.

Weber, M.M. (2002). *Measuring supply chain agility in the virtual organization.* Under review.

Yankee Group. (2003, February 7). SAP R/3 product description. Retrieved May 1, 2003, from http://www.yankeegroup.com/public/products/research_note.jsp?ID=9551.

Chapter V

B2E SAP Portals:
Employee Self-Service Case Study

Andrew Stein
Victoria University, Australia

Paul Hawking
Victoria University, Australia

David C. Wyld
Southeastern Louisiana University, USA

Abstract

The global ERP industry that blossomed in the 1990's automating back office operations has made moves to introduce a "second wave" of functionality in ERP systems. In 2002/3 there was an expanded focus on mysap.com, small to medium enterprises and the expansion into "second wave" products. Companies around the world are exploring various Internet business models to evaluate their business potential and risk implications and a number of companies have realised the relatively quick gains with low associated risks that can be achieved through the business-to-employee (B2E) model. Employee Self Service (ESS) is a solution based on this model that enables employee's access to the corporate human resource information system, and Australian companies are increasingly implementing this solution. This chapter presents the findings of a research project that looks at the changing nature of Human Resources (HR) in modern organisations and the development of an HR ESS portal in a major Australian organisation.

Introduction

Companies around the world are exploring various Internet business models, mostly B2B and B2C, to evaluate their potential and business implications. A number of Australian companies have realised the relatively quick gains with low associated risks that can be achieved through the business-to-employee (B2E) model. Employee Self Service (ESS) is a solution based on the B2E model that enables employees' access to the corporate human resource information system. The global ERP industry, including the market leader SAP, blossomed in the 1990s, automating back office operations has made moves to introduce a "second wave" of functionality in ERP systems. These products were basically enhancements to the ERP software and included Business Information Warehouse (BW), Knowledge Warehouse (KW), Strategic Enterprise Management (SEM), Customer Relationship Management (CRM), Employee Self-Service (ESS) and Advanced Planner and Optimisation (APO). Table 1 presents SAP's Asia-Pacific implementations of some of the second wave products presented with user segment and key market identified.

The change in demand for the second wave products is shown in the purchase patterns for 2001 and 2002 (Bennett, 2002). In Australasia in 2001, Supply Chain Management (SCM) accounted for 15% and CRM for 20% of SAP

Table 1. Second wave implementations by year (Bennett, 2001).

Software	Implementations	User Segment	Key Market
CRM	70	>50	AU/NZ
e-Procurement	56	>50	AU/JP/SG
BW	263	1-20	AU/JP
APO	73	1-20	AU/NZ
ESS	33	>20	AU
Workplace	122	>20	AU/Korea

sales revenue. In 2002 SCM accounted for 22% of revenue with CRM 21%, Portals 11% and Supplier Relationship Management (SRM) exchanges 11%.

There are several reasons for this diversification of ERP systems: integration of business processes, need for a common platform, better data visibility, lower operating costs, increased customer responsiveness and improved strategic decision making (Iggulden, 1999). This slowing in demand for core ERP systems has resulted in added functionality installed, like Employee Self Service (ESS), to prepare organisations for e-business. Many of Australia's larger companies and public sector organisations are implementing ESS functionality as an adjunct to their enterprise resource planning (ERP) systems. These types of systems are enterprise-wide and are adopted by companies in an attempt to integrate many of their human resource business process and provide better data visibility. They claim to incorporate "best business practice" and it is understandable the growth in companies implementing ESS solutions has been significant (Webster Buchanan Research, 2002). The return on investment of ESS applications has been substantial (Lehman, 2000), with ESS transforming labour intensive paper based HR forms to digital enabled forms, allowing a 50% reduction of transaction costs, 40% reduction in administrative staffing, 80% reduction in management HR duties and a 10-fold speed-up of HR processes (Workforce, 2001).

Approximately 320 of Australia's top companies have implemented SAP's ERP system (SAP R/3), and of these approximately 150 have implemented the HR module, with 33 implementing the ESS component. These companies include Toyota, Westpac, RMIT, National Australia Bank, Siemens, Telstra, and Linfox. In recent times there has been a plethora of research associated with the impact and implications of e-commerce. Much of this research has focused on the various business models such as business-to-business and business-to-consumer with the importance of developing customer and partner relationships being espoused. There has been little attention paid to the potential of business-to-employee (B2E) and the role that B2E systems can play in improving business-to-employee relationships. This chapter looks at the development of the human resources (HR) ESS portal and presents the findings of a case study of a leading Australian telecommunications company that has implemented a "second wave" ESS portal. A model based on work by Eckerson (1999) and Brosche (2002) depicting portal maturity is presented and analysis shows that the ESS portal can be categorised as first generation with an "Access Rich" focus. Planned developments for moving the portal to second generation with a content focus are presented.

From HRM to HRMIS to eHR

The function of human resource management has changed dramatically over time. It has evolved from an administrative function primarily responsible for payroll to a strategic role that can add value to an organisation. Companies have now realised the importance of this function and are investing resources into supporting Human Resource Information Systems (HRMIS). The evolution of HR to eHR has been accelerated by the convergence of several organisational forces. The internal process of HR is changing its role from support to a more strategic place in the organisation. The role has developed from being primarily administrative to support, and then to the role of a business partner. At the same time HR is a stable, reliable business process that has high recognition within the organisation and touches every employee. This high recognition gives HR a rapid acceptance when being given the "e" treatment. Another important force acting on HR is the "adding value" imperative. Organisations are involved in a "war on talent" (Link, 2001) and organisations see eHR as an important technological tool in winning the war. HR has seized this change in organisational focus and adopted the B2E model to further enhance the business partner role. Internet technology continues to shape the way that HR information is being delivered to employees.

There are three main delivery platforms – Customer Service Representative (CSR), Interactive Voice Response (IVR) and Web applications – however, the frequency of use is changing. Customer service usage (CSR) and interactive voice response (IVR) gain 20-30% of employee enquiries, with Web applications gaining 50% of employee enquiries (Anonymous, 2002). The customer service representative is still the dominant access method for complex transactions. Web access is replacing IVR as preferred self-service method in large organisations.

Many of the world's leading companies are using ERP systems to support their HR information needs. This is partly due to the realisation of the integrative role HR has in numerous business processes such as work scheduling, travel management, production planning and occupational health and safety (Curran & Kellar, 1998). The B2E model involves the provision of databases, knowledge management tools and employee related processes online to enable greater accessibility for employees (Deimler & Hansen, 2001). They believe that there are large savings to make from implementing B2E solutions.

Figure 1. The employee relationship management landscape (Hamerman, 2002).

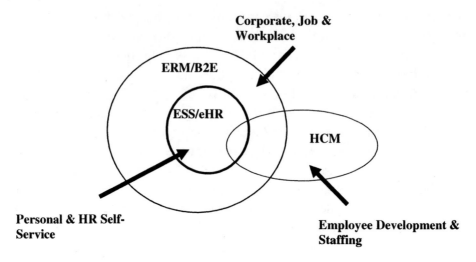

Business-to-Employee (B2E) Models

With advances in network and browser technology companies have been moving more and more of their corporate information resources to Web based applications, making them available to employees via the company intranet. Originally these applications only allowed employees to view and browse electronic versions of existing documents. Companies found that there was a saving in publication costs and an empowerment of employees through the increased availability of corporate procedures and knowledge to enable them to perform their day-to-day tasks. The increased familiarisation of employees in the use of browser technology and the maturing of this technology within companies has resulted in these applications evolving to incorporate transactional interactions. This has a number of benefits, including the move towards paperless transactions and the implied reduction in administrative overheads and the provision of better level of service to employees. Hamerman (2002) sets the Employee Relationship Management (ERM) landscape with corporate, personal and employee elements set out in a diagram (see Figure 1). Hamerman (2002) sees ERM suites as being platforms for information delivery, process execution and collaboration in the organisation. The advantages in empowering employees through an ERM suite include:

- Multiple value propositions,
- Consistent portal GUIs,
- All employee 24x7,
- Real-time dynamic information delivery, and
- Comprehensive collaborative work environment.

Employees can now access a range of information pertinent to themselves without having to rely on others. They can compare pay slips for a number of given periods and they can view their superannuation and leave entitlements and then apply for leave online. Human resources (HR) for many companies are evolving from the traditional payroll processing function to a more strategic direction of human capital management (Malis, 2002). As HR has evolved, the level of associated administrative duties has increased proportionally, with some research estimating that as much as 70% of HR personnel time is spent on administrative duties (Barron, 2002). This has been estimated to represent a cost of up to $US1700 per employee per year (Khirallah, 2000). It has been estimated (Wagner, 2002) that HR paper forms cost $20-$30 to process, telephone based HR forms cost $2-$4 to process but Internet based HR forms cost only 5-10 cents. In an attempt to exploit these cost differences companies have looked to the Internet for the solution.

B2E: Employee Self Service

B2E Employee Self Service (ESS) is an Internet based solution that provides employees with a browser interface to relevant HR data and transactions. This enables employees' real-time access to their data without leaving their desktop. They can update their personal details, apply for leave, view their pay details and associated benefits, view internal job vacancies and book training and travel. The benefits of this type of technology have been well documented (Alexander, 2002, McKenna, 2002; Webster Buchanan Research, 2002; Wiscombe, 2001). They include reduced administrative overheads and the freeing of HR staff for more strategic activities, improved data integrity, and empowerment of employees. One report identified a major benefit as the provision of HR services to employees in a geographically decentralised company (NetKey, 2002). Tangible measures include reductions in administrative staff by 40% and a reduction in transaction costs of 50% (Wiscombe,

2001) and the reduction of processes from two to three days to a few hours (NetKey, 2002). A recent study of UK top 500 firms revealed that the majority of B2E solutions were still at a basic level and have focussed on improved efficiency and electronic document delivery (Dunford, 2002). Ordonez (2002) maintains the theme of information delivery in presenting ESS as allowing employees access to the right information at the right time to carry out and process transactions; further, ESS allows the ability to create, view and maintain data through multiple access technologies. Companies such as Toyota Australia are now extending this functionality beyond the desktop by providing access to electronic HR Kiosks in common meeting areas.

The Cedar group (Cedar Group, 1999, 2000, 2001, 2002) carry out an annual survey of major global organisations and their B2E intentions. The survey covers many facets of ESS including technology, vendors, drivers, costs and benefits. The average expenditure in 2001 on an ESS implementation was $US1.505 million. This cost is broken down:

- Software 22%,
- Hardware 18%,
- Internal implementation costs 18%,
- External implementation costs 17%,
- Marketing 10%, and
- ASPs 17%.

Looking at this cost from an employee perspective sees the average cost of ESS implementation ranging from $US32/employee for a large organisation (>60,000 employees), to $US155/employee for a medium size organisation (7,500 employees). The funding for the HR ESS comes from the HR function in North American and Australian organizations, whereas the Head Office funds them in European organisations. The main drivers for ESS are:

- Improved service (98%),
- Better information access (90%),
- Reduced costs (85%),
- Streamlined processes (70%), and
- Strategic HR (80%).

Employees can use a variety of applications in the ESS, and the main ones identified in the Cedar survey are employee communications (95%), pension services (72%), training (40%), and leave requests (25%), along with many others. Managers use self-service differently in the three regions of the survey. North American managers use MSS to process travel and expenses (42%), European managers to process purchase orders (48%) and Australian managers to process leave requests (45%). Employee services can be delivered by a variety of methods, and the Web-based self-service (B2E) is undergoing substantial planned growth from 42% in 2001 to 80% planned in 2004. The trend is for implementing HRMIS applications from major vendors like SAP or PeopleSoft. ESS implementations show overwhelming success measures, with 53% indicating their implementation was successful and 43% somewhat successful. The value proposition for ESS includes:

- Average cost of transaction (down 60%),
- Inquiries (down 10%),
- Cycle time (reduced 60%),
- Headcount (70% reduction),
- R.O.I. (100% in 22 months), and
- Employee satisfaction (increased 50%).

The culmination of the Cedar group reports lists the barriers to benefit attainment and critical success factors in ESS applications. North America and Australian organisation both list cost of ownership/lack of budget as the main barriers, whilst European organisations perceive lack of privacy and security as the main barriers. Other barriers include: lack of technical skills, unable to state business case, low HR priority and HRMS not in place. As with other complex IT application projects, executive commitment, internal collaboration and availability of technical skills to implement the application are all considered important success factors.

Web Portals

The term "portal" has been an Internet buzzword that has promised great benefits to organisations. Dias (2001) predicted that the corporate portal would become the most important information delivery project of the next decade. The term "portal" takes a different meaning depending on the viewpoint of the participant in the portal. To the business user the portal is all about information access and navigation; to a business the portal is all about adding value; to the marketplace the portal is all about new business models; and to the technologist a portal is all about integration. The portal was developed to address problems with the large-scale development of corporate intranets.

Corporate intranets promised much but had to address multiple problems in the organisation (Collins as reported in Brosche, 2001, p. 14). On the user side employees must make informed and consistent decisions and are being implored to access multiple information sources on the Web. On the technology side Intranet sites in organisations have proliferated, resulting in an increase in search complexity for corporate users. Early versions of portals were merely Web pages with extensive document linkages, a gateway to the Web. These early versions have been replaced by more advanced portal versions. Eckerson (1999) proposed four generations of portals (see Table 2) and he proposed that portals can be analysed by the information content, information flow and the technology focus that make up the portal. Just as the Intranet proliferated within organizations, portals are now starting to multiply. The mega portal is being developed in the hope of addressing the unfettered expansion of function specific portals. The portal management system or the mega portal is being developed to take control of portal proliferation and has the aim of enhancing

Table 2. Portal generations (Eckerson, 1999).

Generation	Descriptor	Features
First	Referential	Generic Focus Hierarchical catalogue of pages Pull Flow Decision support
Second	Personalised	Personalised Focus Push and Pull Flow Customised Distribution
Third	Interactive	Application Focussed Collaborative Flow
Fourth	Specialised	Role Focussed Corporate Applications Integrated Work Flow

business process convergence and integration. Shilakes and Tylman (1998) coined the term "Enterprise Information Portal" (EIP), and this definition encompassed information access, application nature and Internet gateway that are apparent in the second and third generations of organisational portals. One area that is being developed via portal technology is employee relationships. We have already looked at ESS as an example of a B2E system; some additional employee applications are M2E (Manager-to- Employee), E2E (Employee-to-Employee) and X2E (external-to-Employee). Taken together, all these relationships are considered part of the ERM strategy (Doerzaph & Udolph, 2002). An ERM strategy is made up of the following components: self-service technology, collaboration tools, communication tools, knowledge management techniques, personalisation focus and lastly, access technology. The access technology can encompass employee interaction centres like hotlines or helpdesks or enterprise portals. General Motors is one of the leading HR portals implemented in the world and they have proposed three generations of HR portals (Dessert & Colby, 2002).

The three phases are presented in Table 3 and are presented in five organisational dimensions. A model of portal architecture is proposed by Brosche (2002, p.19) and depicts a portal having core, key elements and specialisation components. The components proposed by Brosche (2002) can be further categorised as having an information focus, technology focus or a process

Table 3. Generations of HR portals (Dessert & Colby, 2002).

Dimensions	1st Generation	2nd Generation	3rd Generation
User Stickiness	Static Web High Usage Search	Dynamic Personalised Robust Search	Anywhere Access Analytics Dashboard
Communications & Collaboration	News Chat Jobs	Unified Messaging Targeted Push versu Pull Role-Based	e-Learning e-Culture Broadcast Media
Information Access	Online Publications Links Launching Pad	Dynamic publishing Native Web Apps Content Integration b/w functions	Online Publishing Int Content
Services	Travel expenses Payroll E-Procurement	Life/Work Events Communities e-Health	Role Based Online Consulting
Technology	Web/App servers Unsecured Basic login	Content Management LDAP Int e-mail, chat, IM,	Federated services Wireless Multi-media Broadband

Figure 2. Portal generations by Brosche categories.

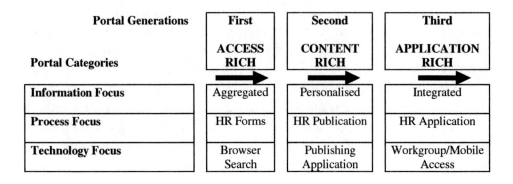

Portal Generations	First ACCESS RICH	Second CONTENT RICH	Third APPLICATION RICH
Information Focus	Aggregated	Personalised	Integrated
Process Focus	HR Forms	HR Publication	HR Application
Technology Focus	Browser Search	Publishing Application	Workgroup/Mobile Access

focus. We can further combine Eckerson generations with Brosche portal model and analyse an organisation's portal by its information focus, technology focus and process focus and categorise it as being first, second or third generation (see Figure 2).

Using this proposed categorisation of portals we will analyse the ESS portal of a major Australian organisation and locate the stage of portal development it is currently in.

Case Study

Auscom B2E Solution

The move to B2E ESS portals is detailed through the use of a case study. Case study research methodology was used as the chapter presents an exploratory look at implications of ESS implementations. Yin (1994, p. 35) emphasises the importance of asking "what" when analysing information systems. Yin goes further and emphasises the need to study contemporary phenomena within real-life contexts. The etic or outsider approach was used in this case study. This approach emphasises an analysis based upon an outsider's categorisation of the meanings and reading of the reality inside the firm. The analysis is based upon objective methods such as document analysis, surveys and interviews. Assumptions that were gleaned in the analysis of maturity of portal development were queried and clarified by interview. Walsham (2000, p. 204) supports case study methodology and sees the need for a move away from traditional information systems research methods such as surveys toward more interpretative case studies, ethnographies and action research projects. Several works have used case studies (Benbasat et al., 1987; Chan & Roseman, 2001; Lee, 1989) in presenting information systems research. Cavaye (1995) used case study research to analyse inter-organisational systems and the complexity of information systems. A single company was chosen for case study research in attempt to identify the impact of an ESS implementation and the associated development along the ESS to Portal path. The chosen company attended a forum on ESS conducted by the SAP Australian User Group (SAUG). The case study company was chosen because it is a leading Australian organisation with a long mature SAP history and had implemented SAP ESS module. Initially, information was collected as a result of the company's presentation at the ESS forum in June 2002. Interviews were conducted firstly by e-mail with two managers from Auscom; one manager was from Corporate Systems and the other from Infrastructure Services. These predetermined questions were then analysed and enhanced and formed the basis of the interviews supported by observations through access to the ESS system. Interviews were transcribed and follow-up queries and clarification of points were conducted by telephone. Project documentation and policy documents were also supplied. The initial case study was commenced in October 2002 by Engleby, Nur and Romsdal (2002) and then refined and extended in December by the authors of this chapter. The name of the case study organisation has been withheld due to conditions set in the case study interview.

Australian Communications Organisation (Auscom)

Auscom is Australia's leading telecommunications company. It was privatised in 1997 and currently has 40,000 full-time employees, 20,000 contractors, 2,000 information systems and 50,000 desktops (Greenblat, 2002). It offers a full range of communications and information services products, including local, long distance, mobile, Internet and subscriber television. In the year ending June 2002 it had $AUD 20 billion of sales and a profit of $AUD 3 billion. Auscom's vision is to be a world-class, full service telecommunications by delivering company-wide process improvement, productivity gains and cost efficiency (Auscomvision, 2002). It could be viewed in the same strategic light as say, a leading European telecom, Deutsche Telecom AG. One of the areas that Auscom had analysed and felt was able to better deliver their vision was HR. The existing HR system was cost bloated, process fragmented and had poor data access. Auscom wanted to explore the strategic aspects of HR, especially the concept of "employer of choice," and instigated "People Online" in May 2001. The project was to be developed in three phases: Phase 1 introduced ESS to provide simple HR employee based transactions and information search facilities. Phase 1 had two components, MyDetails, the simple employee HR ESS and PeopleSearch, the information search component. Phase 2 would introduce workflow for both HR and non-HR processes. Phase 3 would provide additional features, but is really "over the horizon" at this stage. Phase 1 was rolled out in May 2002 and phase 2 was scheduled to be rolled out in November 2002 with Deloitte consulting the development partner. The business case for phase 1 identified four groups of benefits: quantifiable cost savings, increased data integrity, enabling process re-engineering and e-enabling the workforce. Details of the benefit metrics were not available due to commercial in confidence. Four months after the implementation an external organisation carried out a review and analysed the business requirements, performance, implementation and project management of PeopleOnline. An analysis of the review is presented with reference to the portal generations in Figure 2.

Information Focus

Information stickiness refers to the ability of the ESS to draw and retain the user. The Mydetails application did provide enhanced stickiness but PeopleSearch did not. The review team found that the needs of super/power users in switchboard/reception, who use PeopleSearch extensively, had not been analysed enough in the initial business requirements analysis. There was also a problem when cost considerations created a scope and software change and project requirements of the special power users was not re-visited after this change. There was also an operational problem where service level agreements did not have adequate time/penalty clauses and or metrics built in, thereby causing performance problems to be neglected. Overall, the Mydetails component did enhance stickiness as it provided the full range of typical "PULL" ESS features: personal details, pay, leave, bank and benefit packages. This type of ESS site is typically a first generation "ACCESS RICH" site with predominately "pull" features (Static Web, High Usage). The information provided to the user was limited to HR or employee based information. There was no process information, business transaction information or product information provided. There was no across-function information flows. The access focus of the portal would indicate that the portal was immature and still first generation.

Process Focus

This dimension looks at the extent that the portal reaches out to other areas of the organisation and the extent that the portal enables collaboration and cross-integration business process operations, like e-procurement, travel expenses authorisation, payroll, time and HR data management. The services provided by the Phase 1 project was limited to HR type data including payroll. The extension into other areas of the organisation and across business units is scheduled for Phase 2. The Peopleseach component enhanced communications by providing one-stop search facility in the whole organisation. It was important that this communication tool should have been aligned to the corporate intranet look and feel. There was little collaboration built into this phase. Again this type of portal with moderate communications but limited collaboration features is a first generation "ACCESS RICH" HR portal.

Technology Focus

The IT model of the HR infrastructure was based around SAP R/3 with ESS added functionality for self-service and SAP's WhosWhos application for search capability. Halfway through the business requirements analysis Auscom dropped WhosWhos and replaced it with an in-house search package. The risk of upgrading the Internet browser from IE4 to IE5 created major problems to the extent that the system was written to IE4 compatibility. There was no content management, publishing capability, workgroup, collaboration or e-mail access. Again, looking at the Figure 2 the technology dimension is clearly first generation "ACCESS RICH" portal.

Conclusion

"MSS and ESS are the 'killer applications' of the HR world. They represent a pivotal point in the technology of HRMS" (Johnston, 2001)

ESS has proven to provide a number of quick wins in the business-to-employee e-business model. It provides a number of benefits to companies and stream-lines many of the HR processes while at the same time empowering employees. A recent Tower Perrin report (2002) showed that ESS portals have been or are being adopted by 73% of organisations and that eHR has taken hold in organisations. David White from Deloitte Touché (2002) confirmed the accep-tance of eHR portals into the lexicon of e-enablement:

"A Successful technology-enabled HR strategy combines business strategy with emerging technologies and existing infrastructure to produce an integrated, comprehensive plan for how HR will deliver services, provide information, and process transaction."

Compared to other e-business solutions it has a relatively low impact on the organisation, employees and processes. The risks are minimal as it provides a Web interface to an existing system and improves data integrity, as employees are responsible for much of their own data. However, as with most IT projects, ESS portals do promise to provide extended functionality into and across the organisation. Many companies such as GM USA (Dessert & Colby, 2002) are now evolving their ESS solutions into employee portals where the HR function-ality is just another tab that appears on their Web page with their business transactions, corporate data, calendar and e-mail functionality. ESS should eventually disappear as a term as Web interfaces become standard in corporate portals where the employee has one interface to carry out all business related transactions. We can analyse the relative positions of Auscom and GM portal maturity by referring to Table 4. Auscom developed their first generation portal to be primarily an information pull application with the main focus on traditional HR forms. Little collaboration or communication applications were developed in the first release and as such this place the Auscom portal firmly in the "access rich" type. The next version of the portal was looking at the online routing of standard HR transactions, online recruitment, talent management and an enhanced emphasis on training. This development would move the Auscom portal into the "content rich" and partially into the "application rich" phases. The GM portal, as shown in Tables 3 and 4, has moved beyond this "access rich" phase into the content and application phase. Auscom seem to be moving in the right direction, if somewhat behind GM. There seems to be no doubt that the technology exists to move an organisation like Auscom from first generation "access rich" to second generation "content rich" and onto third generation "application rich" portal.

Future work developed from this chapter could include looking at organisations that have implemented B2E HR portals and seeing if they can be categorised into the three generations of portals as depicted above. Another important aspect would be to look at the drivers and obstacles in developing portal solutions together with implementation issues and problems. It would also be important to chart the development of portal resources, including content, "portlets" and portal communities. There are many terms used to describe the move from traditional HR to the "e-enabled" versions of HR: HRMIS, eHR, B2E, ESS, Web enabled ESS, HR portal, ESS portal and several others. What is not vague is the understanding that these are information delivery platforms that have much potential to deliver not only cost focussed savings but the more important strategic HR benefits being sought by modern organisations. The recent Cedar report (2002, p. 1) commented:

> *"HR self-service and portal technologies are maturing as strategic, comprehensive solutions that support building high performance workforces, while sponsored and supported by HR, these technologies are increasingly part of enterprise to employee solutions."*

Table 4. Portal generations by Brosche categories.

Portal Generations	First	Second	Third
Portal Categories	**ACCESS RICH**	**CONTENT RICH**	**APPLICATION RICH**
Information Focus	Aggregated *Auscom Portal*	Personalised	Integrated *General Motors Portal*
Process Focus	HR Forms *Auscom Portal*	HR Publication	HR Application *General Motors Portal*
Technology Focus	Browser Search *Auscom Portal*	Publishing Application	Workgroup/Mobile Access *General Motors Portal*

When a major Australian organisation leads the way with modern e-enabled applications, the stage is set for other Australian organisations to be aggressive followers. We will watch with great interest the march to ESS and then the advancement to HR/corporate/enterprise portals.

References

Alexander S. (2002). HR e-power to the people. *Infoworld.* Retrieved August 2002, from http://staging.infoworld.com/articles/ca/xml/01/02/010212 cahr.xml.

Anonymous. (2002, April). *Trends in HR service delivery.* White paper for Gildner Human Resources Outsourcing Forum. Retrieved March 2003, from http://www.gildner.net/White%20Paper%20-%20HR%20 Service%20Delivery%20Trends.pdf.

Auscomvision. (2002). Auscom's vision & direction. Retrieved October 2002, from http://www.Auscom.com.au/investor/vision.html.

Barron, M. (2002). Retail Web-based self-serve isn't just for customers, it's for employees. *Internet Retailer.* Retrieved September 2002, from http://www.internetretailer.com/dailynews.asp?id=6688.

Benbasat, I., Goldstein, D., & Mead, M. (1987). The case research strategy in studies of information systems. *MIS Quarterly, 113,* 369-386.

Bennett, C. (2001). *SAP Update.* Australian SAP User Group, December Plenary, Sydney, Australia.

Bennett, C. (2002, December 3-5). Keynote address. *Proceedings of the 13th Australasian Conference on Information Systems,* Victoria University of Technology, Melbourne, Australia.

Brosche, C. (2002, May). *Designing the corporate portal.* Masters Thesis, Department of Computer Science, University of Gothenburg, Sweden.

Cavaye, A. (1996). Case study research: A multi-faceted approach for IS. *Information Systems Journal, 63,* 227-242.

Cedar Group. (1999). *Cedar 1999 human resources self-service.* Cedar Group, Baltimore.

Cedar Group. (2000). *Cedar 2000 human resources self-service.* Cedar Group, Baltimore.

Cedar Group. (2001). *Cedar 2001 human resources self-service/portal survey.* Cedar Group, Baltimore.

Cedar Group. (2002). *Cedar 2002 human resources self-service/portal survey.* Cedar Group, Baltimore.

Chan, R., & Roseman, M. (2001). Integrating knowledge into process models - A case study. *Proceedings of the Twelfth Australasian Conference on Information Systems,* Southern Cross University, Australia.

Curran, T., & Kellar, G. (1998). *SAP R/3 business blueprint.* New Jersey: Prentice Hall.

Deimler, M., & Hansen, M. (2001). The online employee. Boston Consulting Group. Retrieved March 2002, from http://www.bcg.com/publications/files/Online_Employee_Aug_01_perpsective.pdf.

Dessert, M., & Colby, E. (2002). General Motor's employee portal – Liftoff plus 1 year: The sky's the limit. *Proceedings of the IHRIM2002 Conference,* Boston.

Dias, C. (2001). Corporate portals. *International Journal of Information Management, 21,* 269-287.

Doerzapf, A., & Udolph, S. (2002). Maximising return on employee telationships. *SAP Insider, 4*(1), 20-29.

Dunford, I. (2002, October 24). B2E: The future looks rosy. Retrieved March 2003, from http://www.computing.co.uk/Analysis/1136393.

Eckerson, W. (1999). Plumtree blossoms: New version fulfils enterprise portal requirements. Patricia Seybold Report. Retrieved March 2003, from http://www.e-global.es/017/017_eckerson_plumtree.pdf.

Engelby, I., Nur, M., & Romsdal, A. (2002, November). *Auscom People Online.* ERP Implementation Seminar, Victoria University.

Greenblat, E. (2002). Auscom hurting on profit of 3.6 billion. Retrieved October 2002, from http://www.theage.com.au/articles/2002/08/28/1030508074093.html.

Hamerman, P. (2002, July). *Extending employee relationships with Web applications.* Presentation to SAPPHIRE Lisbon Conference.

Iggulden, T. (Ed.). (1999, June). Looking for payback. *MIS,* 75-80.

Johnston, J. (2001, April/June). E-HR: What is it. *IHRIM Journal,* 120-122.

Khirallah, D. (2000). Picture this: Self-service HR at Sony. *Information Week*. Retrieved September 2002, from http://www.informationweek.com/811/sony.htm.

Lee, A. (1989). Case studies as natural experiments. *Human Relations, 422*, 117-137.

Lehman, J. (2000, September 26). HR self-service strategies: Lessons learned. *Gartner Research Note*.

Link, D. (2001). How HR can shape corporate portals. *HRMagazine, 46*(9), 131-137.

Malis, E. (2002). Cited in crosswind corporate intranets include automated time & attendance in your HR self service offering. Retrieved September 2002, from http://www.crosswind.com.

McKenna, E. (2002). Empowering employees. *FCW*. Retrieved August 2002, from http://www.fcw.com/fcw/articles/2002/0107/tec-hr-01-07-02.asp.

Netkey. (2002). Unlocking the power of HR self service. *NetKey*. Retrieved September 2002, from www.netkey.com.

Ordonez, E. (2001). MySAP human resources: Human capital management for your business. *SAP*. Retrieved July 2002, from http://www.sap.com.

Shilakes, C., & Tylman, J. (1998). Enterprise information portals. Merril Lynch Report. Retrieved March 2003, from http://emarkets.grm.hia.no/gem/topic7/eip_ind.pdf.

Wagner, M. (2002, June). Saving trees & serving up benefits. *Internet Retailer*.

Walsham, G. (2000). *Globalisation & IT: Agenda for research. Organisational & social perspectives on information technology* (pp. 195-210). Boston: Kluwer Academic Publishers.

Webster Buchanan Research. (2002). HR self service – The practitioners' view. Retrieved August 2002, from www.leadersinHR.org.

White, D. (2001). How portals are enabling HR service delivery success. Deloitte & touché human Capital Advisory Service. Retrieved March 2003, from http://www.deloitte.com/dtt/cda/doc/content/HC%20 Technologies_Portals.pdf.

Wiscombe, J. (2001, September). Using technology to cut costs. *Workforce*. Retrieved August 2002, from http://www.workforce.com/archive/feature/22/29/82/index.php.

Workforce. (2001). HR statistics. *Workforce, 79*(10), 54-61.

Yin, R. (1994). *Case study research. Design & methods* (2nd ed.). Newbury Park: Sage Publications.

Chapter VI

Enterprise Systems and the Challenge of Integrated Change:
A Focus on Occupational Communities

Joe McDonagh
University of Dublin, Ireland

Abstract

While the business press is awash with claims that investing in enterprise-wide systems is the key to delivering superior economic performance, unfortunately it appears that reaping the benefits of such IT investments is fraught with difficulty. Indeed, the introduction of IT into work organisations is generally marred with persistent reports of underperformance and failure. This chapter critiques the nature of this dilemma and in particular explores the role of diverse occupational groups in its perpetuation over time. This dilemma is sustained over time by the behavioural patterns of diverse occupational groups that have vested but divergent, interests in exploiting IT. Executive management tend to view the introduction of IT as an economic imperative while IT specialists tend to view it as a technical imperative. The coalescent nature of these two imperatives is such that the human and organisational aspects of IT related change are frequently marginalised and ignored. Achieving a more integrated approach to the introduction of IT is inordinately difficult since the narrow perspectives embraced by the executive and IT communities do not naturally attend to change in an integrated manner.

Introduction

While the business press is awash with claims that investing in enterprise-wide information systems is the key to delivering superior economic performance, unfortunately it appears that reaping the benefits of such investments is fraught with difficulty. Indeed, the introduction of enterprise systems in work organisations is generally marred with persistent reports of underperformance and failure. This chapter critiques the nature of this dilemma and in particular explores the role of occupational communities in its perpetuation through time. The chapter concludes by way of noting that effecting an integrated approach to the introduction of enterprise systems that accounts for economic, technical, human, and organisational facets of change is inordinately difficult since the requisite knowledge and expertise are widely dispersed among diverse occupational communities.

A Historical Dilemma

Undoubtedly, the influence of computer based information systems has been pervasive throughout the last four decades. A brief historical tour bears witness to such pervasiveness: from electronic data processing in the 1950s, data processing in the 1960s, management information systems in the 1970s, strategic information systems in the 1980s, to enterprise systems, electronic business, electronic commerce, and electronic government in the 1990s and 2000s. Each decade has witnessed rapid advances in technological innovation which when combined with pivotal administrative innovations have offered the promise of major benefits at multiple organizational and inter-organizational levels.

It is indeed fair to say that what best characterises this present era of computer based information systems from earlier eras is the dominant focus on the promise of extending the reach of the enterprise (Champy, 2002; Davenport, 2000; Hammer, 2001; Porter, 2001), enabled by significant advances in information and communication technologies (PriceWaterhouseCoopers, 2001). Should we eagerly nurture the fulfilment of this promise or should the many claims about espoused benefits cause us to embrace a more cautious response? A cautious response may be advisable!

Consider recent evidence that confirms that realizing the benefits of enterprise-wide information systems poses a formidable challenge for many private and public sector organizations alike. For example, in a survey of 117 firms across 17 countries, only 34% of respondents confirmed that they were very satisfied with their investments (McNurlin, 2001). Furthermore, in excess of 90% of enterprise systems implementations overrun in terms of cost or time or both (Sammon et al., 2001). Research conducted by the Standish Group confirms that 28% of enterprise systems implementations are abandoned for a variety of reasons (Crowe et al., 2002).

Evidence of the nature outlined above is not new. Reflecting briefly upon organizations' experiences with information technology (IT) throughout the last four decades, it appears that the much-vaunted promise of IT investment yielding significant gain has regularly failed to materialize (Clegg et al., 1996; McDonagh, 1999). Indeed, many organisations appear to experience significant underperformance and failure with regard to their IT investments as opposed to the promise of superior performance so frequently claimed in the business press. Consider for a moment a number of high profile cases where the introduction of IT has been a fiasco.

- After a total of $125 million dollars had been invested, Hilton Hotels Corporation, Marriott Corporation and Budget Rent-A-Car Corporation cancelled what had become a major IT failure (Oz, 1994).

- FoxMeyer Drug, a large Texas-based pharmaceutical company, filed for bankruptcy in August 1994 as a consequence of a $65 million dollar enterprise system investment that went devastatingly wrong (James, 1997).

- The California Department of Motor Vehicles embarked on a major project to revitalise its driver's licence and registration applications process. By 1993, after $45 million dollars had been spent, the project was cancelled (Johnson, 1995).

- Having invested £600 million, the Child Support Agency in the United Kingdom admitted that its new system was a failure and was being abandoned (Jones, 1997).

- After seven years and about $500 million dollars trying to implement the mainframe-based SAP R/2 enterprise software package, Dow Chemical scrapped the project and started from scratch with a client/server version instead (Cambridge Information Network, 1999).

- Having invested £878 million on a magnetic stripe card that never saw the light of day, the UK Government admitted that its PATHWAY initiative was a failure and was being cancelled (Ranger, 2000).

There is significant evidence to suggest that failures of the nature outlined above are a constant feature of the IT landscape (McDonagh, 2000; Ranger, 2000; Sabbagh, 1998). A recent analysis of 27 sources of evidence between 1979 and 1998 concludes that around 50% of IT initiatives fail or are completely abandoned, while another 40% are delivered late and over budget (McDonagh, 1999). Unfortunately, the percentage of initiatives that deliver business value is as low as 10% (Clegg et al., 1996; Johnson, 1995; Kearney, 1990; McDonagh, 1999).

Learning from Failure

Considering that such poor outcomes from IT investment initiatives has been a pervasive theme both in management literature and organisational practice throughout the last four decades, how can one readily account for such outcomes? To understand the persistent nature of this phenomenon one must understand the essential nature of the challenge involved in the introduction of IT into work organisations. That challenge necessitates fostering an integrated approach to the management of change, an approach that concurrently co-ordinates and integrates economic, technical, human and organisational facets of change. Recognising the systemic nature of this challenge it is disappointing then to find that most IT-enabled change initiatives are dominated by economic and technical considerations to the relative exclusion of human and organisational considerations (Lunt & Barclay, 1988; More, 1990). The tangible nature of this dilemma readily manifests itself when one considers that extant empirical research supports the assertion that economic and technical considerations are unlikely to feature prominently when IT fails to deliver (Clegg et al., 1996).

What then are the consequences of failing to nurture a systemic approach to change that concurrently accounts for economic, technical, human, and organisational aspects of IT? Indeed, they appear rather grave since failing to attend to human and organisational facets of change are considered to be the root of much IT-related underperformance and failure (Benyon-Davies, 1997; Lucas, 1975). Lucas (1975) states that the difficulties with IT are primarily of a behavioural nature, a view well supported by Bariff and Ginzberg (1982). Other writers have succinctly noted that 90% of the problems encountered in IT-enabled change are of a human and organisational nature (Clegg et al., 1996; Isaac-Henry, 1997; Long, 1987).

Recent literature on enterprise-wide information systems provides potent confirmatory evidence that failure to address the human and organisational aspects of change all too frequently contributes to rather poor outcomes in such investments (Esteves & Pastor, 2001; Sarker, 2000; Sedera et al., 2001; Smyth, 2001).

A brief examination of the human and organisational factors frequently marginalizsed in IT-enabled change initiatives suggests major areas of concern (McDonagh, 1999):

- Lack of guiding business and technology strategies
- Lack of attention to organisation structure, design, and culture
- Lack of attention to job design, task design, and the nature of work
- Lack of attention to existing procedures, practices, and systems
- Lack of attention to management style
- Lack of attention to industrial relations
- Lack of attention to education, training, and awareness
- Lack of fit between the system and the organisation
- Lack of attention to knowledge, skill, experience and attitude of executives, experts, and users
- Lack of attention to IT specialists' limited cognitive skills, social skills and human codes
- Lack of attention to users' capabilities including cognitive style, stress adaptation, motivation and commitment

- Lack of appropriate systems development and project management methods

- Lack of attention to the underlying assumptions that drive the systems development process

- Lack of user participation and user ownership in the systems development process

- Lack of attention to systems implementation

- Lack of attention to the composition and effectiveness of project teams

- Lack of organisational resources and support

Considering the wide array of evidence that suggests that human and organisational aspects of change are routinely marginalised and ignored in IT-enabled change initiatives, it is worth considering why this dilemma persists through time. Are organisational actors genuinely unaware of the human and organisational facets of change, or in a more sinister sense, do they wilfully collude to marginalise and ignore these key dimensions of change? While the themes of both individual and collective learning are chic in the field of management and organisation studies, one could be excused for believing that organisations learn little, if anything, from their difficulties with IT-enabled change. In the words of Andriole and Freeman (1993), "we seem to learn relatively little from our mistakes ... we are not learning from our experience".

An Occupational Quandary

Reflecting on such poor outcomes from IT investment initiatives, it is hardly surprising that the introduction of IT into work organisations offers a potent arena in which organisational actors are regularly drawn into a milieu of intense discord. Evidence of such discord abounds. Many IT specialists are considered lacking in the core skills required to integrate IT with the business (Martin et al., 1995). Company directors have little faith in the business judgement of their IT counterparts, even though IT is recognised as critical to corporate success (Stammers, 1997). Bosses tend to accuse IT colleagues of hiding behind techno-babble to cover their lack of business acumen (McGinn, 1997). IT people are often aloof and uncooperative, uncomfortable with teamwork and unable to listen effectively to users (Vora, 1997). Indeed, a recent survey of 340 CIOs (chief information officers) in the United States, the UK, Germany and France noted that CIOs show a lack of business acumen and shrewdness and are generally perceived as geeks and not business professionals (Korn/ Ferry International, 1998).

Conversely, a UK survey of 1,000 full-time IT professionals and 200 IT employers carried out by Harris Research revealed that 32% of IT professionals felt that "senior management did not fully appreciate the role of IT in their business" (Briggs, 1996). Similarly, a survey of the UK's top IT directors carried out by the Butler Group revealed that 73% did not think their business managers were IT focused (Briggs, 1997). IT specialists accuse management of profound ignorance when it comes to new technology (McGinn, 1997). Those who work in IT often complain that their non-IT colleagues do not really understand the true potential of technology. This is held to be especially true of directors, who can seem radically out of touch (Hallahan, 1998). Golden (1997) sums it up when he says that all too often there is a yawning gap of understanding between business management and IT professionals.

Castigations of the nature outlined above have persisted throughout recent decades (Fitz-enz, 1978; Oliver & Langford, 1987). Consider the assertion made two decades ago that the average software engineer "is excessively independent – sometimes to a point of mild paranoia. He is often eccentric, slightly neurotic, and he borders upon a limited schizophrenia" (Fitz-enz, 1978). While Oliver and Langford (1987) note that such discord is rooted in ill-understood differences in cognitive style it remains that such polarisation is not uncommon.

It is of interest to note from the above that much of the discord surrounding the introduction of IT in work organisations appears to manifest itself in the polarisation of diverse occupational groups, namely executive management and IT specialists. "Information technology has a polarising effect on managers; it either bedazzles or frightens. Those who are afraid of it shun it, while bedazzled IT departments frequently become prisoners of their own fascination, constructing elaborate technology architectures and enterprise information models" (Davenport, 1994). The level of inter-group dissent highlights the need for a deeper understanding of how such groups separately and collectively influence the process of introducing IT into work organisations.

On closer inquiry, it emerges that the plight with IT is of an enduring nature sustained by the behavioural patterns of polarised occupational groups who have vested, but divergent, interests in exploiting IT (McDonagh, 1999). Executive management view the introduction of IT as an economic imperative, while IT specialists view it as a technical imperative. The coalescent nature of these two imperatives is such that human and organisational considerations are regularly marginalised and ignored during the process of introducing IT into work organisations (McDonagh, 1999; McDonagh & Coghlan, 2000).

Reflecting more closely on the manner in which the executive community shapes the introduction of IT in work organisations, it becomes increasingly apparent that this worldwide community of practitioners has a potent effect on IT-enabled change (McDonagh, 1999).

- Many senior executives see people as costly impersonal resources that generate problems rather than solutions.

- Many senior executives embrace a narrow economic focus on IT believing that IT merely offers an opportunity for rationalisation and cost reduction.

- Many senior executives see IT as a cost-pit rather than a strategic capability.

- Many senior executives embrace a short-term focus on IT and exert inordinate pressure to achieve rapid payback and short-term gain.

- IT executives charged with delivering business value from IT are more often than not excluded from boards of management, executive management teams, and the corporate strategy process.

- Many senior executives fail to commit to the IT strategy process.

- The clear separation of managerial and technical work serves to reinforce and invigorate the divide between business and IT.

In a similar vein, IT specialists, as a worldwide community of practitioners, have a profound impact upon the introduction of IT in work organisations (McDonagh, 1999).

- Much of the community embraces a technical focus on IT, attending primarily to the task and technology components of work organisations into which IT is being introduced.

- The tools, techniques, and methods used by the community of practitioners sustain this narrow techno-centric agenda.

- Much of the community is genuinely unaware of the human and organisational factors that account for the majority of IT-related under-performance and failure.

- There is no apparent incentive for the community of practitioners to embrace a more holistic perspective on IT-related change.

Conflict and discord between the executive and IT communities is undoubtedly a predictable outcome considering the manner in which each community shapes IT-enabled change. Each community assumes a limited perspective on IT-enabled change, executives assuming an economic focus and IT specialists assuming a technical focus. Each community shares a predilection to design people out of rather than into systems. Similarly, each community shares a genuine lack of knowledge concerning the human and organisational aspects of IT. The dominance of these foci regularly results in a "task and technology" approach to the introduction of IT in work organisations (Blackler & Brown, 1986).

A Paucity of Action

It remains unclear then as to whom is responsible for nurturing a more integrated approach to IT-enabled change that concurrently attends to economic, technical, human and organisational considerations. Clegg and Kemp (1986) and Clegg (1995) note that IT specialists see their job as being complete once the software application has been developed. Similarly, Markus and Benjamin (1997) note that

> *"Deeply held beliefs that IT can cause change lead both line managers and IT specialists to restrict their own efforts as change agents. With everyone assuming that change management is the job of someone – or something – else, there is often no one left to perform change management tasks. Change then fails, and lack of learning about the root causes of failure promotes future failures."*

Considering the power and influence that both the executive and IT communities exert on the process of introducing IT into work organisations, the challenge of embracing a more integrated approach seems daunting. In light of this, and without being prescriptive, how can organisations influence the process of introducing IT to ensure that human and organisational issues are given equal consideration with economic and technical ones? One distinct possibility is to consider the involvement of organisation development (OD) expertise since such expertise is generally well grounded in the human and organisational factors that must be addressed for change to be effective (Burke, 1994).

OD focuses upon the process of planned change and as such focuses on "people, and groups that operate inside organizations and on the processes associated with teamwork, change and integration" (Worley et al., 1996, p. 3). Furthermore, organization development "gives equal standing to both the strategic and business issues that define an organization's performance potential and the human and organizational issues that ultimately determine whether the performance is fully realized" (Worley et al., 1996, p. 13). This elaboration on the nature of organisation development suggests that as a field of theory and practice it is ideally suited to addressing the challenge of integrated change, with a particular emphasis on human and organisational aspects of such change.

Reflecting upon the earlier argument about the manner in which diverse occupational communities shape the introduction of IT in work organisations, it would appear that attempts to shape a more holistic approach to IT-enabled change must confront two key challenges. The first challenge involves legitimising a systemic approach to change in the knowledge that key stakeholders appear to place inordinate emphasis on economic and technical considerations to the detriment of human and organisational considerations? Creating legitimate space for attending to human and organisational factors, as a part of a systemic approach to change, is a rather formidable task in its own right.

The second challenge involves creating an environment in which behavioural science knowledge and expertise are perceived to be as legitimate as technical knowledge and expertise. Crafting such a balance appears difficult as organisations appear readily willing to make major investments in acquiring IT competencies with rather scant attention given to OD based competencies. Consider large financial services organisations where one is likely to find IT specialists in their thousands and OD specialists in their tens.

Notwithstanding the above challenges, over the last two decades, various writers within the disciplines of OD and IT have advocated a potential role for OD-based expertise. Despite such advocacy, it remains that the IT and OD communities are equally polarised with respect to their perspectives on change. IT specialists pursue a technocentric agenda, ignoring the human and organisational consequences of that agenda (McDonagh & Coghlan, 2000). Similarly, OD specialists pursue an explicitly humanistic agenda and do not consider the IT domain as one to which they can naturally contribute (Burke, 1997; McDermott, 1984).

The potential role for a humanistic focus in the process of introducing IT is a central theme for neither the OD community nor the IT community. While some elements in both communities have pointed to the need for an integrated perspective on IT-related change, the reality remains that the IT community does not understand OD and the OD community does not understand IT (Markus & Benjamin, 1997a, 1997b). Considering the lack of understanding between these communities, should we be surprised to find that IT-related change remains, for the most part, technically driven?

Conclusion

As noted earlier, outcomes from investments in enterprise systems appear no better or no worse than outcomes from investments in IT in general. While the process of introducing IT into work organisations warrants an integrated perspective on economic, technical, human and organisational aspects of IT, it appears that technical and economic considerations dominate the practitioner landscape. Paradoxically, when IT fails to deliver as it so often does, human and organisational considerations are the prime determinants of such underperformance and failure. Recent literature on enterprise systems provides potent confirmatory evidence that failure to address the human and organisational aspects of change all too frequently contribute to rather poor outcomes in such investments (Esteves & Pastor, 2001; Sarker, 2000; Sedera et al., 2001; Smyth, 2001). This poses an intractable dilemma for many organisations.

The dilemma is of an enduring nature, sustained by the behavioural patterns of polarised occupational groups who have vested, but divergent, interests in exploiting IT. Executive management tend to view the introduction of IT as an economic imperative while IT specialists tend to view it as a technical imperative. The coalescent nature of these two imperatives is such that human and organisational considerations are regularly marginalised and ignored during the process of introducing IT into work organisations.

Implementing a more integrated approach to the introduction of IT that accounts for economic, technical, human, and organisational considerations is inherently difficult since the requisite knowledge and expertise are widely dispersed among diverse occupational groups (Andriole & Freeman, 1993; Clegg et al, 1996, 1997; Coghlan & McDonagh, 1997; McDonagh &

Coghlan, 1999, 2000). This calls for expertise that cuts across the social, behavioural, computer, mathematical, engineering, management, and even physical sciences (Andriole & Freeman, 1993). Those who understand the technology tend not to appreciate the wider organisational issues, and those who have the knowledge of these are often technically naive. This places a very high premium on finding ways of integrating different forms of knowledge and expertise (Clegg et al., 1996).

References

Andriole, S.J., & Freeman, P.A. (1993). Software systems engineering: The case for a new discipline. *Software Engineering Journal, 8*(3), 165-179.

Bariff, M.L., & Ginzberg, M.J. (1982, Fall). MIS and the behavioural sciences: Research patterns and prescriptions. *Data Base,* 19-29.

Benyon-Davies, P. (1997). *Information systems failures and how to avoid them.* London: FT-Pitman.

Blackler, F., & Brown, C. (1986). Alternative models to guide the design and introduction of the new information technologies into work organisations. *Journal of Occupational Psychology, 59,* 287-313.

Briggs, P. (1996, September 12). Bosses fear IT, say staff. *Computing, 33.*

Briggs, P. (1997, February 6). Managers fall down on basics. *Computing, 35.*

Burke, W.W. (1994). *Organization development: A process of learning and changing* (2nd ed.). Reading, MA: Addison-Wesley.

Burke, W.W. (1997, Summer). The new agenda for organisation development. *Organisational Dynamics,* 7-20.

Cambridge Information Network. (1999, May 27). Business feels the ERP heat. *Computing,* 37-40

Champy, J. (2002). *X-engineering the corporation – Reinvent your business in the digital age.* London: Hodder & Stoughton.

Clegg, C.W. (1995). Psychology and information technology: The study of cognition in organisations. *British Journal of Psychology, 85,* 449-477.

Clegg, C.W., & Kemp, N. (1986). Information technology: Personnel, where are you? *Personnel Review, 15*(1), 8-15.

Clegg, C.W., Axtell, C. et al. (1996). *The performance of information technology and the role of human and organisational factors.* Report to the Economic and Social Research Council. United Kingdom.

Clegg, C. W., Waterson, P.E. et al. (1997). Software development: Some critical views. *Behaviour and Information Technology, 16*(6), 359-362.

Coghlan, D., McDonagh, J. (1997). Doing action science in your own organisation. In T. Brannick & W. Roche (Eds.), *Business research methods – Strategies, techniques and sources* (pp. 139-161). Dublin: Oak Tree Press.

Crowe, T.J., Zayas-Castro, J.L. et al. (2002). Readiness assessment for enterprise resource planning. *The Eleventh International Conference on the Management of Technology.*

Davenport, T.H. (1994, March-April). Saving IT's soul: Human-centered information management. *Harvard Business Review,* 119-131.

Davenport, T.H. (2000). *Mission critical – Realizing the promise of enterprise systems.* Boston: Harvard Business School Press.

Esteves, J., & Pastor, J. (2001). Towards the unification of critical success factors for ERP implementation. *Tenth International BIT Conference,* Manchester, England.

Fitz-enz, J. (1978, September). Who is the DP professional. *Datamation,* 125-128.

Golden, T. (1997, February 23). Does your IT manager make any sense? *The Sunday Business Post,* 4.

Hallahan, S. (1998, February 19). Short-sighted attitude. *Computing,* 164-166.

Hammer, M. (2001). *The agenda.* London: Random House.

Isaacc-Henry, K. (1997). Management of information technology in the public sector. In K.P. Isaac-Henry & C. Barnes (Eds.), *Management in the public sector - Challenge and change* (pp. 131-159). London: International Thomson Business Press.

James, G. (1997, November). IT fiascoes and how to avoid them. *Datamation,* 84-88.

Johnson, J. (1995, January). Chaos: The dollar drain of IT project failures. *Application Development Trends,* 41-47.

Jones, R. (1997a, April 3). CSA plans to replace the 'heartache' system early. *Computing,* 1.

Kearney, A.T. (1990). *Barriers to the successful application of information technology.* London:Department of Trade and Industry.

Korn/Ferry International, K.F. (1998). *The changing role of the chief information officer.* London: Korn/Ferry International in conjunction with the Financial Times.

Long, R.J. (1987). *New office information technology: Human and managerial implications.* London: Croom Helm.

Lucas, H.C. (1975). *Why information systems fail.* New York,: Columbia University Press.

Lunt, P.J., & Barclay, I. (1988). The importance of organisational considerations for the implementation of information technology. *Journal of Information Technology, 3*(4), 244-250.

Markus, M.L., & Benjamin, R.I. (1997a). The magic bullet of IT-enabled change. *Sloan Management Review, 38*(2), 55-68.

Markus, M.L., & Benjamin, R.I. (1997b). IT-enabled organisational change: New developments for IT specialists. In C. Sauer, P.W. Yetton et al. (Eds.), *Steps to the future: Fresh thinking on the management of IT-based organisational transformation* (pp. 115-142). San Francisco: Jossey-Bass Publishers.

Martin, B.L., Batchelder, G. et al. (1995, September/October). The end of delegation? Information technology and the CEO. *Harvard Business Review,* 161-172.

McDermott, L. (1984, February). The many faces of the OD professional. *Training and Development Journal,* 15-19.

McDonagh, J. (1999). *Exploring the role of executive management in shaping strategic change: The case of information technology.* Unpublished PhD Dissertation, University of Warwick, England.

McDonagh, J., & Coghlan, D. (1999). Can OD help solve the IT dilemma? OD in IT related change. *Organisation Development Journal, 16*(4).

McDonagh, J., & Coghlan, D. (2000). Sustaining the dilemma with IT-enabled change – The fortuitous role of academia. *Journal of European Industrial Training, 24*(5), 297-304.

McGinn, J. (1997, December 18). Men of faction. *Computing,* 28-29.

McNurlin, B. (2001). Will users of ERP stay satisfied? *Sloan Management Review, 42*(2).

More, E. (1990). Information systems: People issues. *Journal of Information Science, 16,* 311-320.

Oliver, I., & Langford, H. (1987). Myths of demons and users: Evidence and analysis of negative perceptions of users. In R.D. Galliers (Ed.), *Information analysis* (pp. 113-123). Addison-Wesley Publishing Company.

Oz, E. (1994). When professional standards are lax: The confirm failure and its lessons. *Communications of the ACM, 37*(10), 29-36.

Porter, M.E. (2001). Strategy and the Internet. *Harvard Business Review, 79*(1), 63-78.

PriceWaterhouseCoopers. (2001). *Technology forecast: 2001-2003.* California: PriceWaterhouseCoopers Technology Centre.

Ranger, S. (2000, October 12). Why government IT projects fail. *Computing,* 1.

Sabbagh, D. (1998, July 9). Pathway hits the buffers – The £1bn project to automate benefit payments through the post office is in trouble. *Computing,* 15.

Sammon, D., Adam, F. et al. (2001). ERP dreams and sound business rationale. *Seventh Americas Conference on Information Systems.*

Sarker, S., & Lee, A. (2000). Using a case study to test the role of three key social enablers in ERP implementations. *International Conference on Information Systems,* Brisbane, Australia.

Sedera, W., Rosemann, M. et al. (2001). Process modelling for enterprise systems: Factors critical to success. *Twelfth Australasian Conference on Information Systems.*

Smyth, R.W. (2001). *Challenges to successful ERP use: Research in progress.* European Conference on Information Systems, Bled, Slovenia.

Stammers, T. (1997, March 27). Business doesn't rate IT staff. *Computing,* 10.

Vora, M. (1997). A change of title is not enough. *Information Strategy, 2*(1), 58.

Worley, C.G., Hitchin, D.E., & Ross, W.L. (1996). *Integrated strategic change: How OD builds competitive advantage.* Reading, MA: Addison Wesley.

Section III

Implementation and Management of SAP Systems:
Issues and Challenges

Chapter VII

A Successful ERP Implementation Plan:
Issues and Challenges

Linda K. Lau
Longwood University, USA

Abstract

This chapter commences with a brief description of Enterprise Resource Planning (ERP), followed by a discussion of the benefits provided by an integrated ERP system. Next, the chapter describes several critical issues that managers must consider before making the final decision to integrate all the business functions in the organization. These issues are categorized under fundamental issues, people, the organizational change process, and the different approaches to implementing ERP. A well-defined plan is the first step to a successful ERP implementation. Therefore, the chapter concludes with a flow chart, depicting many of the activities that must be included in an ERP implementation plan.

Introduction

The vision of an integrated information systems started in the 1960s, evolving from the inventory tracking systems to Materials Requirements Planning

(MRP), and finally to Enterprise Resource Planning (ERP) (Brady, Monk & Wagner, 2001). Today, almost every organization integrates part or all of its business functions together to achieve higher efficiency and productivity.

ERP is the process of integrating all the business functions and processes in an organization to achieve numerous benefits. First, a single point of data entry helps to reduce data redundancy while saving employees time in entering data, thereby reducing labor and overhead costs (Jacobs & Whybark, 2000). Second, the centralization of information, decision-making, and control leads to increases in efficiencies of operations and productivity, as well as coordination between departments, divisions, regions, and even countries. This is especially true for multinational corporations (MNC), in which global integration could result in better communications and coordination around the world. The global sourcing and distribution of parts and services could also provide appropriate benchmarks for operations around the world. Third, the sharing of a centralized database provides business managers with accurate and up-to-date information to make well-informed business decisions. Further, it reduces data redundancy while improving data integrity at the same time. Fourth, functional integration will consolidate all sorts of data, such as financial, manufacturing, and sales, to take advantage of bulk discounts. ERP is especially important for companies who are "intimately connected" to their vendors and customers, and who use electronic data interchange (EDI) to process sales transactions electronically. Therefore, the implementation of ERP is exceptionally beneficial to businesses such as manufacturing plants that mass produce products with little changes (Brady, Monk & Wagner, 2001). Nevertheless, the revolutionary and innovative ERP software system quickly expands into other business areas such as finance and retailing. ERP also provides companies with a competitive advantage over their competitors.

Important Issues to consider before Implementation

Before integrating business functions, managers must consider several important issues that will help them decide whether an ERP integration is the right choice for their organization (Lau, 2003). These pertinent issues are classified under the following categories: fundamental issues, organizational change process, people, and the different approaches to implementing ERP.

Fundamental Issues

First, managers must consider the fundamental issues of system integration by analyzing the organization's vision and corporate objectives (Jacobs & Whybark, 2000). For instance, does management fully understand its current business processes, and can it make implementation decisions in a timely manner? Is management ready to undertake drastic business process reengineering efforts to yield dramatic outcomes? Is management ready to make any changes in the structure, operations, and cultural environment to accommodate the options configured in the ERP system? Is the organization financially and economically prepared to invest heavily in an ERP implementation?

Next, management needs to decide on the key related implementation and business issues and how to proceed. Certainly, ERP is not suitable for companies that are experiencing rapid growth and change in an unstable environment, are undergoing change in the corporate management and philosophy, or that will be experiencing merger or liquidation in the near future. Understandably, there will be more foreseeable system integration problems if one of the merging companies is in the midst of an ERP upgrade because it must deal with scalability, a new IT infrastructure, and a different corporate culture simultaneously (Radcliff & LaPlante, 1999). Further, ERP integration is not recommended for companies which require a lot of flexibility to succeed or which manufacture products that are constantly changing (Jacobs & Whybark, 2000). Similarly, companies that have very little experience with formal information systems or have constantly changing information systems requirements will not benefit from an ERP implementation.

Finally, organizations need to exploit future communication and computing technology to integrate the ERP system with e-business applications. Often times, additional new hardware and specialized professionals are needed to run the powerful software system. Depending on the size of the company and the modules installed, the cost of implementation can range from one million to five hundred million dollars, and will take as long as two years for a mid-size company and seven years for a large, multinational corporation to complete.

People

People-related issues such as corporate philosophy and leadership style can play an important role in the ERP implementation process. Research has concluded that active top management support and commitment are essential to the success of any system implementation. Frequently, executive councils and steering committees consisting of top managers are developed to plan and manage the IT initiatives (Ross & Weill, 2002). Such senior managerial involvement tends to increase the optimization of IT business values.

Employees can be quite wary of any kind of change in the business processes, particularly during periods of economic downturn. Ill-trained employees who fight the changes in the business process tend to be poor performers. Therefore, to increase the chance of a successful ERP implementation and to reduce users' resistance to change, end users, especially those who are very knowledgeable with the operations, must be involved in all stages of the implementation process. Employees must also be educated about the ERP installation. Such educational endeavor should include a concise introduction to the basic concepts and architecture of ERP systems, including actual screen shots of the function modules. During these training sessions, it is important to discuss the managerial issues involved and to build a basic understanding of the integration concepts prior to the actual installation of the ERP system. Further, any business-to-business initiatives, reengineering projects, alliances, and the introduction of new technologies should also be addressed.

Project managers must take charge of the implementation process at all times. They must oversee the reengineering of the key business processes, reassign job responsibilities, restructure the organization's chart, and redefine work relationships. Further, they must also learn how to manage the software vendors and any outside consultants.

The Organizational Change Process

ERP implementation requires organizations to reengineer their key business processes in fundamental ways, revamping old ways of conducting business, redefining job responsibilities, and restructuring the organization. For major multinational corporations (MNC), the ERP systems must be customized to address global issues where different countries have different ways of doing business, and to incorporate country-specific business practices pertaining to accounting, tax requirements, environmental regulations, human resources, manufacturing, and currency conversion into the integrated systems. While integrating the information systems across various countries, three types of misfits (relating to data, process, and output) can occur due to incompatibilities between software functionality and organizational requirements as well as differences in cultural and regulatory environments (Soh, Sia & Tay-Yap, 2000). The unique context of each country in which an organization operates must be carefully enmeshed into the traditionally Western-biased business practices inherent in the ERP systems.

Diese et al. (2000) describe an eight-level process that managers can use to manage change. The first step is to create a comprehensive change vision and to make the vision operational. Then, a change strategy is defined to assess readiness change within the organization, to select the best change configuration, and to establish change governance. The third process is to develop leadership, in order to lead the change program and to develop leadership capability. Commitment from teams is built through communication, managing resistance, and transferring of knowledge and skills. The fifth process is to manage employee and stakeholders' performance by establishing needs, and implementing performance management and people practices. Business benefits are delivered through the building of business cases, and quantifying and sustaining benefits. The next process is to develop culture in the organization by understanding the current culture, and then to design the target culture and to implement cultural change. The final process is to design the organization by understanding the current organization, and then to design the target organization and to implement organizational change.

Different Approaches to Implementing ERP

Another important question for managers to consider is how much to implement. Depending on the tasks and processes involved in the installation process, there are several approaches to implementing ERP. For instance, is the organization embarking on an ambitious journey of revamping the whole enterprise using a complete integration, or is the organization employing a franchising strategy of implementing a partial integration across a few divisions with uncommon processes (Koch, 2002)? The complete integration approach was quite popular during the 1990s among the Fortune 500 corporations because ERP implementation was touted as the perfect solution to the Y2K problem. On the contrary, the franchise approach is employed by large or diverse companies that do not have many common processes across the organizations. Individual ERP software packages with their own database are installed in each business division, while common processes sharing common information are installed across the organization. This is a good strategy for companies who would like to ease into ERP implementation, by starting with a pilot installation and slowly moving into other business units. Another approach is for small companies interested in experimenting with ERP, by starting with a few key processes or a particular module. Such "canned" processes would require little reengineering, thereby maintaining minimal disruption to the daily business operations. However, such IT endeavors seldom result in extensive benefits to the organizations.

The bigger the organization, the more complex the business processes are and the greater the difficulties in implementing the ERP system (Brady, Monk & Wagner, 2001). Organizations considering a partial implementation must deal with the problems associated with using multiple vendors. They also need to consider simultaneous versus piecemeal implementation because of the ripple effect caused by decisions made in one module. In general, in order to maintain a smooth transition of the business processes and operations, simultaneous integration of the whole system, instead of functional or departmental integration, is highly recommended.

The ERP Implementation Plan

The flowchart in Figure 1 depicts several activities that must be performed before implementing an ERP system. First, managers must conduct a feasibility study of the current situation to assess the organization's needs by analyzing the availability of hardware, software, databases, and in-house computer expertise, and make the decision to implement ERP where integration is essential (Buck-Emden, 2000). They must also set goals for improvement and establish objectives for the implementation, and calculate the break-even points and benefits to be received from this expensive IT investment. The second major activity involves educating and recruiting end users to be involved throughout the implementation process.

Third, managers will form a project team or steering committee that consists of experts from all functional areas to lead the project. After a decision is made, a team of system consultants will be hired to evaluate the appropriateness of implementing an ERP system, and to help select the best enterprise software provider and the best approach to implementing ERP. In most situations, the consultant team will also recommend the modules that are best suited to the company's operations (manufacturing, financials, human resources, logistics,

Figure 1. The ERP implementation plan.

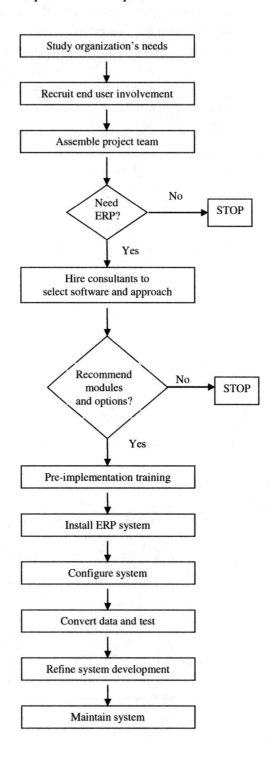

forecasting, etc.), system configurations, and business-to-business applications such as supply-chain management, customer relationship management, e-procurement, and e-marketplace.

The importance of adequate employee and manager training can never be overestimated. IT analysts usually recommend that managers reserve 11% of the project's budget for training. Different kinds and different levels of training must be provided to all business stakeholders, including managers, end users, customers, and vendors, before the system is implemented. Such training is usually customized and can be provided by either internal or outside trainers.

The system installation process will address issues such as software configuration, hardware acquisition, and software testing. Data and information in the databases must be converted to the format used in the new ERP system and servers and networks need to be upgraded. This is also the time to refine systems development, and ensure that the business functions are aligned with IT needs. An ongoing system maintenance will address issues and problems that arise during operations. A post-implementation review is recommended to ensure that all business objectives established during the planning phase are achieved. Needed modifications are tackled during this phase too.

Conclusion

An ERP implementation is a huge commitment from the organization, costing millions of dollars, and can take up to several years to complete. However, when it is integrated successfully, the benefits can be enormous. A well-designed and properly integrated ERP system allows the most updated information to be shared among various business functions, thereby resulting in tremendous cost savings and increased efficiency. When making the implementation decision, management must considered fundamental issues such as the organization's readiness for a dramatic change, the degree of integration, key business processes to be implemented, e-business applications to be included, and whether or not new hardware need to be acquired. In order to increase the chance of user acceptance, employees must be consulted and be involved in all stages of the implementation process. Providing proper education and appropriate training are also two important strategies to increase the end-user acceptance rate. The organization is also going through a drastic change, with changes in the way businesses are conducted, the organization being restructured, and job responsibilities being redefined. To facilitate the change process, managers are encouraged to utilize the eight-level organizational change process recommended by Diese et al. (2000). Managers can implement their ERP systems in several ways, which include the whole integration, the franchise approach, and the single-module approach. Finally, the chapter concludes with a flowchart, depicting many of the activities that managers must perform to ensure a proper ERP implementation.

References

Brady, J., Monk, E., & Wagner, B. (2001). *Concepts in enterprise resource planning.* Boston, MA: Course Technology.

Buck-Emden, R. (2000). *The SAP R/3 system: An introduction to ERP and business software technology.* Reading, MA: Addison-Wesley.

Diese, M. et al. (2000). *Executive's guide to e-business: From tactics to strategy.* New York, NY: John Wiley & Sons, Inc.

Jacobs, R., & Whybark, C. (2000). *Why ERP? A primer on SAP implementation.* New York, NY: Irwin McGraw-Hill.

Koch, C. (2002, February 7). The ABCs of ERP. http://www.cio.com/research/erp/edit/erpbasics.html

Lau, L. (2003). Implementing ERP systems using SAP. In M. Khosrow-Pour (Ed.), *Information technology and organizations: Trends, issues, challenges, and solutions* (pp. 732-734). Hershey, PA: Idea Group Publishing.

Radcliff, D., & LaPlante, A. (1999, November 29). When merger mania hits ERP. *Computerworld, 44.*

Ross, J., & Weill, P. (2002). Six IT decisions your IT people shouldn't make. *Harvard Business Review, 87.*

Soh, C., Sia, S., & Tay-Yap, J. (2000). Cultural fits and misfits: Is ERP a universal solution? *Communications of the ACM, 43*(4), 47.

Chapter VIII

Benefit Realisation with SAP:
A Case Study

Graham Blick
Curtin University of Technology, Australia

Mohammed Quaddus
Curtin University of Technology, Australia

Abstract

SAP is one of the dominating enterprise resource planning (ERP) software, which is used as an essential part of enterprise-wide information systems. While it can significantly contribute towards an organization's competitiveness by increasing efficiencies across various functional units, it can, on the other hand, bring about disasters if implemented incorrectly. Literature presents both implementation successes and failures. This chapter presents a successful SAP implementation in the WATER CORPORATION in Western Australia. A "Benefit Realisation Strategy and Realisation Process" was considered to be the key success factor in the implementation of SAP. The chapter describes the benefit realisation structure and process and discusses how SAP was implemented successfully within this framework. The benefits realisation and its impact are presented. Finally, future directions are highlighted.

Introduction

The current wave of Information Technology (IT)-enabled change appears to be just the beginning. The expected long-term impact of information technology is routinely compared to such technologies as electricity, the internal combustion engine, the printing press, and even the wheel. Literature suggests that its arrival represents an economic and social transition as fundamental as the shift from rural agriculture to urban industry 200 years ago, during the first Industrial Revolution. Information technology is capable not only of enabling a new economic infrastructure for industry, but also of transforming society – how people work, shop, play, and go to school. For example, advanced information and networking systems are changing the way we do research, communicate knowledge, learn, publish, and manage intellectual property. Information technologies are combining the engineering power of mass production with the intellectual capabilities of the modern library, publishing, and broadcasting systems (Thorp, 1998).

At the moment, however, there is a big practical problem. The track record of information technology to date is uneven and it is hard to figure out what makes for a successful IT investment. In practical terms, it is difficult for even large corporations to predict how major investments in new information systems will turn out, or how many months and years will go by before these investments produce solid economic returns, if they ever do. Few of the executives approving these multimillion-dollar investments have a clear idea of the results that they expect to get, or whether they actually achieved the benefits when the money is spent. This is not a technology problem – it is a business problem. It is about realising the potential value of information technology to the organisation. Understanding how to deal with this problem is an imperative for all business managers, and for those who are embarking on the acquisition and implementation of SAP it is fundamental (Thorp, 1998).

SAP is a complex system. It therefore needs a different approach for its implementation and benefits to be realised. It brings about its own culture, which needs to be adapted within the existing organisational culture (Krumbholz & Maiden, 2001). At the heart of the problem is a fundamental change in how organisations are using SAP and the information provided by that technology. Unlike other IT applications, implementation of SAP needs fundamental change in the business process and essentially involves "change management implementation" (Mandal & Gunasekaran, 2003). Unfortunately, it is not always easy to achieve. Krumbholz and Maiden (2001) point out that ERP implementation projects were, on average, 178% over budget, took two and half times longer than intended, and delivered only 30% of promised benefit. Crux of the problem was an improper implementation.

This chapter presents a case study on the successful implementation of SAP R/ three in the WATER CORPORATION of Western Australia (WA). As a result of a major long-term information management planning, the corporation adopted a plan to implement SAP R/3 in order to integrate its various functional areas. Sensing that major changes are needed in its business processes, the corporation came up with a benefit realisation strategy and realisation process in order to implement SAP successfully. The thrust of this chapter is to describe how this benefits realisation program was structured and implemented in order to successfully implement the SAP R/3.

In the next several sections we first provide background literature on ERP and SAP with respect to their implementations. The WATER CORPORATION of WA case is then presented. The benefit realisation structure and process are then described in detail with respect to SAP implementation in the corporation. The expected benefits, benefit realisation and its impact are next presented. Finally, conclusions are presented.

Background Literature

Implementation of information systems has been widely researched over the last two decades (Cooper & Zmud, 1990; Kwon & Zmud, 1987; among many others). A number of high-level factors, such as individual, structural, techno-logical, task-related, and environmental, have been found to affect the success-ful implementation of information systems (Kwon & Zmud, 1987). Most of these studies were, however, conducted in the context of traditional functional information systems. Enterprise resource planning (ERP) software, of which SAP is the market leader, brings extra complexities in the implementation process. ERP needs a deep appreciation of both operational and strategic impacts on the organisation, and very often that successful implementation often results in a cultural shift. In what follows we present a brief review of some past literature on the implementation of ERP/SAP.

Nah et al. (2001) conducted a comprehensive review of the literature and found 11 factors that are critical in the successful implementation of ERP systems. These are: ERP teamwork and composition; change management program and culture; top management support; business plan and vision; business process reengineering with minimum customisation; project management; monitoring and evaluation of performance; effective communication; software development, testing and troubleshooting; project champion; and appropriate business and IT legacy systems. It is noted that monitoring and evaluation of performance is one of the 11 critical factors, which is the subject of this chapter. Al-Mashari et al. (2003) developed a taxonomy of critical success factors of successful ERP implementation. It is also noted that performance evaluation of ERP systems is one of the most important factors suggested by the authors. In another study, Umble et al. (2003) presented a list of nine critical success factors for ERP implementation, such as: clear understanding of strategic goals, commitment by top management, excellent project management, great implementation team, data accuracy, extensive education and training, focused performance measures, and multi-site issues. It is noted that these factors overlap to a great extent with the factors presented by Nah et al. (2001). The authors also presented a case study and discussed how the nine factors were addressed by the company in implementing an ERP system. Hong and Kim (2002) identified critical success factors of ERP implementations in terms of "organizational fit of ERP" and "contingency variables". Based on a cross-sectional survey the authors concluded that ERP implementation success significantly depends on the organisational fit of ERP and certain contingency variables.

Mabert et al. (2003b) studied the ERP implementation process in US manufacturing companies. The authors stated that a typical ERP implementation took anywhere from one to five years. They also did a comparative analysis of on-time and on/under-budget with late and over-budget ERP implementations using logit (logistic) regression models. The results indicated a number of factors to be significant, including pre-implementation planning and system configuration. In a related study, Mabert et al. (2003a) conducted a two-phased study of ERP implementations (case studies followed by survey) of US manufacturing companies. Key finding of this study was that companies of different sizes approach ERP implementations differently, and the benefits realised are also dependent on company size. The authors found that "larger companies report improvements in financial measures, whereas the smaller companies report better performance in manufacturing and logistics". Abdinnour-

Helm et al. (2003) did an interesting study. The authors wanted to find out if pre-implementation involvement and training in ERP result in acceptance and effective implementation of ERP systems. Based on survey in a large aircraft manufacturing organization in the USA, the authors concluded that, "contrary to conventional wisdom, extensive organizational investments in shaping pre-implementation attitudes do not always achieve the desired effects" (Abdinnour-Helm et al., 2003). However, it must be recognised that the study was conducted only in one organisation, and at one point in time, thus limiting its generalisation. In a longitudinal study, Hutton et al. (2003) examined the impact of ERP adoption on firm performance. The authors found that over a three-year period ERP adopting firms showed significantly better financial performance compared to the non-adopters. Also, during the same time, financial performance of the non-adopters decreased, while it stayed steady for the adopters.

Rajagopal (2002) studied the implementation of ERP taking an innovation diffusion perspective. He examined implementations of ERP in six manufacturing firms via qualitative research process using the six-stage model proposed by Kwon and Zmud (1987). The author developed a comprehensive model of ERP implementation, which needs to be tested in a large sample of firms. In a comprehensive study, Stratman and Roth (2002) developed eight ERP competency constructs that are posited to result in improved business performance after the ERP system is operational in an organisation. The authors used the high level confirmatory factor analysis (CFA) technique to test the reliability and validity of the constructs. Their study, however, did not extend to test the impact of these constructs on the improved business performance due to ERP implementation. Sarker and Lee (2002) presented three key social enablers – strong and committed leadership, open and honest communication, and a balanced and empowered implementation team – as the precursors of successful ERP implementation. Taking a positivist case study approach, the authors, however, found that only strong and committed leadership could be established as a necessary condition of successful ERP implementation. The authors call for more research in this area to establish facts.

In a comprehensive survey of 158 Swedish manufacturing firms, Olhager and Selldin (2003) identified a list of 10 benefits that the firms experienced due to ERP implementations. Topping the list were "quickened information response time" and "increased interaction across the enterprise". The authors also reported the importance of pre-implementation process, implementation experience, and ERP system configuration. Mandal and Gunasekaran (2003) reported their experiences of ERP implementation in a WATER CORPORA-

TION in Australia. The authors found three distinct phases of pre-implementation, implementation, and post-implementation strategies to be significant in the success of ERP implementation in the corporation. The authors also offered specific strategies to be followed in any future implementation of ERP systems. In an interesting study, O'Leary (2002) investigated the use of knowledge management, specifically case-based reasoning, across the entire ERP life cycle. The author reported how case-based reasoning can be effectively used in ERP system choice, implementation and use. A prototype system was also presented. Krumbholz and Maiden (2001) highlighted the need for adapting ERP systems to fit with the organisational and national culture. Based on an empirical study in a large pharmaceutical organization in Scandinavia, the authors reported the evidence of a strong association between organisational culture and successful ERP implementation.

This review is not comprehensive. It is observed, however, that most of the studies on ERP implementations primarily deal with identifying (and sometimes testing) various critical factors. The range of studies varied from theoretical opinion-based to deep model building and testing quantitatively in a sample of firms. The notion of "benefit" came across in almost all the studies, either directly or indirectly. No formal study, however, was available to realise the benefit in an effective way, nor was the benefit notion used in any study as a means to implement ERP successfully.

This chapter addresses this gap and presents a case study of a benefit realisation program to implement ERP successfully in the WATER CORPORATION of Western Australia.

The WATER CORPORATION of Western Australia

The WATER CORPORATION of Western Australia (http://www.watercorporation.com.au/) is the only organisation in WA that provides water, wastewater, drainage and irrigation services to 1.7 million people throughout Western Australia. The Web site of the corporation describes its services as follows:

"The Water Corporation is one of Australia's largest and most successful water service providers with nearly A $9 billion invested in water services infrastructure. The Water Corporation enjoys an excellent performance record, benchmarked against world standards, and we use our 100 years of commercial and technical expertise to provide the most cost effective and suitable business solutions for our customers.

We are one of the world's more unique water utilities, providing world class water and wastewater services to the burgeoning city of Perth and hundreds of towns and communities spread over 2.5 million square kilometres. We also provide drainage and irrigation services to thousands of households, businesses and farms across the State.

We take pride in the leading role our organisation has played in developing the vast and diverse State of Western Australia particularly in the areas of customer service, planning, technology, and our corporate wide commitment to our environmental responsibilities." (http://www.watercorporation.com.au/, accessed on May 19, 2003)

The WATER CORPORATION was increasingly facing some major challenges in the form of tighter regulation and competition, in one form or another. International utilities are expected to actively seek opportunities in the Australian market, and are already competing in some instances. The Corporation's direction as outlined in its Strategic Development Plan, and its active pursuit of performance improvement are clear indications that the Corporation seeks to ensure its competitiveness by adopting "best practices" throughout the organisation. There is overwhelming evidence that the Corporation will simply be unable to meet the requirements of a regulated competitive environment while it continues to rely on the management information provided to it by its current systems (Water Corporation of W.A. –1997 A).

In May 1997 the WATER CORPORATION completed a major information management planning initiative (the "Corporation Information Management Strategy") to identify the strategic information needs of the WATER CORPORATION through 2002. In doing this, consideration was given to the Corporation's current information systems and technology environment, to identify a program of work aimed at positioning the Corporation to make cost effective use of information and information technology in undertaking its business. A key finding of the plan was that the existing suite of information systems lacked the functionality to support both current and emerging business requirements. In particular:

- The current systems comprise a combination of "in house" developed solutions and commercial packages. The majority of the existing systems are more than 10 years old and require significant ongoing maintenance and support;

- The systems utilise individual databases with data being exchanged through a set of complex interfaces; as a consequence data are frequently entered separately in different systems, resulting in duplication of effort and inconsistencies in the data;

- As a result of the lack of integration between systems, implementation of procedural or data changes in any system requires similar manual changes to be made in other relevant systems;

- No existing corporate systems are in place to support project management or contract management activities; this represents a major shortcoming given the magnitude of Corporation expenditure on capital investment and service delivery contracts;

- As a result of the system limitations, access to management information on many key business processes is limited, with data frequently being unreliable and out of date.

In the light of the above, a key recommendation of the Corporate Information Management System was to investigate the feasibility of replacing existing corporate applications with an integrated contemporary solution (Water Corporation of WA, 1997a – 1997d). In December 1997, a decision was therefore made by the board of the WATER CORPORATION to implement and integrate key business systems using the SAP R/3 packaged software as part of the "System 2000 project". The Corporation's implementation of SAP R/3 was considered to be much more than the upgrading of systems to meet Year 2000 requirements. It was an essential strategic step to enable the Corporation to succeed against the competition that will emerge in the next several years.

Benefit Realisation Program

Business Case for SAP R/3

The "Systems 2000 Project" of the WATER CORPORATION prepared a business case for SAP R/3. It included a detailed cost justification for the implementation of all of the functionalities of SAP R/3.

The Case was built around a structure identifying the major sources of costs and benefits from implementing SAP as the Corporation's information system (over a life of eight years). SAP Implementation and On-going Costs (Costs), net of Avoided Legacy System Costs (Avoided Costs) are subtracted from the Process Improvement Benefits (Benefits) resulting from the SAP implementation, to reach the Net Savings. The Costs, Avoided Costs and Benefits were analysed using accepted WATER CORPORATION investment financial models to form the basis for decision-making (assistance was sought from the "Commercial Division" of the WATER CORPORATION in vetting all models and assumptions used).

There were assumptions behind each primary area's Costs, Avoided Costs and Benefits, which were detailed in the full report. For example, one important assumption was the implementation timeline used in the business case. The timeline was subject to adjustments that will affect the timing of costs. To cater for such uncertainties a contingency had been included in the project budget.

The results from the business case indicated an *after-tax* Net Present Value (NPV) of A $22.01 million based on costs of A $39.76 million over an eight-year period. The NPV equated to an internal rate of return of 33% and investment payback in three years. Most of the costs would occur during the first two years of implementation and were more than offset by the benefits resulting from implementation of SAP in the following years. Internal and consulting resources accounted for 66% of the one-off costs. Other ongoing costs such as annual licence fees and configuration and application development (ABAP) support were also a significant component of total costs. The main avoided costs related to not having to repair existing systems, including financials. The two areas with the largest percentage of total benefits were Projects (Capital Works)—44% and Finance—23%.

This report recommended that the WATER CORPORATION proceed with the SAP implementation based not only on the quantifiable benefits, but also the qualitative benefits that will accrue. Such qualitative items included improved organisational decision-making; improved issue resolution through system integration and user-friendliness; and enhanced service to external and internal customers. The initiative was in alignment with the Corporation's strategic information technology plan (CIMS) and would tightly integrate information within the firm's mission-critical and reporting functions.

Benefit Realisation Structure

Services of Deloitte ICS consulting were used to implement the operational aspects of SAP R/3. It was felt, however, that to reap maximum benefit there needed to be a culture-shift and associated behavioural changes in the Corporation's management and staff. It is this supporting program of cultural change that will ultimately ensure the realisation and continuous reinforcement of the benefits identified for each of the process streams. SAP R/3 alone will deliver only a fraction of the benefits identified if the implementation is not complemented by vigorous executive leadership. Fundamental cultural changes are required to bring about a commercially aware and operationally astute WATER CORPORATION of the future.

A project management approach was therefore undertaken to implement SAP. Literature reveals that in order to implement complex systems like ERP software a project and program management approach must be undertaken formally (Ribbers & Schoo, 2002; Weston, Jr., 2001). In WATER CORPORATION's case a formal project was defined for SAP implementation and within this project a "Benefit Realisation Strategy and Realisation Process" was considered to be a critical factor in order to deal with the change management process and thus maximise the implementation prospects of SAP. It was also recognised that the benefits identified for the business case would need refining, and discussion on "Redesign" of the business process proceeded and the impact of the new processes became more clearly understood. In other words benefit realisation for SAP is not static; it is very much dynamic. The end users must be aware of the benefits of SAP in a formal and ongoing way.

The benefit realisation program of the corporation was considered to be vital for the successful implementation of SAP. It was structured as follows.

The Benefits Management Office

A Benefits Management Office was established to maintain stewardship of the benefits realisation process, the resulting documentation and knowledge assets arising across all process streams. The office had four full-time and three part-time employees. The roles included:

- Supporting the creation of business cases and funding proposals for out of scope initiatives and new initiatives, by interpretation of the associated benefit implications, that is, dollars, timing, resources and so forth.
- Monitoring the identified intangible benefits for review and reporting to the WATER CORPORATION as part of the ongoing process of cultural change.
- Revising the preferred realisation scenario to reflect the latest information on realised benefits as well as continuing any proposed initiatives.
- Communication to all stakeholders about benefits delivered.

The Benefits Register

A benefit register was created. Following sign-off of the benefit initiatives, it was appropriate to formally register the benefits. This required the creation of a base record in the Benefits Register database. The Benefits Register became the basis for the formal tracking of the benefit realisation for each of the agreed initiatives. The register was maintained by the Benefits Management Office, and contained the following sections:

- **Register of Initiatives** – contained all data related to the benefits, their measurement and assigned accountabilities for realisation.
- **Benefits Realisation Status** – contained information related to physical tracking of registered initiatives. This would include projects undertaken, progress reports, benefits generated, and costs incurred.

Benefit Realisation Process

Figure 1 shows an overview of the benefit realisation process, which was undertaken at the WATER CORPORATION.

It consists of three phases:

- **Define the Benefits Rationale** – This phase established the overall context for the change that was proposed through the implementation of SAP R/3.
- **Define the Plan** – Having defined the rationale, the approved benefits realisation initiatives were planned in terms of activities, responsibilities and timing. The plan was primarily outcome focused. Benefits arising were measured at the major initiative level. The focus was on the explicitly identified segments that provided the greatest measurable payback.
- **Monitor and Realise the Benefits** – Benefits realisation plan progress was monitored on an ongoing basis. Accountability for realising the benefits rested with the Process Owners, supported by a Benefits Management Office. The benefits achieved were monitored via a Benefits Register (as described earlier). When unexpected issues arose, the impact was analysed and as a result downstream plans might change. This phase used to begin with the commencement of sign-off, and continued through the entire realisation process.

Figure 1. The benefit realization process.

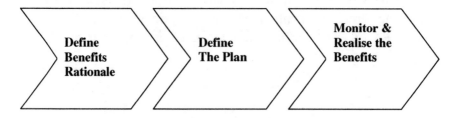

Defining the "Realisation Plan"

Defining the "Realisation Plan" was considered to be an involved process. As indicated earlier it involved finding the activities, responsibilities and timing, and it was outcome focused. Figure 2 shows the process that was followed in order to develop the "Realisation Plan".

The process involved three major phases: set the current baseline ("as-is" position), develop target baseline ("to-be" position), and prepare the realisation plan (implementation framework) (see Figure 2). The benefit realisation builds on prior work undertaken for the business case and seeks, with the benefits of additional information and analysis, to validate the findings of the business case and identify additional benefits. Finally, a realisation plan is developed to set out how the Corporation will realise the benefits and what initiatives must be put in place in order to achieve them. The work plan incorporates a number of inputs, including the results of the "Visioning and Targeting phase of Systems 2000," the incorporation of world's "best practices" and "benchmarking" data, the outputs of the "process redesign workshops" and "interviews" with WATER CORPORATION staff.

Figure 2. Process for realization plan.

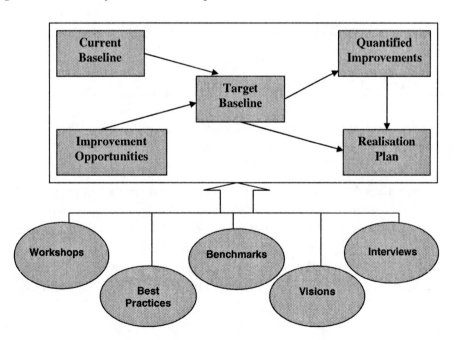

Expected Benefits and Impact of Benefit Realisation

Expected Strategic Benefits with SAP

Before SAP was implemented a detailed list of "expected" benefits were worked out. The project team along with outside consultants identified the following strategic benefits:

- Increased customer satisfaction
- Faster response to regulatory reporting demands
- Increased competitive advantage
- Support alliances, mergers, and acquisitions
- Improved business decisions
- Process integration and improvement
- Improved access to information
- Integrate culture
- Improved flexibility/adaptability
- Benchmark partnerships
- Improved employee flexibility

Expected Operational Benefits

The expected operational benefits were centered on the following areas: Projects, Finance and Materials management.

In the area of projects, the WATER CORPORATION of WA spends approximately A$275 million dollars per annum on its capital program. For a number of reasons including approved scope changes, land access problems, latent construction conditions and resource availability, projects are often not completed within their estimated timeframes. This contributes to project cost over runs. In addition, the current lack of systems integration, caused by the existence of a number of disparate systems (Works, CIP, General Ledger,

Primavera P3), generates inefficiencies in the management and administration of projects and contracts. The implementation of SAP R/3 was expected to benefit the Corporation by providing tools that will enable project managers and support staff to focus their efforts on delivering quality outcomes rather than expending effort on the current cumbersome reporting and administration process. This should result in:

- Lower project management costs and/or an improved focus on quality project outcomes.
- Improved project-reporting information highlighting the causes of estimate variations and providing a means for taking corrective action and a basis of continuous improvement.

This would allow the Corporation to realise quantifiable benefits (net of costs) that equate to A$24.85 million in present value terms over an eight-year time horizon.

In the Finance area, SAP functionality would enable a significant amount of process change to occur as a result of:

- Streamlining of processing effort,
- Streamlining of data gathering, compilation, and presentation,
- Reduction in data validation and error correction,
- Elimination of duplicate data entry points,
- Consistency of information enabling efficient information sharing,
- Consistent practices and business rules enforced through the system,
- Visibility of information across functional boundaries, and
- Improved data interrogation capabilities.

This would allow the Corporation to realise quantifiable benefits (net of costs) that equate to A$13.03 million present value terms over an eight-year time horizon.

In materials management, SAP functionality would enable the Corporation to realise quantifiable benefits in two key areas:

- Discounts through supplier rationalisation and strategic contracts.
- Improved inventory management.

In the area of supplier rationalisation and strategic contracts, the use of SAP functionality and tools would assist the Corporation in selecting the suppliers it wishes to enter into contracts with by providing vendor evaluation and flexible reporting from summary to detailed level. The decision support capability provided by SAP will need to be supplemented by additional resources to negotiate and set up contracts.

In the area of improved inventory management, strong integration with Project schedules and Works Management schedules would provide the opportunity to use the integration of SAP to alter the requisition dates in the Material Management Module to reflect slippage in Projects, thereby reducing the risk of unnecessary stockpiling of inventory.

This would allow the Corporation to realise quantifiable benefits (net of costs) that equate to A$11.50 million in present value terms over an eight-year time horizon.

Besides the above quantifiable benefits the project team also came up with a list of intangible benefits for various functional areas that will come about due to SAP implementation.

Benefits Realisation and Its Impact

A structured approach to develop "target baselines" (see Figure 2) and benefits for each SAP sub-system was effected, and was undertaken by external consultants and internal business representatives. The outcomes included a series of recommended business changes to maximise benefits from SAP, such as centralising HR/Payroll, Logistics Management, Finance and Controlling, and the processing functions associated with Plant Maintenance.

Process Management principles were developed in the Visioning Phase of the SAP Project by adopting the "Industry Process Print". The process Model was further developed and accepted during the current Benefits Realisation phase. This paved the way for breaking down cross-functional organizational barriers that hindered change and placed responsibility on Process Owners for leading the implementation of change initiatives.

SAP is also being used by the business as a process improvement tool. For example, an HR Service Centre was implemented, where a new central function was created to reduce transactional staffing numbers Corporation-wide along with improving the process. Shared business support functions may also be reviewed to improve operational effectiveness, achieve savings for the business, and reduce staffing numbers, such as Logistic Services (Material Management Process). There is potential for similar benefits in the Plant Maintenance Process from centralising transactional functions associated with Work Order feedback and employee Daily Time Sheets.

System functionality and integration has provided the business with opportunities to commercially benefit from centralising some of its functions. There is no reason why this should not continue, if there are sound commercial opportunities, and no negative impact on business performance.

The Benefits Realisation process has focused on a long-term view in contributing to the development of a cultural change in the business. It has done this by developing processes and tools, including:

- Benefits Delivery Implementation Process and Tools, incorporating:
    - Operating Principles For Leading Organisational Change
    - Communication and Stakeholder Enrolment Strategy
    - Benefits Realisation Group Relationships
    - High Level Generic Implementation Plan and Time Line
    - Low Level Generic Implementation Plan and Time Line
- A requirement for a structured methodology to deliver process improvements and process re-engineering business gains.
- A Benefits Realisation Strategy incorporated in any change process and business case.
- An ongoing employee education and development strategy is in place.
- Accountability for the delivery of benefits by Process Owners, Custodians and Managers are defined and agreed prior to the implementation of any change process to assist them to drive full realisation of benefits within an established time frame.
- The Benefits Realisation Group providing the tools and support to enable Process Owners to lead the implementation of initiatives.

- The Benefits Realisation process focusing on providing a consulting, facilitation, and advisory service, including the provision of business processes and tools.

- Integration, coordination, and cooperation between all impacted sectors of the business from commencement of the change process.

- Business savings being recorded and reported.

- Process Custodians and Process Managers monitoring and reporting regularly to the executive on tangible and non-tangible business benefits as a result of change initiatives.

Survey

To measure the impact of benefit realisation and SAP implementation, a benefit survey was undertaken to get a view from the end users. Outcomes of the survey were intended to provide the following:

- An appreciation within divisions, regions, and between SAP processes of the system's impact on the business and work practices;

- Information to assist with the planning and implementation of a SAP version upgrade and associated delta teams; and

- A baseline upon which future productivity improvements of SAP implementation and the upgrade could be measured.

The Benefits Realisation Group designed the SAP Benefits Survey, which was administered throughout the Corporation (across all strategic business units of the WATER CORPORATION) in November 2000. The survey used a Likert scale for various benefit measures. Twelve hundred end users were distributed with the questionnaire. The response rate was 37.5%, with a satisfactory level of participation from most areas of the business, including an alliance partner Serco, Australia.

Overall Survey Outcomes

The overall findings from the SAP Benefits Survey are summarised in the following:

- SAP technology has been embraced by the business.
- There has been a significant positive change in work practices.
- SAP offers greater access to information, better integration and design than legacy systems.
- Infrequent users find SAP to be complex and not very user friendly, thus having a high demand for system support, reliance on others, and training.
- An increase in productivity and time spent on innovative solutions to work problems.
- More time spent at work, mainly due to increased workloads and staff reductions.
- Training provided has been satisfactory.
- 86% of respondents had attended a SAP overview course.
- 73% had attended SAP module-specific training.
- Reporting is difficult, causes frustration and does not support business needs. Respondents indicated that the difficulties associated with generating reports inhibited their ability to meet performance targets.
- High degree of confidence in the accuracy of information from SAP.
- Level of duplication in work.
- Employees are confident in their understanding, application and optimisation of SAP; however, they are not fully aware of the potential of SAP.
- Infrequent users rely on support staff to operate SAP as it is difficult to master if not used regularly; that is, the system is not very user friendly.
- Quality and effectiveness of SAP have outweighed other information technology and business related problems.

Significant Results

Considering the responses to the survey questions, and from the comments provided, respondents have specifically identified opportunities for the Corporation to improve in the following areas:

- Better reporting facility.
- Remote access for country users.

- Advanced training, job specific training, tailored to employee groups, and more time to learn.

- Better interface between SAP and other corporate computer systems, for example, Grange.

- Less duplication between SAP and manual processes.

- Improve the "friendliness" of SAP – system down time, lock outs, passwords, cheat sheets, short cuts.

- The amount of time spent on IT problems.

- Reduce bureaucracy.

Conclusions and the Future

Organisations have struggled over the years to implement SAP successfully. Although the literature is full of case studies on factors and variables, operational studies on successful SAP implementation is relatively scarce. This chapter presents an operational case study on how SAP was successfully implemented in the WATER CORPORATION of Western Australia. A benefit realisation program was embedded in the project of implementing the SAP. This benefit realisation program was considered vital in the successful implementation of SAP.

The chapter discusses the structure and process of the benefit realisation program. It also presents how the business case for SAP was successfully built for the WATER CORPORATION. Finally, the chapter presents the expected and actual benefits that were realised due to the implementation of SAP via survey on the users of SAP.

After successfully implementing SAP and monitoring its operations for about two years the WATER CORPORATION decided to formally close the benefit realisation group and integrate it into the business. This was done via the delivery of a training program to senior line managers on the benefit realisation methodology and toolsets. The responsibility of delivery of benefits was incorporated in the corporate accountability model and reporting on benefits was transferred to management accounting. At the time of its closure the benefit realisation group achieved a total savings of A\$14.91 million for the WATER CORPORATION in about 14 months. More importantly, it also helped to develop a "benefits" culture within the corporation and maintained a constant focus on benefits delivery and key issue resolution.

References

Abdinnour-Helm, S., Lengnick-Hall, M.L., & Lengnick-Hall, C.A. (2003). Pre-implementation attitudes and organizational readiness for implementing an enterprise resource planning system. *European Journal of Operational Research, 146,* 258-273.

Al-Mashari, M., Al-Mudimigh, A., & Zairi, M. (2003). Enterprise resource planning: A taxonomy of critical ractors. *European Journal of Operational Research, 146,* 352-364.

Cooper, R.B., & Zmud, R.W. (1990). Information technology implementation research: A technology diffusion approach. *Management Science, 36*(2), 123-139.

Hong, K.K., & Kim, Y.G. (2002). The critical success factors for ERP implementation: An organizational fit perspective. *Information and Management, 40,* 25-40.

Hutton, J.E., Lippincott, B., & Reck, J.L. (2003). Enterprise resource planning systems: Comparing firm performance of adopters and non-adopters, *International Journal of Accounting Information Systems, 55,* 1-20.

Krumbholz, M., & Maiden, N. (2001). The implementation of enterprise resource planning packages in different organizational and national cultures. *Information Systems, 26,* 185-204.

Kwon, T.H., & Zmud, R.W. (1987). Unifying the fragmented models of information systems implementation. In R.J. Boland & R.A. Hirschheim (Eds.), *Critical issues in information systems research* (pp. 227-251). Wiley.

Mabert, V.A., Soni, A., & Venkataramanan, M.A. (2003a). The impact of organization size on enterprise resource planning (ERP) implementations in the US manufacturing sector. *Omega,* 31, 235-246.

Mabert, V.A., Soni, A., & Venkataramanan, M.A. (2003b). Enterprise resource planning: Managing the implementation process. *European Journal of Operational Research, 146,* 302-314.

Mandal, P., & Gunasekaran, A. (2003). Issues in implementing ERP: A case study. *European Journal of Operational Research, 146,* 274-283.

Nah, F.F., Lau, J.L., & Kuang, J. (2001). Critical factors for successful implementation of enterprise systems. *Business Process Management Journal, 7*(3), 285-296.

O'Leary, D.E. (2002). Knowledge management across the enterprise resource planning system life cycle. *International Journal of Accounting Information Systems, 3,* 99-110.

Olhager, J., & Selldin, E. (2003). Enterprise resource planning survey of Swedish manufacturing firms. *European Journal of Operational Research, 146,* 365-373.

Rajagopal, P. (2002). An innovation-diffusion view of implementation of enterprise resource planning (ERP) systems and development of a research model. *Information and Management, 40,* 87-114.

Ribbers, P.M.A., & Schoo, K.C. (2002). Program management and complexity of ERP implementations. *Engineering Management Journal, 14*(2), 45-52.

Sarker, S., & Lee, A.S. (2002). Using a case study to test the role of three key social enablers in ERP implementation. *Information and Management,* 1-17.

Stratman, J.K., & Roth, A.V. (2002). Enterprise resource planning (ERP) competence constructs: Two-stage multi-item scale development and validation. *Decision Sciences, 33*(4), 601-628.

Thorp, J. (1998). *The information paradox.* Toronto: McGraw-Hill.

Umble, E.J., Haft, R.R., & Umble, M.M. (2003). Enterprise resource planning: Implementation procedures and critical success factors. *European Journal of Operational Research, 146,* 241-257.

Water Corporation of WA. (1997a). *System 2000 – Proposal for the replacement of the corporation's financial systems – Version 01.* Water Corporation of WA, Perth, Australia.

Water Corporation of WA. (1997b). *Business case executive summary – Implementation of key business information systems.* Water Corporation of WA, Perth, Australia.

Water Corporation of WA. (1997c). *Business case – Part A formal submission - Implementation of key business information systems.* Water Corporation of WA, Perth, Australia.

Water Corporation of WA. (1997d). *Business case – Part B benchmark comparisons - Implementation of key business information systems.* Water Corporation of WA, Perth, Australia.

Weston, F.C., Jr. (2001). ERP implementation and project management. *Production and Inventory Management Journal,* 3rd/4th Quarter, 75-80.

Chapter IX

The e-ERP Transformation Matrix

Colin G. Ash
Edith Cowan University, Australia

Janice M. Burn
Edith Cowan University, Australia

Abstract

A model of e-business transformation is developed for ERP enabled organisations, based on the findings of a longitudinal multiple case study analysis of SAP sites. The model is represented as a matrix along three stages of e-business growth. The theory embedded within the matrix recommends that successful e-business transformation with ERP systems occurs when B2B value propositions are realised through integration and differentiation of technologies, used to support new business models for delivering products and services online. In addition, the management focus evolves through employee self-service and empowerment towards extensive relationship building with e-alliances. The matrix can be used by ERP business managers to guide their strategies for organisational transformation but also highlights critical stages of change.

Introduction

This chapter presents the results of a longitudinal analysis of e-business implementations through ERP (e-ERP). This involved a study of 11 international organisations over a four-year period using multiple interviews and extensive secondary data collection. Three separate research models were used to analyse different stages of e-business growth and the results of this multi-stage analysis consolidated into a model of e-business transformation. This brings together the antecedents of e-business success using the findings from case analyses against three separate research models: B2B interaction, e-business change, and virtual organising.

A single model of e-business transformation (eBT) is proposed that focuses on realising the benefits of B2B interaction from virtual organising by utilising the facilitators of successful e-business change. This model of eBT represents a comprehensive view of e-ERP as the fusion of the three research models, mapped into various stages of e-business development: integration, differentiation, and demonstration of value propositions. The authors argue that successful e-business transformation with ERP occurs when *value propositions* are realised through *integration* and *differentiation of technologies* used to support new *business models* to deliver *products and services* online. The associated management focus evolves through self-service, care and empowerment towards extensive relationship building with e-alliances.

Theoretical Framework

A comprehensive model of e-ERP implementations may be presented simply as the fusion of three interrelated models. Figure 1 illustrates e-ERP as a primitive composite view of the three research models: *Benefits of B2B, e-Business Change, and Virtual Organising,* where:

- Benefits of B2B are illustrated by a two-dimensional model (1) where value returns are directly proportional to the level of integration of e-business activity across a set of B2B models (Carlson, 1995). B2B refers to the class of business-to-business (B2B) models that include business-

Figure 1. Three views of e-ERP implementation.

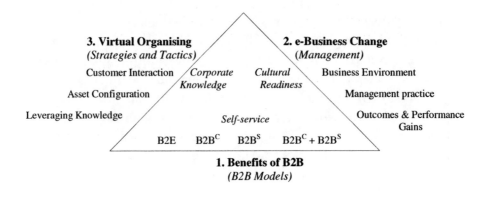

to-supplier (B2B^S), business-to-employee (B2E), business-to-consumer B2C and business-to-corporate customer (B2B^C) (Ash, 2001).

- e-Business Change is illustrated by a flat model (2) in which progress is across 11 interrelated components within three broad dimensions based on relevant research in the areas of "strategic management innovation, organisational change, and e-business evaluation" (Guha et al., 1997). These models overcome a purely techno-centric view.

- Virtual Organising is illustrated by a three-dimensional model (3) of e-business activity that is "applicable to any company." Progress is along the three dimensions of "customer interaction, asset configuration, and leveraging knowledge" (Venkatraman & Henderson, 1998).

Each research model represented in Figure 1 reflects a different business focus covering organisational theory, strategy, change management, and work practices. These models were evaluated at different stages of the study through a composite case based method as shown in Figure 2.

Figure 2. Stages of composite case-based research method.

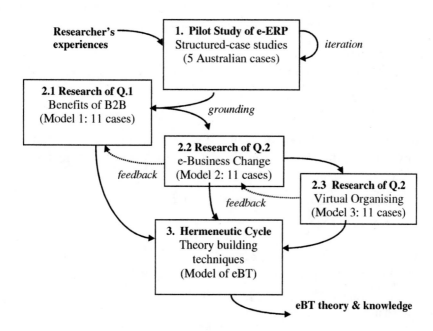

Methodology: Triangulation of Research Models

A pilot case study of five Australian SAP sites helped ground the theory for the study of e-ERP. This was followed by a three-stage study of 11 international SAP sites within a diverse industry context. The final conceptual framework is described in terms of e-business transformation (eBT), a term previously used by Lehmann (2001) and Soni (2001).

Data Collection and Analysis

Data were gathered from three sources; primary, secondary and tertiary:

- *Primary data* – from semi-structured interviews conducted November 1999, June 2000, and June 2001 in 11 international SAP organisations.

- *Secondary data* – from company documents collected or sent via e-mails.

- *Tertiary data* – from case research papers written by third party consultants.

In all cases the focal point for contact was a SAP project manager in the company who was directly responsible or integrally involved with the project

Table 1. Data collection and analysis matrix.

Key Questions	Data Collection Instrument	Data Analysis
1. How do organisations maximise benefits from e-ERP implementations?	1st Interview instrument - semi-structured Questionnaire.	Content analysis of interview data within CF_1 model developed from the Pilot Study.
2. What factors facilitate and/or inhibit the success of e-ERP implementations?	2nd Interview instrument - semi-structured Questionnaire constructs of components of e-ERP projects.	Cross-case analysis of constructs to determine the components that contribute to success or failure; using exemplar cases.
3. Do e-ERP projects fit the strategy of virtual organising?	1st and 3rd Interview instrument - semi-structured Questionnaire and industry presentations.	Map content of all cases to demonstrate the vector interdependence maximum benefits from VOing

Table 2. Business-to-business cases.

Case Organisation	Industry	B2E Interaction	e-Business Project Title	No. of Users
1. Halliburton	Engineering	Intranet access to	"Employee Tracking Intranet"	~1100 staff
2. UBS	Banking	SAP data	"Employee Networking"	~40,000 emps
		B2C Interaction		
3. Wine Society	Retailing	Internet access to SAP data	Online Ordering by Members	~60 staff
4. UNICEF Aust.	National Charity	Internet access to SAP by ASP	1st Australian Charity Web site	~35 employees +30 volunteers
		B2B Interaction	**(B2B^S and B2B^C)**	
5. Biotech	Biotechnology	SAP to supplier	Staff research procurement	~240 staff
6. Novartis	Chemical	catalogues and	Sales Order and Rapid Delivery	~22,000
7. Bertelsmann	Media	Intranet access	Simple Ordering e-catalogue	~28,000
8. Statoil	Oil and Gas	to SAP data	Staff travel procurement	~18,000
9. Employee-Nat	Employment		Simple Ordering e-catalogue	~14,000
10. FSC - Fujitsu Siemens computer	Computer	Corp. customer access to SAP data	Order Request System extended to an e-Mall of 3 companies	~11,000
11. Dell corp with LSI Logic corp	Computer ------------------ Electronics	non-ERP with SAP	Customised online sales integrated with corporate customers MRO procurement	~27,000 ~14,000

from beginning to end. To eliminate any bias by a single respondent, attempts were made to ensure triangulation of data from multiple sources in the organisation. Most of the interviewees were either sponsors of the e-ERP or major team members who had a good, objective, and knowledgeable view of the project. The questions and collection instruments are summarised in Table 1. In Table 2 the profiles of the case SAP-based organisations that participated in the study are shown.

The findings are presented by categories of the three interactive B2B models summarised as:

- *Business-to-employee* (B2E), to harness the flow/sharing of corporate information, via intranets.
- *Business-to-consumer* (B2C), to access a 24x7 global consumer base, via the Web.
- *Business-to-Business* (B2B^S and B2B^C), to support supply chain management between partner organisations.

Within each classification the case findings are presented in order of increasing e-business application sophistication (Perez et al., 1999).

The case material collected was used to verify all the essential characteristics of an e-business transformation. The case findings were distilled into a single comprehensive "3x3" matrix as the essential part of a new theory or model of e-Business Transformation (eBT), developed to guide managers through different stages of e-business implementation.

Model of E-Business Transformation

The concept of eBT is defined as realising the benefits from virtual organising within complex B2B interactions by utilising the facilitators of successful e-business change. To develop a precisely defined theory of eBT, we begin by identifying the basic research themes, displayed as a model in Figure 3.

Figure 3 represents eBT as a comprehensive business architecture that focuses on three interdependent dimensions of online business: *ICT technologies, Products and Services, Business Models* (Osterwalder et al., 2002), where:

- *ICT Technologies* – refers to the convergence of technologies for information flow within and between organisations, for example e-ERP implementations;
- *Products and Services* – refers to asset and competency sourcing for providing cheaper, faster, and improved quality of products and services;
- *Business Models* – refers to the architecture of the firm and its network of partners for creating, marketing and delivering value.

Figure 3. e-Business transformation model.

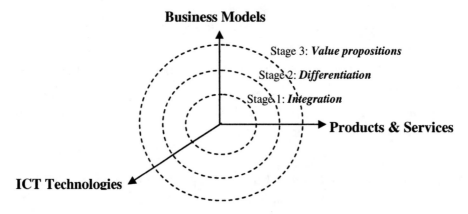

Stages of e-Business Transformation

Each dimension of the eBT model is further detailed at three stages of greater e-business commitment to integration, differentiation, and demonstration of value propositions. Progress in the first stage focuses on *integration* for achieving efficiency gains in task units such as customer service, purchasing, and new product development. In stage 2 the focus is on *differentiation* through selecting the most effective resourcing and marketing activities. The third stage focuses on demonstration of *value propositions* within an inter-organisational network to design and leverage multiple interdependent communities to create superior economic and virtual value (Singh & Thomson, 2002; Venkatraman & Henderson, 1998).

The model of eBT shows business focused at three stages of development with outcomes and performance gains of greater virtual progression:

Figure 4 illustrates the interrelatedness of the three stages of eBT as:

Figure 4. Three stages of e-Business transformation.

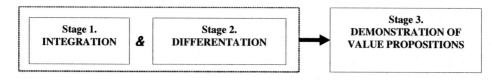

e-ERP Transformation Matrix

Table 3 represents a map of the issues distilled from the findings of this longitudinal three-stage study. This table is referred to as the e-ERP transformation matrix and forms the next level of abstraction in the eBT model. It identifies the essentials of eBT and is constructed to illustrate the interdependence of the dimensions of eBT and the stages of progression. The results of the analysis were mapped along the e-business stages of growth: integration of e-business technologies for e-malls and B2B commerce, differentiation of products and services for e-business positioning, and the realisation of value propositions of the e-partnerships.

Table 3. e-ERP transformation matrix.

| | Stages of e-Business Transformation | | |
	(1999 -)	(2000 -)	(2001 -)
Business Dimensions	**Stage 1: Integration**	**Stage 2: Differentiation**	**Stage 3: Demonstration of Value Propositions**
Technology (virtual infrastructure)	*** <u>ICT</u> ERP with e-Sales & e-Procurement applns.**	Differential Resourcing ASP versus cost of ownership on the outsourcing spectrum	Innovative Technologies ERP and non-ERP networks for e-marketplaces
Products & Services (virtual experience)	e-Malls e-Mall integration and information exchange	*** e-Branding Customisation versus standardisation; Brand identity & integrity**	e-Communities Foster customer, supplier, and employee expertise; Emerging collaborative online communities
Business Models (virtual B2B interactions)	e-Commerce Integration B2B Integration of e-Sales & e-Procurement systems $B2B^C + B2B^S$	e-Positioning B2B positioning within a range open to private e-marketplaces	*** e-Enterprise One2Many versus One2One; Distinct focus of One2One partnerships**
Examples	Remote experience of e-catalogues. More tasks, "group ware" skills for online communication.	Assemble and coordinate assets through effective use of online services	Business network to design and leverage interdependent e-communities. Dependent on relationships

* The arrows represent real organisational transformation with e-business

In Table 3 the three diagonal cells* in the e-ERP matrix (3x3) indicate the 'critical' elements that involve a cultural shift for a real organisational transformation. The other cells identify the elements that contribute to the organisation's competitive advantage. Transition along the diagonal or critical elements of the matrix, represents real organisational transformation with e-business. This was observed to occur within a culture of e-business readiness of the organisation and partner organisations.

Case Analysis for e-ERP Transformation Matrix

The case findings were analysed to identify and code the elements within the stages of the e-ERP transformation and by the business dimensions.

Stage 1: Integration

Technologies: e-ERP (Essential to Stage 1)

The findings show that "back-end" to "front-end" enterprise application integration is essential to achieve savings and cost reduction. Integration of the system architecture is made possible through a variety of "back-end," "sell-side" and "buy-side" systems; all 11 cases demonstrated this, but specifically Statoil and Siemens with their standardised ERP platform and e-business applications.

Products and Services: e-Malls

In a study of Australian e-malls, Singh and Thompson (2002, p.308) concluded: "it is apparent that for effective B2B exchange in Australia, standards for interoperability between business partners, and technology integration for information exchange on goods and services is essential". For example, Fujitsu Siemens Computers (FSC) achieved integration of the online sales systems for three companies.

Business Models: e-Commerce B2B Integration

The integration of e-business models, $B2B^C$ with $B2B^S$ is essential to maximise efficiency gains from supporting technology infrastructure, so that people can get the job done efficiently. Two cases of B2B e-business integration with a global computer supplier and its largest corporate customer demonstrate a more complex model. These exemplar cases demonstrate the integration of ERP and non-ERP systems with other ERP systems, using Web-based technologies to provide the infrastructure required to optimise the overall B2B value chain. Also, the study emphasises the synergistic benefit stream from B2B integration and the interaction of inter-organisation e-business solutions, for example Dell and FSC.

Stage 2: Differentiation

Technologies: Differential Outsourcing

Segev and Gebauer (2001, p. 249) argue that "the mid points of the outsourcing continuum are the most challenging." From case observations they describe the continuum as a wide range from "do it yourself" to complete outsourcing, with an increasing number of possibilities. The one case study where the complete management of an e-ERP project was outsourced to an ASP demonstrates the challenge for UNICEF Australia to balance the loss of control against the cost of ownership, whereas FSC partially outsourced their online sales systems to Siemens Business Systems quite successfully.

Products and Services: e-Branding (Essential to Stage 2)

The e-business tactics for positioning in the virtual space were to:

- Differentiate between corporate customers and end consumers; for example, UNICEF and Dell,
- Deliver customised products and services using standard components; for example, Dell and FSC,

- Differentiate between brand identity and brand integrity, where "e-branding becomes a critical issue" (Venkatraman & Henderson, 1998, p. 34); for example Bertlesmann, UNICEF, Wine Society, Dell and FSC.

Business Models: e-Positioning

Biotech and Novartis repositioned themselves with their largest corporate suppliers. FSC repositioned itself into the computer industry through e-sales. The tendency of these pioneers was to start with development of public relationship building and then shift to private relationship building between suppliers and buyers. This is observed to be more than a passing phase. Further, had the product lines been high technology-based, for example Dell and FSC, then it is likely the level of e-business readiness would have been too low to realise and sustain a value proposition.

Stage 3: Demonstration of Value Propositions

Technologies: Innovative Technologies

Halliburton's HR Intranet ERP system demonstrated a B2E value proposition. Their technology innovation was bottom-up driven and from both sides of B2E and B2G of the value chain. This bottom-up approach provided a model for the company's global e-ERP infrastructure.

Employee-Nat demonstrated the integration of ERP and non-ERP systems with Web technologies (Fan et al., 2000). Wine Society found problems with a lack of internal expertise with implementing Web-based innovations with their ERP system.

Products and Services: e-Communities

Statoil and UBS used Intranet employee self-service applications to develop a practice of industry-based e-communities. Dell has competence centres where customers can validate system design and configuration without disrupting their live computing network. These facilities act as collaborative online network to provide customers with systems design and application tuning support, allowing them to test various hardware and software configurations before making a purchase decision; for example Dell and FSC.

Business Models: e-Enterprise Model (Essential to Stage 3)

A pilot approach demonstrating a value proposition is shown in the One2One relationship formed by Dell and LSI. Also, the case emphasises the synergistic benefit stream from B2B integration and the interaction of inter-organisation e-business solutions. In the short term, it may be better to adopt e-commerce implementations (e-sales and e-procurement) with new customers and suppliers. This has the capability of persuading existing customers and suppliers that are more resistant to e-business change of the win-win value propositions; for example FSC with SAP, Dell and LSI. In these two "twin" case studies the focus was on building a "One2One" relationship. The creation of a "win-win" value proposition was observed to be a model for other B2B partnering.

In Table 4 complementary benefits are identified with FSC's online B2B partners.

Table 4. Complementary benefits from B2B integration.

FSC Benefits	Partner Benefits
Ordering times optimised through online connection Shorter and therefore faster ordering times Incorrect orders reduced to minimum Presentation of configurable products on the Internet Information management for CRM	Available 24 hours a day, 7 days/wk. Simpler ordering, resulting in savings in cost and time Automatic online information on order changes and delivery notifications Tracking of orders at any time Pre-testing of products Customised service

Changing Management Objectives in E-Business Transformation

The changing management objectives across the stages in the e-ERP transformation matrix are classified in Table 5 and are viewed as interdependent and

Table 5. Changing management objectives in the e-ERP transformation matrix.

	Stage 1	Stage 2	Stage 3
Management focus	Self-service	Empowerment	Relationship building
Change Management focus	Top-down Training Internal	Bottom-up Self-learning External	Visionary Value enhancement Community
Outcomes and Performance Gains	Improved operating efficiency (ROI)	Effective resourcing (QWL)	Virtual and economic value added (EVA)

Key: Return on investment (ROI), Quality of working life (QWL), Economic value added (EVA)

supportive of each other. This is especially so in the area of outcomes and performances objectives where efficiency through employee self-service and effectiveness through empowerment in customer care is used to support value adding activities for sustained competitive advantage.

Management focus is on the exploitation of employee self-service, the empowerment of individuals, and the extensive relationship building with multiple alliances.

Outcomes and performance gains were identified as: efficient operations, effective resourcing, and virtual value adding.

Management Focus in e-Business Transformation

The conceptual model in Figure 5 brings together key management issues and their relationships into e-business transformation. This model illustrates how change in industry practices and e-ERP developments relate to B2E, B2C and the B2B^S, and B2B^C models (Ash & Burn, 2002). It identifies the accelerated symbiotic relationship between e-business technologies and business improvement caused by a shift in customer demand. The arrows connecting customers, employees, and suppliers indicate the business interactions through self-service, care and empowerment towards extensive relationship building with multiple alliances.

To realise the benefits from the symbiosis of e-ERP developments and business practice, organisations are optimising B2B models:

Figure 5. Relationships building cycle model from staged growth of e-business.

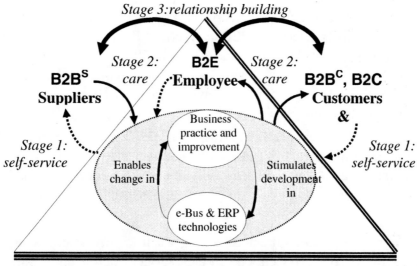

Stage 2: care through empowerment

- *Stage 1* – To offer cheaper products with efficient service by utilising customer **self-service** in B2B^C, and consumer **self-service** in B2C, and to procure standard materials faster through e-procurement agreements by utilising employee **self-service** in B2B^S.

- *Stage 2* – To provide customised service in B2B^C, by utilising employee and supplier **empowerment** in B2E and B2B^S.

- *Stage 3* – To generate value enhanced **alliances** through B2E, B2B^C and B2B^S, with all players in an e-ERP network.

In addition, Figure 5 represents a complete view of the foundations of this study: e-ERP technology, e-business practice, and multiple relationships building. One indicator of a successful comprehensive e-business implementation is the widespread acceptance by employees of using B2B e-procurement for their own office equipment and supplies.

Change Management Focus in e-ERP Transformation

The model for e-business change management represents a comprehensive tool for assisting managers in diagnosing the key facilitators and inhibitors of successful e-ERP projects for B2B interaction. The results confirm that the more successful projects were found to have facilitators in all components of the eBC framework. The framework specifically explores the areas related to the successful learning organisation where the key issues remain as people oriented organisational issues.

The nature of change was reported to be participative change resulting in an evolutionary change tactic. This was viewed as a "waterfall" progression of change, starting with an alleviation of dissatisfaction by employees and eventually working towards a well-managed e-business implementation:

- *Stage 1* – Top-down directed learning of self-service for efficiency gains to offer cheaper products with efficient service by utilising customer self-service in B2B^C, and customer self-service in B2C, and to procure materials cheaper through e-procurement agreements by utilising employee self-service in B2B^S.

- *Stage 2* – Bottom-up self-directed learning focuses on external partner effectiveness. e-Readiness and emergent change management are two key factors for influencing people working effectively with new e-business environments. Barua et al. (2001) found that the success of a company's e-business initiatives comes in part from the readiness of customers and suppliers to engage in electronic interactions; for example Dell had to wait for LSI to be "e-business ready" for the B2B integration project to be implemented. To address complexities of change, each component must be aligned, along with the enabling technology, to the strategic initiatives (Statoil's Data Quality Manager; Hesterbrink, 1999, p. 5). An important ingredient in the right cultural mix for successful eBC is leadership from the top and initiatives from employees, together with an atmosphere of open communication, participation, committed cross-functional. In the new business environment, organisational change is becoming more complex, and training is shifting to self-directed learning.

- *Stage 3* – Visionary sense of value enhancement utilising e-community to generate effective **alliances** through B2E, B2C, B2B^C and B2B^S with all players in the e-ERP environment; for example Dell with LSI. Organisations attempting to change performance radically seem to require some "sense of urgency" in their business activities and situation, translating, in turn, into a compelling vision that is espoused throughout the organisation.

To overcome pockets of reluctance to change, an organisation's vision for change must provide an atmosphere of communication where concerns about eBC are not seen negatively but rather welcomed:

(i)   Achieving this requires continuous articulation and communication of the value of reporting results and monitoring each individual's contribution and accountability to the overall company's change effort. At this individual level, concern should be placed on how the eBC will improve employee satisfaction and the quality of work life.

(ii) Measurement is a means to success. A well-defined transparent management approach should include a documented methodology of change; use objective and quantified metrics showing the value of change; continuously communicate process metrics to senior management; and possess a well-documented rollout of the new e-business design.

(iii) Further to the findings, there is a case to be argued on how and why change management is changing. For the issue of change management, we observe a shift towards a learning organisation (Vering & Matthias, 2002, p. 159). In support of the claim that "change management" is changing, they argue there is:

 •   a new generation of system users,

 •   a constant or continuous nature of change,

 •   a demand for both top-down and bottom-up change.

(iv) However, change still requires that resources be matched to the business objects and tasks. What is new is that the Workplace now offers tools and opportunities for implementing change. An organisation that designs its systems in terms of roles for end users can drive organisational change through workplace implementation. The workplace not only delivers best practices, "as ERP systems do," it provides an understanding of roles and organisational responsibilities that go along with them, "as ERP systems do not" (Vering & Matthias, 2002, p. 164).

Outcomes and Performance Gains in e-ERP Transformation

The stages of eBT, identified in Table 5, are viewed as interdependent and supportive of each other, as in Figure 3. This is especially so with respect to the *business focus* and the *performances objectives* where *efficiency* through employee self-service and *effectiveness* through empowerment in customer care is used to support *value adding* activities for sustained competitive advantage.

In Table 5 the e-ERP matrix classifies the generic outcomes and performance objectives as:

- improved efficiency in decreased order times, automatic approvals to reduce costs,
- greater effectiveness means improved decision making, greater responsibilities,
- value adding refers to complementary benefits realised for all network partners along the value chains when doing business online (Figure 6).

To achieve the outcomes from e-ERP projects, organisations are utilising three B2B models. They offer customers cheaper products with efficient service by exploiting self-service in B2B^C and B2C. They source materials cheaper and more efficiently through procurement agreements in B2B^S and utilisation of employee self-service in B2E. They now optimise processes in B2B^S with B2B^C for customised service by utilising employee self-service in B2E.

Figure 6 illustrates the generic outcomes and performance gains and the relationships between them. The performance gains for e-procurement were

Figure 6. Outcomes and performance gains criteria for e-ERP matrix.

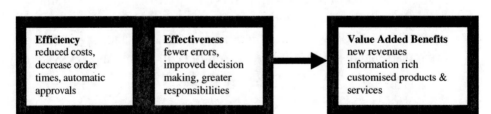

achieved from two sources: cost savings, and reduced cycle time from customer access (24x7) to supplier data. These projects enabled efficiency gains from minimising of delays in customer orders, and effectiveness gains from optimising employee/staff time. The cost savings through operational efficiencies of all equipment resourcing compare favourably to those cost savings (efficiencies) in other e-procurement case studies. However, the improvement in staff QWL appears to be from learning of new skills, understanding of processes, and acceptance of new responsibilities with greater flexibility.

By taking a more holistic approach, executives can turn these facets of a company's operations into the drivers of e-business excellence. So the central task for senior managers lies in understanding what drives operational excellence in the e-ERP realm, and then committing the necessary resources (structures, training, responsibilities) to the development of the drivers.

To this end, managers should assess the company's operations by looking at both the traditional and e-business measures. For example, Dell and some Siemens companies used the same internal performance measures in both e-business and traditional business operations.

Virtual organising proposed by Venkatraman and Henderson (1998) extends the findings from the case studies to a measure for inter-organisation or B2B activity. This suggests a measure for successful relationships building.

Figure 7 identifies the measures for outcomes and performance gains and the relationships between them within the e-business change research model. These measures intersect the measures of the proposed e-ERP transformation matrix described in Table 3. They canvass the measures at the level of employee performance.

Figure 7. Measures for outcomes and performance gains.

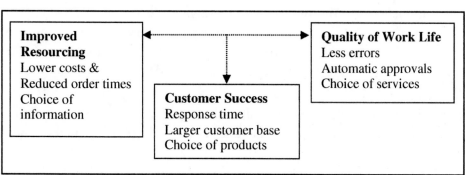

An indicator of a successful comprehensive e-business implementation is the widespread acceptance by employees of using B2B e-procurement for their own office equipment and supplies.

To realise the superior benefits, the following essential factors were found to apply:

(i)   continuous improvement of the quality of the Web interface for the end user,

(ii)   formalising agreements with partners on a common IT platform,

(iii) standardising purchasing agreements with suppliers, and

(iv)   communicating the business strategy to employees.

Strengths and Limitations of the Model

The proposed model of e-business transformation can be used as a detailed criterion to direct and evaluate the progress in the virtual space for traditional organisations or new entrants. The nature and value of the model is based on a set of exemplar SAP-based organisations (innovators) that pioneered e-business implementations through their ERP systems for sustained competitive advantage.

Although limited to discrete snapshots of each organisation's e-business transformation, the proposed model of eBT nevertheless serves the purpose of demonstrating the transition rather well; that is, a model that represents a documented comprehensive and long-term plan that should assist managers of ERP-based organisations in migrating their company towards a successful e-business organisation. Similar to virtual organising, the eBT model offers a foundational perspective of strategies, tactics and performance objectives for e-ERP implementations. As a theory, its strength is based on the synthesis of case snapshots. It is seen as evolutionary in nature and content driven. The triangulation of the research frameworks provides a method for study at appropriate levels of complexity.

Claims of external validity must await further examination with a wider sample of projects with different contexts and motives. Extra case material was gathered to validate the final research framework and to confirm the factors for success of an e-business implementation.

Conclusion

The conceptual framework of e-business transformation (eBT) captures the stages of growth in which improvement is along the three dimensions of business activity: *integration* is tempered by *differentiation* for realising B2B *value propositions*. It identifies the antecedents of successful e-business implementations within ERP environments (e-ERP). As a final research model of e-ERP phenomena, it represents a triangulation of three interdependent research models: virtual organising through e-ERP, e-business change with critical success factors and facilitators, and complementary benefits from B2B interaction. Each model exhibits attributes that have varying influences at different stages of e-business implementation.

The e-ERP matrix represents the stages of growth development of a comprehensive and iterative plan that should assist managers of ERP-based organisations in migrating their company towards a successful e-business organisation. The model offers a foundational perspective of strategies, tactics and performance objectives for e-ERP implementations. The strength of the theory lies in the synthesis of multiple case analyses using three different lenses over three separate time periods. The triangulation of the three research frameworks provides a method for study at appropriate levels of complexity for e-business implementation with SAP systems.

References

Ash, C.G. (2001). e-Business with ERP: A primary study of e-ERP implementations. *Proceedings of the 2ⁿᵈ Working of e-Business Conference* (pp. 364-375). Perth, Australia: Edith Cowan University.

Ash, C.G., & Burn, J.M. (2002). Exploring the benefits from B2B implementations through ERP. *Proceedings Xth European Conference of Information Systems ECIS2002* (pp. 184-193). Gdansk, Poland: University of Gdansk.

Barua, A., Konana, P., Whinston, A.B., & Yin, F. (2001, Fall). Driving e-business excellence. *Sloan Management Review,* 36-44.

Carlson, D.A. (1995). Harnessing the flow of knowledge. Retrieved April 20, 1998, from Ontogenics Web site: http://www.ontogenics.com/research/papers/default.htm, pp. 4, 9.

Fan, M., Stallaert, J., & Whinston, A.B. (2000). The adoption and design methodologies of component-based enterprise systems. *European Journal of Information Systems, 9*(1), 25-35.

Guha, S., Grover, V., Kettinger, W.J., & Teng, J.T.C. (1997). Business process change and organisational performance: Exploring an antecedent model. *Journal of Management Information Systems, 14*(1), 119-154.

Hesterbrink, C. (1999). e-Business and ERP: Bringing two paradigms together. Retrieved September 15, 1999, from PriceWaterhouse Coopers Web site: http://www.pwc.com/, pp. 1, 9.

Lehmann, H. (2001). e-Business transformation challenges for an airline maintenance and engineering organization. *1st International SAP Research & Curriculum Congress.* San Diego, CA: SAP America.

Osterwalder, A., & Pigneur, Y. (2002). An e-business model ontology for modeling e-business. *Proceedings of 15th Bled Electronic Commerce Conference* (pp. 569-582). Bled, Slovenia: University of Maribor.

Perez, M., Hantusch, T., & Matzke, B. (1999). *The Sap R/3 System on the Internet* (pp. 33-42). Harlow, UK: Addison-Wesley, Pearson Edn.

Segev, A., & Gebauer, J. (2001). B2B procurement and market transformation. *Information Technology and Management, 2*(1), 242-260.

Singh, M., & Thomson, D. (2002). eReality: Constructing the eEconomy. *Proceedings of 15th Bled Electronic Commerce Conference* (pp. 293-307). Bled, Slovenia: University of Maribor.

Soni, A. (2001). Transforming from bricks-and-mortar to a clicks-and-bricks enterprise: A case study of one successful company. *1st International SAP Research & Curriculum Congress,* San Diego, pp. 18-20.

Venkatraman, N., & Henderson, J.C. (1998). Real strategies for virtual organising. *Sloan Management Review,* 33-48, Boston: MIT.

Vering, R., & Matthias, R. (2002). *The e-business workplace: Discovering the power of enterprise portals.* New York: John Wiley & Sons, pp. 112-114.

Chapter X

ERP II &
Change Management:
The Real Struggle for ERP
Systems Practices

Paul Hawking
Victoria University, Australia

Susan Foster
Monash University, Australia

Andrew Stein
Victoria University, Australia

Abstract

Enterprise Resource Planning (ERP) systems have become an essential information systems infrastructure for large organisations. Organisations are now looking for ways to leverage their ERP investment by introducing new functionality; however, no matter how many implementations these companies have undertaken the same people issues still provide barriers. This research looks at the change management practices of Australian companies and identifies the main success factors and barriers associated with implementing change management strategies. The chapter presents the results of a survey of 35 major Australian organisations that have implemented an ERP system. Many of these organisations have long histories of ERP usage and multiple ERP implementations and upgrades. The main findings indicate that the respondents considered change management crucial to successful ERP implementations, yet their organisations did not perform change management very well. The main success factor to change management was provision of adequate resources, with the main barrier being lack of communication up and down the organisation.

Introduction

ERP sales have represented a significant proportion of total outlays by business on information technology infrastructure. The global market for ERP software, which was $16.6 billion in 1998, is estimated to have had 300 billion spent over the last decade (Carlino, 2000). The level of their sales and penetration reinforces the importance of these types of systems. A survey of 800 U.S. companies confirmed that almost half of these companies had installed an ERP system and that these systems were commanding 43% of the company's application budget (Carlino, 2000). The market penetration of ERP systems varies considerably from industry to industry. A report by Computer Economics Inc. stated that 76% of manufacturers, 35% of insurance and health care companies, and 24% of federal government agencies already have an ERP system or are in the process of installing one (Stedman, 1999). The major vendor of ERP systems is SAP with approximately 50% of the market (McBride, 2003).

Although ERP systems have the potential to deliver a number of benefits (Table 1), initially many companies implemented an ERP system as a technological solution to the Y2K issue (Deloitte, 1999). Companies were forced to initiate business process engineering for the purpose of "gap analysis" to determine what either had to change in their company or in the ERP to facilitate an effective implementation. Some companies initially struggled with their ERP implementation for many reasons, including: inexperience with projects of this scope, underestimating the impact the system would have on their organisation, and lacking skilled resources. For some companies these barriers have been insurmountable (Calegero, 2000).

Table 1. Top 10 ERP benefits (Davenport et al., 2002).

Benefit
Improved management decision making
Improved financial management
Improved customer service and retention
Ease of expansion/growth and increased flexibility
Faster, more accurate transactions
Headcount reduction
Cycle time reduction
Improved inventory/asset management
Fewer physical resources/better logistics
Increased revenue

In a worldwide CSC (2001) study, 1009 IS managers identified as their main priority "optimising enterprise wide systems". Companies are revisiting their ERP implementations in an attempt to leverage their investment by attaining the purported benefits. In the landmark Deliotte's study (1999), 49% of the sample considered that an ERP implementation is a continuous process, as they continue to gain value propositions from their system. This is a reasonable expectation as companies attempt to realise previously unattained benefits, and additionally, as companies evolve, their ERP system must also evolve to support new business processes and information needs.

The process of achieving additional benefits from an ERP implementation is referred to as "*second wave*" implementations (Deloitte, 1999). Deloitte Consulting (1999) describe a number of post implementation phases organisations adopt (Figure 1). In the Stabilise phase companies familiarise themselves with the implementation and master the changes that occurred. The Synthesise phase is where companies seek improvements by implementing improved business processes, add complimentary solutions, and motivate people to support the changes. In the final stage, Synergise, process optimization occurs, resulting in business transformation.

Figure 1. Deloitte (1999) implementation phases.

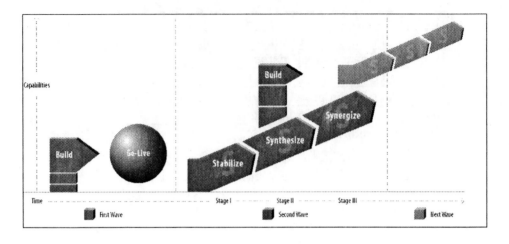

Barriers to Benefit Realisation

Recent research by Hawking and Stein (2002) identified the expected ERP benefits and level of realisation of these benefits in 48 Australian companies. Their research indicated that although the companies gained a number of benefits from their ERP implementation they did not attain the expected level of benefits. The sample was asked to rate on a seven-point likert scale the barriers to benefit realisation of their current ERP implementation. Each barrier was categorised as per the Deloitte Consulting (1999) study: People, Process or Technology (Table 2).

The respondents indicated obstacles that limited benefit attainment for their ERP implementation had little to do with lack of software functionality or major technical issues, but were predominately people related issues. Five of the top seven obstacles could be classified as people issues. It is interesting that two of the top three issues are related to change management. It is important to note that Australian companies have been working with their ERP systems for a number of years, resulting in a level of maturity; however, even though they have been through a number of implementations they still consider the change management issues' impact on implementation success and benefit attainment.

Nah et al. (2001) documented 11 critical success factors (CSFs) that have proved to be vital to a successful ERP implementation. Other researchers have

Table 2. Barriers to benefit realisation (N=48).

Current R/3 Barrier/Obstacle	Mean	Deloitte Category
Lack of Discipline	4.4	P
Lack of Change Management	4.3	P
Inadequate Training	4.2	P
Poor Reporting Procedures	4.2	T
Inadequate Process Engineering	3.9	PR
Misplaced Benefit Ownership	3.8	P
Inadequate Internal Staff	3.3	P
Poor Prioritisation of Resources	3.0	T
Poor Software Functionality	2.9	T
Inadequate Ongoing Support	2.7	T
Poor Business Performance	2.4	PR
Under Performed Project Team	2.3	P
Poor Application Management	2.2	T
Upgrades Performed poorly	1.6	T

identified similar critical success factors and have stressed the importance of change management (Somer & Nelson, 2001).

Change Management

Change management strategies vary from company to company. Change management can be defined as:

> *"the effort to manage people through the emotional ups and down that inevitably occur when an organisation is undergoing massive change"* (Nah & Sieber, 2001).

In the context of the organization, Goff (2000) defines change management as

> " *a planned approach to integrating technological change. This includes formal processes for assessing the impact of the change on both the people it affects and the way they do their jobs. It also uses techniques to get users to accept a change caused by technology and to change their behaviour to take advantage of the new IT functionality*".

This statement implies that information technology projects require change management practices in order to fundamentally change the way people work and behave within an organisation and across organisational boundaries. Other authors refer to the concept of resistance: an expression of reservation that invariably results as a response or reaction to change (Block, 1989, cited in Sohal & Waddell, 1998). Turbit (2002) goes further by describing change management in terms of setting expectations to alleviate the resistance to change by people within organisations.

Current research points to the failure of most ERP implementations as being due to resistance to change by users in the organisations (Aladwani, 2001). A fairly simplistic framework that classifies the types of user resistance to innovations like ERP implementation by source of resistance is that of Sheth (1981) cited in Aladwani (2001). The framework demonstrates that there are two fundamental sources of resistance to innovations: perceived risk and habit. Perceived risk refers to one's perception of the risk associated with the decision to adopt the innovation; that is, the decision to accept the ERP system, while habit refers to current practices that one is routinely doing. Sheth (1981) argues that in order to reduce employees' resistance to ERP implementation, top management of the organisation must analyse these sources of resistance and employ the appropriate set of strategies to counteract them. This argument implies that resistance is a negative influence on and in conflict with the organisational strategy. Therefore it is seen as something to be managed and ultimately eliminated. Others argue, however, that resistance should be recognised as something to be utilised to support a successful change management initiative (Mabin, Foreson & Green, 2001).

There are numerous prerequisites for change to be successful. The list includes a clear vision for change, communicating that vision articulately and clearly from a top-down perspective, preparing a culture for change, setting strong leadership and providing an environment for participation. Developing a vision, describing a picture of the future shape of an organisation, gaining commitment to that vision and synchronisation of purpose and effort are clearly seen as important leadership qualities. This development of vision and mission clearly sets the scene for organisational change (Hamel & Prahalad, 1994; Senge & Roberts, 1994, cited in Mabin et al., 2001). Once the direction for organisational change has been established, the next important step in the change process is influencing the culture of the organisation. Organisational culture is the shared understanding of how an organisation works, and has a major impact and influence on successful change initiatives (Handy, 1996; Schein, 1988; McAdams, 1996). A culture that has shared values and common aims is conducive to success.

Organisations should aim to have a strong corporate identity that is open and willing to change (Nah et al., 2001). Communication and strong leadership play a vital role in preparing any organisation for change and in guiding the organisation through the upheavals that result from changes. The ability to create trust by developing an environment where the people who make up an organisation feel change is required and then commit to that change process are two of leadership's most important qualities (Carlzon, 1989; Schermerhorn, 1989; Zand, 1997). Creating trust can be achieved through the sharing and discussion of issues and ideas.

Although much has been written in regards to change management up to this date, limited research has occurred in regard to change management practices in Australian ERP implementations. Recommendations from previous research (Hawking et al., 2003), which identified change management as one of the major barriers to benefit realisation, indicated that further research was required to identify successful change management practices. The SAP Australian User Group commissioned this research, which reflects relevance of the findings to Australian companies.

Research Method

The primary objective of the study was to survey a range of information systems professionals to seek responses regarding current and historical ERP implementation details and change management success factors and practices originating from these implementations. More specifically, the research posed the following questions:

- What is importance of change management programs to ERP implementations?

- What are the change management success factors and barriers that exist in ERP systems implementations?

- What change management practices do companies employ?

Research Design and Methodology

In order to identify change management practices a survey instrument involving 30 questions covering four areas: demographics, change management metrics, success factors and change management practices was developed. Closed questions were used with Yes/No and seven-point Likert scale responses. Open-ended questions sought responses from the cohort allowing for qualitative data to be collected.

The survey was distributed through the use of an e-mail directing the respondent to a Web site that incorporated a Web based survey delivery platform. Several studies (Comley, 1996; & Sivadas, 1995; Stanton & Rogelberg, 2000) have compared e-mail and Web based survey methods versus mail information collection methods and have proposed that e-mail surveys compare favourably with postal methods in the areas of cost, speed, quality and response rate. It was necessary to preen the e-mail address book to remove and amend e-mail that had bounced back.

Sample

The sample was made up of key contacts from member companies of the SAP Australian User Group. SAP is the leading vendor of ERP systems in Australia with approximately 70% of the market (McBride, 2003) and the User Group is representative of approximately 65% of the SAP customer base. The original e-mail listing contained 166 potential respondents. A number of e-mails were undeliverable due to members of the cohort moving positions, having incorrect e-mail addresses, changing e-mail addresses or automatic out-of-office responses. There were two unusable replies, leaving a total of 35 usable responses. The overall response rate once removing the undeliverable addresses was 24%.

Results

Demographics

Responses were received from 35 IS professionals and the data were analysed to present position, organisation type, size and procurement spend. A summary of responses are presented in Tables 3, 4 and 5. Respondents were predominantly high in the organisational structure, being either an IS or business manager. As key contacts for the user group, their status within their companies would indicate their involvement in the decision making process with regards to any ERP implementations. Accordingly, they should have an understanding as to the type of information required by the survey. The companies represented most industry sectors and were large in size from both a revenue and employee perspective.

Table 3. Position of respondents.

Position	%
IT Manager	33
CIO	16
IT Development	14
Support & Services Man'er	12
SAP Manager	10
Business Manager	5

Table 4. Companies by industry sector.

Industry Sector	%
Public Service	26
Mining Oil & Gas	16
Energy	15
Utility	15
Manufacturing	14
IT Services	14

Table 5. Size of companies.

Number FTEs	No.	Revenue ($millions)	No
>1001	33	Large(>1000)	21
502-1000	3	Large-Med(750-1000)	8
101-500	8	Med-Large(500-749)	3
<100	1	Medium(250-499)	10
		Small(<250)	6

ERP Profile

Respondents were asked to identify: when the first implementation occurred, providing information about their company's experience with an ERP system (Table 6), number of ERP users (Table 7) and the number of implementations and upgrades which the company had been involved in (Table 8).

Nolan and Norton (2000) argue that it is important to consider a company's history with ERP systems when making any comparisons. They believe that companies can learn from their implementation experiences. Accordingly, they propose a maturity model of ERP implementations by classification type:

- Beginning – implemented SAP in the past 12 months,
- Consolidating – implemented SAP between one and three years,
- Mature – implemented SAP for more than three years.

Table 6. Year of implementation.

Year	No
<=1995	1
1996	6
1997	5
1998	10
1999	6
2000	4
2001	2
2002	3

Table 7. SAP user numbers.

SAP Users	No
21-100	7
101-250	7
251-500	10
Greater 501	13

Table 8. No. of implementations.

Upgrade/Implementations	No
0	1
1	8
2	10
3	8
4	4
5	1

Applying this model to the data indicates that 76% of the sample can be classified in the Mature phase, while 16% are in the consolidating phase and 8% in the beginning phase. This would indicate that the sample should have extensive experience with their ERP implementations. This is reinforced by the fact that the majority of the companies are involved with at least two upgrades or implementations.

Change Management Defined

Respondents were asked to provide a short description or definition of change management in order to assess their understanding of this concept. From an analysis of the definitions, the following keywords were obtained:

Manage/coordinate	42%	Training	16%
Communication	29%	Planning	11%
Transition	29%	Monitoring/Assessment	11%
Processes	18%		

Based on the responses an aggregated definition was developed:

> *Change management is defined as the process of assisting the organisation in the smooth transition from one defined state to another, by managing and coordinating changes to business processes and systems. It involves the effective communication with stakeholders regarding the scope and impact of the expected changes, to assist them to cope and adapt to the transition.*

Change Management Budget Metrics

Respondents were asked to indicate what level of their total implementation budget was allocated to change management and to indicate what percentage of their change management budget was allocated to training (Table 9). The majority of respondents indicated that organisations spend less than 10% on change management practices and a significant number of organisations spend

Table 9.

Change Management Budget (% of implementation budget)	No.	Training Budget (% of change budget)	No.
<5%	2	<20%	13
5-10%	19	21-40%	4
11-15%	5	41-60%	6
>15%	7	61-80%	6
		81-100%	5

Table 10. Change management team.

Team Resource	No.	Size	No.
Hired external consultants as experts or advisors	23	<5	16
Cross-functional team	20	6-10	12
Senior executive steering committee or team	20	>10	5
Department-based team	13		
Involved employees at many levels in the change team	12		
Our company did not designate such a team to manage any of the change	4		

less than 20% of the change management budget on training. At the other end of the spectrum, five companies commit nearly their entire change management budget to training.

Respondents were required to indicate the size and makeup of their change management team (Table 10). The majority of companies used external personnel to assist with their change management strategy, although only two companies relied solely on this resource. The change management team was usually representative of a number of stakeholders supported by external personnel. The size of the change team tends to indicate that the team was responsible for managing change and utilised others to implement the change program. There appeared to be no relationship between the size of the change team and the number of SAP users.

Change Management Importance and Success

Respondents were asked to rate on a five-point Likert scale the degree of importance the organisation placed on the change management strategy (see Table 11) and how successful they considered their change management program (see Table 12). This provided an insight into how respondents viewed the importance of change management and how successful they considered their organisations were in implementing change management strategies.

The respondents gave an overwhelming "yes" when asked if change management was important to their ERP implementation, yet indicated that their organizations were nowhere near world class in change management operations.

Table 11. Importance of change management.

Importance of Change Management				
Not Important			Very Important	
1	2	3	4	5
		1	10	24

Table 12. Company's success with change management.

Company's Ability to Implement Change				
Poor				World Class
1	2	3	4	5
1	8	22	4	0

Change Management Success Factors and Barriers

Respondents were asked to rank (from 1 to 5) the top five change management success factors and barriers for their organisational ERP implementations. The results are displayed in Tables 13 and 14. Whilst adequate resources was rated

Table 13. Change management critical success factors.

Critical Success Factor	Rating
Adequate resources given for the change	2.3
A well-communicated, shared understanding of this need for change	2.2
Open and consistent communications at all levels of the organisation	2.1
Participation and support by all management levels within the organisation	1.7
Visible and continuous executive sponsorship	1.4
Being in touch with those affected by the change	1.4
Sufficient pre-implementation training of those who will deliver the change	1.1
Structured approach to managing change	1.1
Recognizing employees for contributions to the change initiative	0.9
A compelling need for change that is critical for the organisation's success	0.8
Clear channels of safe feedback	0.5
Training to prepare change team members	0.3
Personnel changes to support the new organisation	0.2
Offering small gifts to employees for contributions to the change initiative	0.0
Offering salary bonuses or promotions to employees at key milestones	0.0
Offering some savings to employees for success in cost-saving changes	0.0

Table 14. Barriers for change management.

Barrier	Rating
Lack of communication and channels for feedback	2.7
Employee resistance to change	2.3
Not all management levels were engaged in the change	2.1
Inadequate resources or budget	2.0
Shifting focus or changing priorities too soon	1.6
Executives out of touch with those affected by the change	1.6
Executives sending out inconsistent signals	1.5
Management behaviours are not supportive of the change	1.3
Executives not directly involved with project	1.2

as the top success factor, communication based factors were ranked in three of the next six factors.

Lack of communication was considered the main barrier, with employee resistance, management support and resources the next three barriers.

Table 15. Practices to lessen employee resistance.

Practice	No.
Direct face to face communications about the behaviour	25
Question and answer sessions and open discussions at meetings	23
Team communication meetings and performance reviews	20
Re-communication of goals and needs for change	19
Immediate team or sponsor intervention	18
Open, safe communications channels for feedback	18
Focus on goals and what needs to happen to meet the goals	18
Coaching for performance	10
Development of personal progress plans	6

Employee Resistance

As employee resistance was identified as being an important factor for the successful implementation of an ERP system (Aladwani, 2001), respondents were asked to identify practices used to help lessen this resistance. The results (Table 15) reinforce the importance of communication and a personalised approach.

Discussion

Change Management Success Factors and Barriers

The respondents, in many cases decision makers in their organisations, considered change management to be important yet signaled that overall performance in implementing a change management program was not world class. There was little evidence of a link between the success in implementing change and the level of budget allocation, yet the number one success factor was adequate resources. It is also interesting to note that many of the companies involved in the survey were onto their fourth or fifth ERP implementation or upgrade but were still struggling with the change process.

The respondents to a large extent indicated that the success factors and barriers were mirror images of each other. Communications and management support dominated the success factors. Two-way communications and a need to "be in touch" with those affected by change all signal the feedback nature of implementations. Obstacles to their ERP implementation had little to do with lack of software functionality or major technical issues, but were related to lack of management support for change management strategies and poor communication practices. A number of the respondents commented on the lack of management support and understanding:

> "....Insufficient management awareness of SAP capability, leading to sub-optimal use of SAP in the business."

> "A big part of our issue was lack of management support for implementation due to changes in management team and direction mid-stream."

> "... additionally the culture was not geared for Employee Self Service when it was rolled out. Change Management was poorly handled and this showed in user acceptance of the system."

The practices, which were identified as strategies to address employee resistance, specify many of the successful communication practices. It is interesting to note that the offering of various rewards or incentives was not perceived to be important for implementing change.

Even though Australian companies have been working through a number of major implementations with their ERP systems for a number of years, resulting in a level of maturity, they still consider change management issues' impact on the success and benefit attainment.

Researchers have identified that programs which establish positive attitudes towards the introduction of information systems are critical success factors to their successful implementation (Aladwani, 2001). This has led to companies placing increasing emphasis on change management strategies. Hammer (1999) refers to this process as "organisational reengineering" and argues that an essential precedent to any change management strategy is the fostering of a culture for change. SAP's ASAP implementation methodology places considerable emphasis on change management strategies and includes a number of resources to assist this process. However, even though companies have access to this methodology the question remains: why are companies still signalling change problems? It may be that the very maturity of the organisation may impact on change strategies. Further research is required into the complex issues involved in change management and the evaluation of resources and tools provided to assist in the change process.

Conclusion

Many companies implemented an Enterprise Resource Planning (ERP) system to address a number of immediate problems such as Y2K and disparate or poor systems. These same companies have now moved beyond this initial implementation and are looking for ways to optimise their investment. This includes extending the implemented functionality of their ERP system and or implementing new components such as data warehousing, customer relationship management or advanced planning and optimisation. The purpose of this research was to explore factors and barriers of ERP implementations from a change management perspective. The results indicated that although respondent organisations had been through at least one ERP implementation, they continue to encounter problems with change management. One possible explanation lies in the culture of Australian organisations. Do they accommodate outside expertise in conducting implementation? Do they acknowledge that the Australian character is one of self-reliance almost to the exclusion of the "outside" expert? Are change management practices ignored? Are they given a token treatment or are they considered soft and therefore unnecessary? Is the Australian business culture one that is becoming risk averse, and fearful of change? Further research into the nexus of organisations, culture, change management and global software implementations would help us explore the answers to these questions.

References

Aladwani, A.M. (2001). Change management strategies for successful ERP implementation. *Business Process Management Journal, 7*(3).

Bingi, P., Sharma, M.K., & Godla, J.K. (1999, Summer). Critical issues affecting an ERP implementation. *Information Systems Management, 16*(3), 7-14.

BRW2002. (2002). Business review weekly, The BRW1000. Retrieved October 2002, from http://www.brw.com.au/stories/.

Calegero, B. (2000, June). Who is to blame for ERP failure? *Sunsaver*, June.

Carlino, J. (2000). AMR research predicts enterprise allocation market will reach $78 billion by 2004. Retrieved August 2002, from www.amrresearch. com/press/files/.

Carlzon, J. (1989). *Moments of truth.* New York: Harper & Row.

Comley, P. (1996). *The use of the Internet as a data collection method.* Media Futures Report. London: Henley Centre.

CSC. (2001). Critical issues of information systems management. Retrieved November 2002, from http://www.csc.com/aboutus/uploads/CI_Report.

Davenport, T. (2002). *Mission critical: Realizing the promise of enterprise systems.* Boston: Harvard Business School Press.

Deloitte. (1999). *ERPs second wave.* Deloitte Consulting.

Goff, L.J. (2000). Change management, 2000. Retrieved September 2002, from http://www.computerworld.com/news/2000/story/0,11280,41308, 00.html.

Hammer, M. (1999, November/December). How process enterprises really work. *Harvard Business Review.*

Handy, C. (1986). The gods of management. *Executive Book Summaries, 18*(2), 1-8.

Hawking, P., & Stein, A. (2002, May). The ERP market: An Australian update. *Proceedings of IRMA2002 Conference,* Toronto, Canada, 176-192.

Mabin, V.J., Foreson, S., & Green, L. (2001). Harnessing resistance: Using the theory of constraints to assist change management. *Journal of European Industrial Training,* 168-191.

McAdams, J. (1996). *The reward plan advantage.* San Francisco: Jossey-Bass.

McBride, G. (2003). *SAP partner kick off presentation.* Sydney.

Mehta, R., & Sivadas, E. (1995). Comparing response rates & response content in mail versus electronic mail surveys. *Journal of the Market Research Society, 37,* 429-439.

Nah, F., Lee-Shang, L.J., & Kuang, J. (2001). Critical factors for successful implementation of enterprise systems. *Business Processes Management Journal, 7*(3), 285-296.

Nah, F.H., & Sieber, M. (2001). A recurring improvisational methodology for change management in ERP Implementation. http://www.ait.unl.edu/fnah/sieber&Nah.pdf.

Nolan & Norton Institute. (2000). *SAP Benchmarking Report 2000.* Melbourne: KPMG.

Schein, E. (1988). Defining organisational culture. London: Jossey-Bass.

Schermerhorn, J. (1998). *Management for productivity.* New York: John Wiley & Sons.

Sheth, J. (1981). Psychology of innovation resistance. *Research in Marketing, 4,* 273-282.

Sohal, A.S., & Waddell, D. (1998). Resistance: A constructive tool for change management. *Management decision* (pp. 533-535). MCB University Press.

Somer, T., & Nelson, K. (2001). The impact of critical success factors across the stages of enterprise resource planning systems implementations. *Proceedings of the 34th Hawaii International Conference on System Sciences,* HICSS.

Stanton, J., & Rogelberg, S. (2000). Using Internet/intranet Web pages to collect organizational research data. *Organisational Research Methods, 4*(3), 199-216.

Stein, A., & Hawking, P. (2002). *Continuous business improvement & ERP systems: An Australian survey.* Industry Report commissioned by the SAP Australian User Group.

Turbit, N. (2002). ERP Implementation – The trap. http://www.projectperfect.com.au/info_erp_imp.htm.

Zand, D. (1997). The leadership triad. *Soundview Executive Book Summaries, 19*(6), Part 1, 1-8.

Chapter XI

SAP R/3 Implementation Approaches:
A Study in Brazilian Companies

Ronaldo Zwicker
University of São Paulo (USP), Brazil

Cesar Alexandre de Souza
University of São Paulo (USP), Brazil

Abstract

The approach used to implement an ERP system is an important decision in its implementation project as it greatly affects the configuration of the system, the allocation of resources and the management of the project and its risks. It will also play a decisive role at all the stages of the ERP system's life cycle. This chapter discusses the different ways of "going-live" of ERP systems: big-bang, small-bangs *and implementation in* phases, *and describes their advantages and disadvantages. The chapter also presents results of an exploratory study made in 53 Brazilian companies, which implemented SAP R/3. Based on these results, influences of the companies' characteristics and of the project on the selected method are discussed. The relation of the implementation approach and project time is also presented.*

Introduction

The implementation of ERP systems is considered a difficult task that involves many organizational and technical issues. For example, the need for changes in the processes and in the culture of the organization are problems that are frequently discussed in the literature (Bancroft et al., 1998; Bingi et al., 1999; Davenport, 1998). Less attention has been paid to other equally important questions, such as one of the most critical decisions in the implementation project: the selection of the *implementation approach* (*big-bang*, *small-bangs* or implementation in *phases*). This decision depends on a number of factors such as limitations of resources and time, characteristics of the project team, the number of modules which will be implemented, the number of localities where the implementation will take place, and the risks which the company is willing to take.

This chapter presents an analysis of the elements involved in the choice of the implementation approach of ERP systems. First, the chapter describes the life cycle of ERP systems and analyzes the different implementation approaches related to the life-cycle stages. In this first part of the chapter are identified advantages, disadvantages and other factors that should be taken into account when the choice is made. A brief description of the R/3 evolution in the Brazilian market is also presented. Results of an exploratory survey made in 53 companies that implemented SAP R/3 are then shown. Based on these results, influences of the companies' characteristics and of the project on the approach selected for implementation are discussed, and an attempt is made to establish the relationships between relevant factors and the choice made. Finally, the study analyzes the consequences of the choice in terms of the time taken to implement and stabilize the system.

Life Cycle of ERP Systems

ERP systems are integrated information systems that are acquired in the form of commercial software packages. Markus and Tanis (2000) define them as commercial software packages that enable the integration of transactions-oriented data and business processes throughout an organization. The implementation of an ERP system is carried out in well-defined stages. Souza and Zwicker (2001b) present a model for the life cycle of ERP systems, which includes the stages of decision and selection, implementation, stabilization and utilization. These major stages and their temporal relationship can be seen in Figure 1, which represents the life cycle of ERP systems.

At the decision and selection stage the company decides to introduce an ERP system as the solution for its information systems requirements and selects the supplier. The planning of the implementation follows this choice and is also part of this stage. The planning should include the establishment of the project's scope, goals to be achieved and measuring methods for the verification of these goals, definition of the project team and responsibilities, and the implementation strategy. This will involve the choice of the implementation approach (*big-bang*, *small-bangs* or *in phases*), definition of the activities which will be carried out and the project's schedule, which should take time and resource limitations into consideration.

Figure 1. ERP systems life cycle.

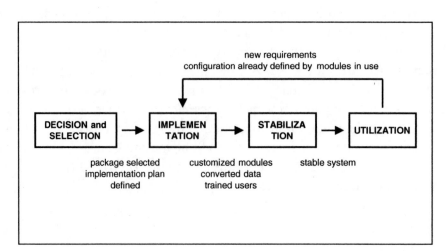

The implementation is the second stage of the proposed life cycle model and may be defined as the process by which the system's modules are put into operation within a company. This stage will involve the adjustment of the business processes to the system, the configuration and customization of the system, the conversion and loading of the initial data, hardware and software configuration and user training. This stage includes all the tasks that are carried out from the end of the implementation planning to the beginning of the system's operation, when the ERP system becomes the company's official information system.

In the first moments after the beginning of the ERP system operation there is a critical stage for the project's success: the stabilization. At this stage the ERP system becomes a concrete object and part of the daily life of the company and of its employees. This is the period when most managerial and technical energy must be devoted to the system. At the beginning of the system operation (similarly to any information system) all kinds of problems arise, such as operational problems, training deficiencies, and bugs in the software, which were not perceived at the implementation stage. At this time the company already depends upon the system for its operations, and thus there is considerable pressure to rapidly solve any problem. The length of this period depends on the company and normally takes about eight weeks (Souza & Zwicker, 2001a).

Finally, at the utilization stage the system becomes an intrinsic part of all company operations. This does not mean that all of its possibilities have been recognized and have been implemented. This knowledge will only be ascertained after a certain period and through the ideas that will emerge in daily use. Thus the utilization stage feeds back the implementation stage with new possibilities and needs, which can be solved through the implementation of new modules, new configurations or new customizations.

Implementation Approaches of ERP Systems

Bancroft et al. (1998) state that the first decisions the company must make after the choice of the ERP package are those of the modules which will be implemented and in which business units or locations this will occur. Deciding the sequence for module implementation defines how the ERP system will be introduced into the company. This choice is vital for the project and influences a series of factors such as deadlines, resources and management requirements. This choice configures what we are calling *implementation approach.*

A number of companies choose to initially implement one module or a group of modules in one or more than one location in the company. Then the project moves to the next group of modules and locations. This is called the *phased* approach. Another alternative is the complete implementation, where all the modules are implemented simultaneously in all companies' locations, and where all modules will be put into operation at the same time. This is known as the *big-bang* approach. The *phased* alternative is safer, as it allows the team to learn from experience before putting important company processes into the new system. However, it requires the construction of interfaces between the old and new systems, a task that requires resources, and the products of these interfaces are mostly discarded at the end of the project.

If the company has more than one business unit or location, there is also a third possibility that is derived from the phased implementation: the *pilot big-bang* or *small-bang.* One business unit or smaller locality will be chosen for the simultaneous starting of the operation just in that locality. It is thus possible to obtain the experience of the simultaneous implementation without excessively harming the business. What follows the *small-bang* could be either simultaneous *big-bang* type implementations in the remaining localities or a series of *small-bangs* or phased module implementations.

Dimensions of an ERP Implementation

One way of analyzing the different ERP implementation approaches is to look at the two dimensions that define the size of each step in the implementation: the functional and the geographical dimensions (also referred as module implementation strategy and physical scope by Parr and Shanks (2000)). The functional dimension consists of the number of modules that will be implemented at the same time, and the geographical dimension consists of the number of localities or business units that will begin to use the system at the same time (Figure 2). For example, the ERP system may be implemented in a number of big stages, each of which involves a certain number of similar modules being adopted simultaneously in various localities. This characterizes a *small-bang* approach

Figure 2. Implementation approach dimensions and company stoppage risk.

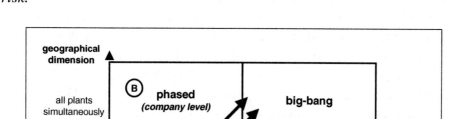

(Region A in Figure 2). On the other hand, the implementation of each module simultaneously in various localities characterizes a *phased* implementation at the company level (Region B in Figure 2).

The arrows in the middle of Figure 2 show, for a given company, the direction of the increase in the risk of the company operations being interrupted as a result of the different strategies used to start the ERP system operation. This risk will be associated to the number of localities that the company has, and to the number of modules that will be implemented. Figure 2 does not compare the risk between different companies, although it can be assumed that, for a given strategy, a company with a greater number of localities and implementing a greater number of modules runs greater risks than a company with fewer localities and fewer modules.

Advantages and Disadvantages of Each Approach

The implementation approach of an ERP system has considerable influence on the various phases of the life cycle, especially the stabilization phase. In the case of the *big-bang* approach there is a clear difference between the implementation and the stabilization phases, differently from the phased or *small-bang* implementation. In *big-bang,* the start of the operation corresponds to initiating the operation of all modules in all locations simultaneously, and therefore the team's full attention is directed towards the stabilization period. On the other hand, in a phased implementation modules at different stages of their life cycle will coexist, and this may result in problems derived from lack of focus of the project team and of top management.

The aim of the implementation stage is to adjust the system to the company in the best possible way. This will require flexibility, constant tests, changes in configurations and development of customizations. On the other hand, the aim of the stabilization stage is to eliminate operational problems as soon as possible, with minimum changes in pre-defined configurations and no new customizations if possible. In a phased implementation this may result in conflicts, because ERP systems are *integrated systems,* and the modification of a module that is being implemented (a desired situation in the implementation stage) may result in modifications in other modules already in use (a situation that is not desired in the stabilization and utilization stages). These conflicts are

Table 1. Risks and advantages of the ways to start the operation.

	Disadvantages/Risks	Advantages
Big-Bang	- risk of company total stoppage - returning to the previous systems in case of problems is almost impossible - requires considerable effort in the stabilization phase - concentration of resources during the project	- smaller implementation time - eliminates the development of interfaces - creates a "sense of urgency" that makes defining priorities easier - better integration of the various modules is obtained
Small-Bang	- risk of total stoppage in specific business units or locations - returning to the previous systems in case of failure is considerably difficult - development of interfaces required	- creates a "sense of urgency" that makes defining priorities easier at the business unit or location - allows learning through experience
Phase	- requires development of interfaces - just part of company is involved - requirements of future modules are ignored - modules being implemented result in changes in modules already stabilized - simultaneity of processes at the implementation and stabilization stages - possible loss of focus of the project	- smaller risk of total stoppage in company - able to return to the old systems in case of problems - less concentration of resources through project - functioning modules will increase confidence in the development of following modules - shorter interval between the design and utilization of each module

clearer in the case of a phased implementation where the stabilization stage begins with the entry into operation of the first module, and only ends when the last module implemented in the last locality of the company is stabilized.

Though considered to be riskier (Bancroft et al., 1998), the *big-bang* option can offer advantages. Souza and Zwicker (2001a) observed in eight case studies that the *big-bang* approach was considered an important motivating factor for the success of the implementation. With *big-bang* a consensus is established in the company that there is no possible return to the previous system. The possibility of a total stoppage of operations in case of a total halt of the system exerts a favorable influence for change and the quick detection of problems, and leads to a joint effort towards the quick solution of the remaining problems in the stabilization stage. O'Leary (2000) presents other advantages for the *big-bang* implementation such as the elimination of temporary interfaces between the system and previous systems, a greater integration between the implemented modules, and less time required for the implementation. Table 1 summarizes the disadvantages and advantages associated with each implementation approach.

Implementation Approaches and the Life Cycle of ERP Systems

The ERP life cycle model presented earlier can be complemented taking into consideration the coexistence of modules at the implementation, stabilization and utilization stages that occur in the *phased* and *small-bangs* approaches.

As shown in Figure 3, the different modules or groups of modules are implemented and stabilized in different phases, at different moments in time (this is represented by the superimposed rectangles in the implementation and stabilization stages). As the modules or groups of modules of each phase go into the utilization stage they are added to the modules already in use (this is represented by the expanding rectangles in the utilization phase, meaning that as each module or group of module starts to be used the scope of the implemented system expands). In the figure, the influence of modification requirements of modules being implemented or stabilized on modules already being used and the restrictions brought about by the modules being used on modules in implementation and stabilization are represented by the dotted line arrows.

Figure 3. ERP systems life cycle model for small-bang and phased implementation.

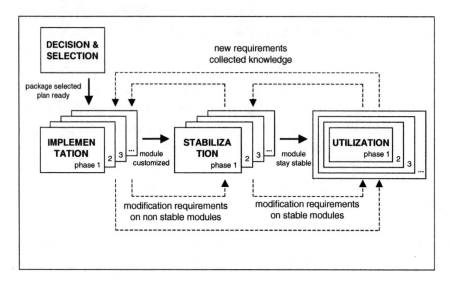

Implementation Approaches Associated Factors

O'Leary (2000) believes that the choice of the implementation approach should be based upon the analysis of the costs and benefits of each option, taking into account the associated risks. Nevertheless, as the costs and risks are difficult to measure, companies end up by basing their decisions on other factors. Thus elements related to the characteristics of the organization and the size of the implementation project usually prevail.

The characteristics of the organization are its size (annual invoicing, number of plants or locations, number of employees and clients) and complexity (characteristics of the product, the productive process and the market supplied). Besides the number of plants or locations, the kind of relationships that exist between them must be considered, as pointed out by Markus et al. (2000). For these authors the different types of relationships among the different business units or locations (ranging from total autonomy of the business units to total centralization of decisions at headquarters) influence project complexity and system configuration, and must be taken into account when planning an ERP implementation and choosing the corresponding approach.

Table 2.   Factors associated with the choice of the implementation approach.

- Project goals
- Advantages and disadvantages of each approach
- Risks of each approach
- Company and business processes complexity
    Company size
    Product and process characteristics
    Market characteristics
    Types of relationships among business units (from total autonomy to total centralization)
- Project complexity
    Number of modules being implemented
    Customization level
    Number of plants or locations
- Project constraints
    Project deadlines
    Financial resources
    Technical and human resources limitations

In principle, smaller and less complex organizations run fewer risks when they opt for a *big-bang* implementation and may achieve the advantages associated with this type of strategy. The number of modules to be implemented and the level of customization the modules will undergo must also be taken into account. A higher number of modules and an increased customization will result in a more complex project, and therefore a phased implementation is preferable.

In the cases analyzed by Souza and Zwicker (2001a) it could be seen that the *big-bang* was used in smaller companies or in companies with clear time restrictions. In larger companies phased implementation was preferable and the *big-bang* was, in some cases, considered totally unfeasible. Table 2 summarizes the various factors associated with the choice of the implementation approach.

SAP R/3 in Brazil

The first implementations of SAP R/3 in Brazil begun in 1995 in large multinational companies (like Pirelli, Bosch and Rhodia). Since then SAP has gained a large share of the ERP market among the big companies in the country (also called the "high-end market"). A recent survey shows that in 333 industrial companies of all sizes, R/3 is present in 33% of the companies classified as "big companies," 3.4% of the companies classified as "medium companies" and no presence in companies classified as "small companies" (Vidal & Souza, 2003). According to the SAP site, in April 2002 there were about 380 clients in Brazil. The second ERP system among the big companies group is supplied by a Brazilian vendor and is used by 20% of these companies.

The first companies that implemented R/3 in Brazil suffered from various problems related to the adjustment of the software to local legislation and business practices (localization). Some of the functionalities needed could not be delivered by SAP, and then the companies used local packages associated with R/3, which caused integration problems. The HR module could not be used until very recently and most companies opted to use Brazilian Human Resources packages. Another problem faced by the companies was the shortage of skilled professionals. This led to a high turnover among companies, as the people involved in implementation projects usually left the companies for higher salaries in consulting companies or other companies that were beginning implementation. (See Souza and Zwicker (2001b) for a description of R/3 implementation cases in Brazil.)

By 2002 most of these problems were solved and presently the software is much more adequate to local needs. Notice that in Brazil there are many and frequent changes in taxes' calculation, which puts considerable workload on SAP to continuously adapt its software, and on the client companies, which have to install the corresponding patches.

Research Methodology

This study presents results of a survey made in 2001 in partnership with ASUG-Brasil (SAP user group in Brazil). The study involved the collection of data through a questionnaire sent to the 254 members of the ASUG in January and February 2001. Fifty-five questionnaires were returned (approximately 21%) of which only two were rejected. Six of the responses were from companies that had not yet started the operation of the system and the information was based on the forecast of the project's end.

The questionnaires surveyed characteristics of the company and of the system implemented, and included specific questions regarding the implementation approach adopted and the length of the project. Using these responses, an exploratory analysis was made, focusing on the implementation strategy (*big-bang*, *small-bangs*, or phased), attempting to check whether and how this strategy was related to the characteristics of the companies and the implementation projects. After this analysis the study attempted to verify whether the chosen form of implementation and the characteristics of the company influenced the duration of the project. The statistical analysis was conducted using the software SPSS for Windows 10.0.

Descriptive and Exploratory Analysis of the Collected Data

Characteristics of the Sample

The distribution of the companies in the sample shows that 71% of them adopted the *big-bang*, 15% the *small-bang*, 8% implementation in phases, and the rest adopted other procedures. Most companies were industrial (78%) and the rest was equally divided between services, utilities and commerce. The high number of companies using the *big-bang* option exceeded the initial expectations that this would be the least popular method. The predominance of industrial companies is characteristic of the market for ERP systems. Companies were equally divided between Brazilian and foreign.

Table 3 presents the statistics and the number of cases with information on each variable of interest. The asymmetry coefficient was calculated using the *skewness* measurement supplied by SPSS divided by its standard deviation. Distributions where this value was situated between -1.96 and 1.96 were considered to be symmetrical (Hair et al., 1998). Only the age of the project (AGEPRJ) could be considered to be symmetrical, as the other factors were positively asymmetrical, which shows that there is a concentration of values at the beginning of the distributions. Nevertheless the median allows us to analyze the characteristics of the companies and their projects. In general, they are large companies with annual invoicing of around US$ 300 million and with more than 1,500 employees. The projects had generally six modules (the "heart" of R/3 is made up of five modules) in four factories with a total of 300 users. The median of the size of the project (MODPLAN) is 18, less than the simple multiplication of modules by plants (6x4 = 24). This shows that some modules are implemented in a centralized form (in fewer plants) and others in a decentralized form (in more plants).

Graph 1 gives an idea of the dispersion of the projects, divided into *big-bang* projects and *others,* according to the number of users and size of the project (axes are on a logarithmic scale). The four largest projects on the graph are those of an auto-parts manufacturer (case 19, 3000 users, 12 modules, seven plants), a chemical company (case 50, 2600 users, eight modules, 32 plants), a food producing company (case 51, 1450 users, five modules, 29 plants) and a cigarette company (case 25, 1200 users, eight modules, 27 plants). Of these cases, just the chemical company used the *big-bang* approach and, in the entire sample, this was the company that took the longest time to introduce the system

Table 3. Characteristics of interest variables.

Variable	Description	Mean	Std. Dev.	Median	Min	Max	Asymm. Coef.	Nr. Cases
TIMPLANT	Length of project in months (*)	16.3	11.2	12	3	48	4.4	53
TESTABLZ	Period of stabilization in weeks (*)	10.5	9.0	8	1	48	3.9	53
AGEPRJ	"Age" of project in months (*)	33.0	14.3	33	4	71	1.3	53
INVOICING	Annual invoicing in US$ million	530.0	858.0	300	20	5,000	10.1	47
NEMPLOYS	Number of employees	4,817.0	8,082.0	1,725	60	40,000	8.6	50
NUSERS	Number of R/3 users	487.0	610.0	300	15	3,000	7.8	53
NPLANTS	Factories with implementation	6.1	7.3	4	1	32	7.5	50
NMODULES	Number of modules implemented	6.8	2.2	6	3	13	2.3	53
MODPLAN	Size of project (*)	32.0	41.4	18	4	256	11.3	50
TOTPROGS	Customized programs develpd. (*)	364.0	428.0	253	31	2,131	7.9	45
ITEMPLS	Number of IT employees	33.4	49.2	17	2	283	9.9	42
(*) see detailed description in Table 4								

Table 4. Description of the variables.

Variable	Detailed description
TIMPLANT	Length of the project in months from its beginning to the initial operation of the final module. In the uncompleted projects the forecast of the end of the project was used.
TESTABLZ	Stabilization time of the system in weeks after entering into operation. Applied only to *big-bang* situations.
AGEPRJ	Measurement of the "age" of the project. The number of months from the beginning of the project to the time the survey was made (Jan 2001).
TOTPROGS	Total number of external programs (including those in ABAP language) and reports (including those generated by the generator) that the company developed up to the date of the survey.
MODPLAN	Measurement of the "size" of the project. For each module the companies informed the number of plants where this module was used. The variable is the sum of these values.

with this approach (21 months). Case 24 is a medium-sized Brazilian chemical company that implemented R/3 in *small-bangs* for a total of 17 users in five plants. Graph 2 shows the distribution of implementation times of the projects in the study.

Graph 1. Projects by number of users and size.

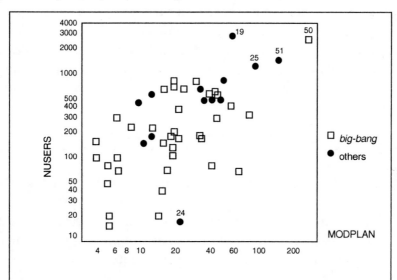

Graph 2. Distribution of project implementation times.

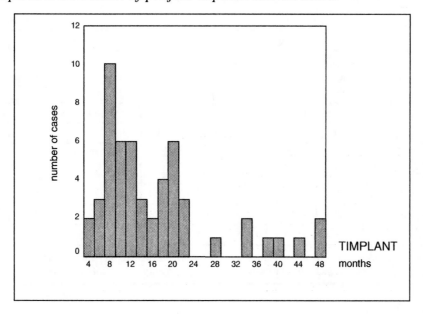

In terms of the stabilization times (TESTABLZ), four companies had much higher values than the rest (40, 30, 28 and 26 weeks). Two factors seem to have contributed to this discrepancy: (1) the concept of stabilization depends on the seriousness of problems that the company considers "normal," and (2) a number of modules stabilize more quickly than others. One of the companies informed that the time needed to regain confidence in the stock control and production costs was 48 weeks, whereas stabilization in the other modules took place much faster (four weeks). In this case the average time was considered to be 26 weeks. If these observations are eliminated, the average time was of eight weeks, similar to that found in the study of Souza and Zwicker (2001a). It should be noted that only those companies that implemented the system using the big-bang approach answered this question.

Relationships Involving the Implementation Approach

In order to verify the relationship between the implementation approach and the remaining variables the sample was divided into two groups: *big-bang* and *others*. This division was made because the number of cases in the other categories (*small-bangs* and *phases*) was small in comparison to the number of cases that used the *big-bang*. As can be seen later on, this division was consistent with the analyses carried out.

Table 5. Results of the t test for the big-bang and others.

variable	Original variable					Transformed variable (*ln*)		
	Signif. of equality of variances	*t*	Signif.	Big-Bang mean value	Others mean value	Signif. of equality of variances	*t*	Signif.
TIMPLANT	.000	-4.070	**.001**	11.9	27.3	.199	-4.789	**<.001**
INVOICING	.001	-1.809	.094	330.6	1053.0	.750	-2.785	**.017**
NEMPLOYS	.000	-2.097	.054	2500.0	10225.0	.228	-2.811	**.007**
NUSERS	.028	-2.149	**.046**	353.3	824.5	.549	-2.671	**.010**
MODPLAN	.689	-1.031	.308	28.4	42.1	--	--	--
MODULOS	.544	-1.079	.286	6.5	7.3	--	--	--
AGEPRJ	.366	-2.335	**.024**	30.2	40.0	--	--	--

Levene's test verifies the equality of the variances of the variable in the two groups. The null hypothesis is the equality of the variances. If the variances are not equal the corrected value of t is presented.

For the nominal variables (nationality and activity sector of the company), the *chi-square* test disclosed whether there was any difference in terms of how the *big-bang* and *others* groups were made up. No significant differences were found in terms of the number of companies that used the *big-bang* or *others* in terms of nationality or activity. Table 5 shows the results of the *t* test, used to check differences in the metric variables between the two groups.

The *t* test is quite robust but depends on the symmetry of the distribution of the variables and on the equality of variances between the groups. In the cases where the variance of the groups was different (based on the Levene test made by SPSS), the results of the *t* test based on the transformed variables are also presented, using the *ln* transformation to compensate for the asymmetry.

The difference in the implementation time between the two groups is statistically significant, with an average of 11.9 months for the companies that implemented the *big-bang* and 27.3 months for those that used other methods. The differences observed in the variables INVOICING and NEMPLOYS (the size of the company) had a significance higher than 0.05, although they ranged within a 0.1 significance. In the case of these variables the transformation allowed for the statistical validation of the differences. The NUSERS variable showed a significant difference while the MODPLAN and MODULOS did not. The remaining variables, which are not included in the table, showed no significant differences.

We can therefore conclude that the *big-bang* was used in projects with lower number of users and which were implemented in a much shorter time. According to the variables of number of employees and annual invoicing, the *big-bang* seems to be linked to smaller companies. The difference shown in relation to the age of the project, where the *big-bang* group had an average of 30.2 months and the *others* group an average of 40.0 months shows that the *big- bang* projects in the sample are more recent than the rest.

Relationships Involving the Nature of the Companies

Table 6 presents the results of the *t* test for the verification of the relationship between TIMPLANT and AGEPRJ to the nationality and the sector of the companies. As can be seen, TIMPLANT did not show any significant difference between the Brazilian and foreign companies or between manufacturing companies and the rest. However, AGEPRJ was significantly greater in the foreign companies in the sample, showing, as expected, that they were the first

Table 6. Results of the t test for nationality and sector of activity.

Variable	Nationality of the company				Sector of activity			
	Value of *t*	Signif. of *t*	*Brazilian average*	*Foreign average*	Value of *t*	Signif. of *t*	*Industrial average*	*Other average*
TIMPLANT	-1.585	.119	13.8	18.7	1.085	.283	17.1	13.0
AGEPRJ	-2.011	**.050**	29.1	36.7	1.662	.108	34.2	28.2
NMODULES	-0.078	.938	6.7	6.7	2.878	**.006**	7.2	5.2

to implement R/3. The number of modules implemented showed a significant difference in relation to the sector of activity, with a higher number of modules in manufacturing companies. The remaining variables did not show significant differences between Brazilian and foreign companies or between those in the industrial sector and other sectors.

Relationships Between Metric Variables

In order to analyze the relationships between the metric variables studied, linear Pearson correlation coefficients were calculated. The values with a coefficient significance lower than or equal to 0.5 are shown in Table 7. The logarithmic transformation (*ln*) of the variables to compensate for the asymmetry did not significantly alter the interpretation of the correlation coefficients, and the original variables were maintained. The exception was the NUSERS variable, which when transformed received the denomination LNNUSERS and is included in the table.

The length of the project (TIMPLANT) was strongly correlated to the age of the project (AGEPRJ). This is interesting as it shows a reduction in the implementation time of the more recent projects. TIMPLANT was also to a lesser degree correlated to INVOICING and this points towards an increase in the implementation time in projects in larger companies. TIMPLANT also showed a correlation to the size of the project, indicated by LNNUSERS.

AGEPRJ is also correlated with MODULES and the total number of programs developed (TOTPROGS). This suggests that after the initial implementation project, the companies continue to implement other modules or customizations in order to complement the system. As was expected, the number of users was

Table 7. Pearson correlation coefficients between the metric variables.

	TIMPLANT	AGEPRJ	TESTABLZ	INVOICING	NEMPLOYS	LNNUSERS	MODULES	MODPLAN	QTSERVDR
AGEPRJ	**.618**								
TESTABLZ									
INVOICING	**.525**								
NEMPLOYS	.328*			**.782**					
LNNUSERS	**.558**	.437**		.421*	.369**				
MODULES	.477**	.410**				.484**			
MODPLAN				.383**		**.519**			
QTDSVDR	.421**			.483**		**.458**	.401**	**.649**	
TOTPROGS	.449**	.344*			.388*	.469**		**.568**	
ITEMPLS	.488**			**.902**	**.742**	.400**			.474**

** significant correlation at the level of 0.01/ * significant correlation at the level of 0.05

reasonably correlated to the size of the project. Also the number of servers is reasonably correlated to MODPLAN and LNNUSERS due to the processing load involved in ERP systems. TOTPROGS is correlated to MODPLAN and LNNUSERS and not directly to the number of modules, as would be expected.

Another finding is the fact that the stabilization time (TESTABLZ) is not correlated with any other factor (for the *big-bang* cases). This probably is due to the fact that after starting the operation in *big bang* there is no alternative for the company other than to stabilize the system in the short-term. If this does not take place, the operations of the company will be affected. This agrees with the "sense of urgency" and the motivation that can be attributed to the *big bang* method of implementation.

Relationships Involving the Number of Users and the Implementation Time

As could be seen, the number of users was significantly different in the *big-bang* and *others* groups. Graph 3 shows the relationship between NUSERS and TIMPLANT and the choice for the method of starting the operation. The graph

Graph 3. Number of users and implementation time.

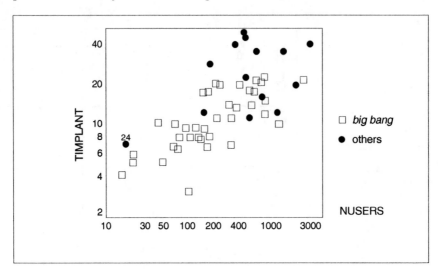

shows that all the companies with less than 150 users chose to use the *big-bang* (with the exception of case 24). When there are more users there are both *big-bang* and *others* projects, and the implementation times of the *others* projects are longer.

Graph 3 clarifies the TIMPLANT distribution presented in Graph 2 and the composition of the projects that have been studied, permitting to recognize the existence of three groups of companies: the *big-bang* companies with up to 200 users; the *big-bang* companies with more than 200 users; and the companies that used phased implementation or small-*bangs*. By projecting the points on the TIMPLANT axis we can see that there is a concentration of the first group around the value of 8 months, of the second group around 20 months, and the third group, which is more disperse, between 12 and 53 months. This exactly reflects the distribution shown in Graph 2.

It is also possible to see that in the case of the *big-bang* companies there is a clearer correlation between NUSERS and TIMPLANT than in the case of the other companies (correlation coefficient 0.700 with a significance of 0.001). By dividing the *big-bang* projects into two groups (up to 200 users and above 200 users), the results obtained for the *t* tests of the variables are presented in Table 8 (with significant differences). As can be seen, this division of *big-bang* projects was quite consistent, with groups distinguished by INVOICING and AGEPRJ. The group of "up to 200 users" comprises smaller companies which implemented the systems more recently.

Table 8. Comparison of variables between the big-bang < 200 and big-bang > 200 user groups.

variables	*t*	Significance	Means for group "big-bang < 200 users"	Means for group "big-bang > 200 users"
TIMPLANT	4.568	< .001	8.9	15.6
AGEPRJ	2.997	.005	25.3	36.3
INVOICING	3.751	.002	139.4	603.6
TOTPROGS	3.111	.003	135.1	490.0
MODULOS	3.585	.001	5.8	7.7

The difference in the number of programs developed and modules implemented may be related to the fact that the projects in the first group are simpler or to the adoption of more standardized solutions by the smaller companies.

The "Market Learning"

Graph 4 shows the relationship between age of the project and implementation time for *big-bang* and *others* projects. The line inserted in the graph helps the analysis and shows a development through time from right to left and an effect

Graph 4. Implementation time and project age.

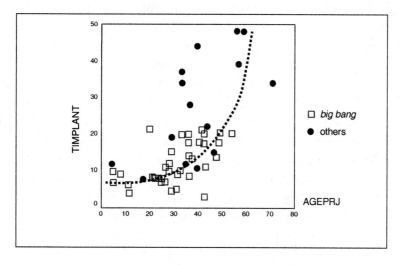

Table 9. Correlations between AGEPRJ, LNNUSERS and TIMPLANT.

	All projects		only *big-bang*	
	LNNUSERS	AGEPRJ	LNNUSERS	AGEPRJ
AGEPRJ Total correlation	.4373**		.4300**	
TIMPLANT Total correlation Partial correlation	.5583** .4075**	.6180** .5010**	.7000** .6126**	.5740** .4233**

of the reduction of time from above top to bottom. It can be seen that more recent projects tend to adopt a *big-bang* strategy and, simultaneously, there is a trend for a reduction of the implementation time.

This may happen because the projects are actually being carried out quicker or because the larger companies with larger projects implemented R/3 before the others. For a clearer analysis of this trend Table 9 presents the total and partial correlations between TIMPLANT, AGEPRJ and LNNUSERS, the latter chosen as an indicator of the project's size. The partial correlation is the correlation between two variables when the effects of other variables are removed (Hair et al., 1998).

As has already been mentioned, the correlation between AGEPRJ and LNNUSERS shows that the more recent projects are smaller, which was also shown in the previous item in relation to the *big-bang* projects. The partial correlation between TIMPLANT and AGEPRJ remained significant, which shows that the most recent projects are implemented quicker even when the effect of the reduction of the number of users in the newer projects is discounted. This effect is greater if all the projects are considered, not just the *big-bang* ones. The partial correlation between TIMPLANT and LNNUSERS also shows, when the age of the project is discounted, that projects with fewer users take less time to implement. In the case of this correlation the effect is greater in the *big-bang* projects. Time reduction of the more recent projects is thus partially associated to a reduction in the size of the projects and partially to a reduction in the time required for implementation.

One possible explanation for the reduction in the implementation time which is not explained by the reduction in the size of the projects is the learning of the consulting companies which implemented the R/3, the professionals on the market, and the vendor itself in relation to the Brazilian implementation projects. This time reduction may also be attributed to improvements in the package, especially in terms of localization (adaptation of R/3 to the Brazilian legislation), which reduced the need for customization. The existence of more information on companies which already implemented as well as the existence of mechanisms of exchanging experiences, such as user groups, may also explain the reduction. All these factors may be interpreted as a "market learning effect" in relation to R/3. However, it is not possible to detect the influence or even the existence of this learning effect only based upon the survey data.

Conclusion

The exploratory survey permitted to observe a number of factors of the implementation of R/3 projects in Brazil. It was initially shown that many projects used the *big-bang* implementation approach, and that these projects are connected to companies with fewer users. It was also observed that the implementation time of these projects was smaller. It was also shown that over time there was an increase in the use of the *big-bang* and a decrease in the implementation time of the projects. This is associated with both a reduction in the size of the more recent projects and a possible effect of "market learning" in relation to the package.

The sample is comprised by part of the companies members of ASUG-Brasil (21%). Although the sample was not random it probably represents this population which, in principle, allows us to generalize the results. According to the April 2002 data of the SAP site there are more than 380 R/3 users in Brazil, of whom 14% are represented in the sample.

As already mentioned, the choice of the method of starting the operation requires many considerations, such as: the risk the company believes to be appropriate, deadlines, budget restrictions, the complexity of the project, the context of the company, and so forth. There are a large number of factors that may interfere and which should be considered. This study did not attempt to set up a normative or explicative model for the choices made during the project and merely attempted to indicate possible relationships between a number of variables which may be directly or indirectly involved in the projects and which may help to improve models to be set up or future studies on the subject.

Finally, it should be noted that ERP systems are a very interesting opportunity for studies in the area of information systems. In studies on the use of information technology in general, the effects of a very important and complex variable are present: the actual information system under study. In the case of ERP systems these effects may be minimized due to the standardization which is incorporated into these systems and which is possibly replicated among the firms studied. This also could help to improve comparisons between companies.

References

Bancroft, N.H., Seip, H., & Sprengel, A. (1998). *Implementing SAP R/3: How to introduce a large system into a large organization.* Manning.

Bingi, P., Sharma, M.K., & Godla, J. (1999). Critical issues affecting an ERP implementation. *Information Systems Management, 16*(3), 7-44.

Davenport, T.H. (1998, July/August). Putting the enterprise into the enterprise system. *Harvard Business Review,* 121-131.

Hair, J.F. et al. (1998). *Multivariate data analysis.* Prentice Hall.

Markus, M.L., & Tanis, C. (2000) The enterprise system experience – from adoption to success. In R. Zmud (Ed.), *Framing the domains of IT research: Glimpsing the future through the past.* Cincinnati: Pinnaflex.

Markus, M.L., Tanis, C., & Fenema, P.C. (2000). Multisite ERP implementations. *Communications of the ACM, 43*(4), 42-46.

O'Leary, D.E. (2000). *Enterprise resource planning systems: Systems, life cycle, electronic commerce and risk.* Cambridge University Press.

Parr, A.N., & Shanks, G. (2000). A taxonomy of ERP implementation approaches. *Proceedings of the 33rd Hawaii International Conference on System Sciences.*

Souza, C., & Zwicker, R. (2001a). Enterprise systems: A multiple-case study in eight Brazilian companies adopting ERP systems. *Proceedings of the 2nd Annual Global Information Technology Management World Conference,* Dallas.

Souza, C., & Zwicker, R. (2001b). ERP systems' life cycle: Findings and recommendations from a multiple-case study in Brazilian companies. *Proceedings of BALAS 2001,* San Diego.

Vidal, A.G.R., & Souza, C. (2003). *Perfil da empresa digital 2000.* Working Paper, University of São Paulo (FEA).

Chapter XII

ERP Systems Management:
A Comparison of Large Sized Brazilian Companies

Cesar Alexandre de Souza
University of São Paulo (USP), Brazil

Ronaldo Zwicker
University of São Paulo (USP), Brazil

Abstract

This chapter investigates the aspects involved in ERP systems management to understand how such artifacts transform the role of Information Technology (IT) areas within the organizations. ERP systems are currently the main component of the information architecture of most large and medium sized companies and the management of these systems has become a critical part of IT teams' every day. Initially is proposed a management model for ERP systems based upon a survey of the literature. Next is presented, based upon the model, the analysis of two ERP systems management cases of large sized Brazilian companies. At the end the cases are compared and important observed differences set up the conclusions of this chapter.

ERP Systems Role in Organizations

During the second half of the nineties the implementation of ERP systems was, on a global scale, one of the central points of attention regarding IT utilization in companies. History shows that implementation of ERP systems is not a simple matter; even some failures were reported. Research on the subject developed as from the end of the decade, which studied mainly the factors governing successful implementation, showed that a process of cultural change is involved. One critical factor for success is to avoid that the endeavor be handled as a "computing" project. Dedication and involvement of top management, strong participation of users and change management were aspects considered essential for the success of these implementation projects.

The issue of benefits achieved with the use of these systems was also researched; however, there are few evaluations of a quantitative nature. ERP systems brought benefits with regard to the integration of the company's internal operations by reducing: raw-material stocks, order taking time, production time and delivery time. Gains in efficiency due to elimination of operations carried out by hand, especially those associated to manual integration between previously isolated departmental systems, were also perceived. Furthermore, these systems use a single database, which adds to the quality of the information available. The availability of real-time information may also contribute to improve the company's decision-making procedures.

In most cases, after implementation, the ERP system becomes the basis upon which the company begins to develop other initiatives, such as: customer relationship management (CRM), supply chain management (SCM) and business intelligence (BI). Also at this stage, called the "ERPs second wave," companies begin to consolidate their process reviews and effectively employ a model of integrated process management.

IT Management: New Challenges

Notwithstanding the ERP phenomenon, the current dynamics of the organizational IT use must also be taken into account. According to Andressen (2002), business units are demanding from the IT area increasingly higher levels of service and IT managers are being forced to review how they carry out their operations, spend their money and plan for tomorrow. To make IT services available "as if they were utilities," which is the case of telephone services, is an approach that is gathering momentum when the discussion is about the form in which IT departments must service the company businesses. Recently, Carr (2003), based upon this approach, caused an intense and polemic discussion when he suggested the decrease of IT importance to the organizations.

For Kayworth (2002), IT departments that traditionally operate as managerial units, focused on the development of transactional systems to enhance the efficiency of the organization, are newly playing a much more strategic role. Furthermore, IT departments have been recast by seemingly endless organizational trends related to how companies interact with their clients, with their suppliers and with their outside partners. Such transformations have taken place in an environment characterized by the rapid evolution and transformation of technology. According to the author it can be argued that, in view of theses changes, the scope and the nature of IT departments' management has radically changed.

Another significant aspect is the growing concern with IT area costs. This can be perceived through the shrinkage of IT investments and the increasing use of valuation methods to assess costs and results of IT use. These now are common in IT context approaches, such as: total cost of ownership (TCO), return on investment (ROI), service level agreement (SLA) and the service level management (SLM). Initially a response of the companies to the economic slow-down which took place as from the year 2000, the tendency to reduce and control investments of the IT area seems to be consolidating and this fact should prevail in the long term. Faced with this scenario, IT departments are compelled to reduce and control their costs; however, on the other hand they are also pressed to offer more extensive, stable and adaptable services in an ongoing adjustment to business shifts.

Management of ERP Systems

Quickly ERP systems developed into the main component of corporate information systems of most large and medium sized companies. This takes place at a time when companies and IT teams are obliged to assure response capability and adjustment capability of their systems to the requirements of business and its relentless changes. In general, the ERP system is a critical resource for the integrated management of the company's diverse areas and for its supply chain. This implies the fulfillment of extreme requisites of availability and performance.

This in principle outlines the meaning of management of ERP systems: it comprises the group of actions carried out to ensure the fulfillment of business requirements, the performance, the availability and the control of maintenance and operation activities. Currently, these activities have become a critical part of the every day of IT teams within the companies.

Experience proves that ERP systems management may be problematic. For instance, Chew (2001) mentions that, after operation start-up of ERP systems, users face high costs of maintenance, poor technical support and "painful" upgrades. A fourth of the companies interviewed in the Chew survey admitted they suffered interruptions in their business due to upgrades of their ERP systems. One-third protested against waiting times longer than those predicted for support services by their suppliers. According to the survey, in reply to such difficulties, the companies must be capable of giving their applications own support. He also suggests that discontent users must take advantage of the next upgrade to consider changing the ERP supplier.

Performance, availability and costs requirements as well as constant adjustment to business needs are also applicable to the other company systems, internally developed or not. However, in the case of ERP systems some of the knowledge needed to meet such requisites is not found in the company. Such knowledge is strongly integrated with the software itself and scattered among the other agents (suppliers and consultants). This entails challenges to the management of ERP systems that differ from those related to the management of systems developed internally. According to Brooks (1995), insofar that a commercial software package sells by thousands the quality, delay for delivery, product performance and support costs become controlling issues instead of the development costs, so crucial in the case of systems developed internally.

According to Kern (2002), when the company choose the use of a package then they must understand that the supplier now controls the introduction of new functionalities in the product. If the internal users ask for functionality changes then it may be possible that they only must wait; however, if the requests are not part of the supplier plans then they possibly do not have any alternative. Inclusively the resolution of performance related problems may demand knowledge not available in the company, since it depends upon the structure of databases and computer programs. Pui-Ng, Chan and Gable (2001) state that because of these aspects, the ERP systems maintenance differs profoundly from the maintenance of systems that are developed internally.

Research Methodology

For O'Brien (2001), IT management encompasses the aspects of strategic management, operations management, resources management, technology management and distributed management. Strategic management must ensure that IT significantly contributes to profitability and the greater objectives of the company. Operations management, which the author divides into development, operations and technical support, includes the activities that must be performed to ensure systems availability and suitable use. Resources and technology management encompass activities related to information resources, hardware, software, networks and IT human resources. Distributed management must deal with the partition of responsibilities pertinent to the information systems among end users and managers.

This taxonomy recommends taking into account aspects of operational management as part of the model that will be used in this work. In this way the development, operation and technical support activities specifically related to

Figure 1. ERP systems management model.

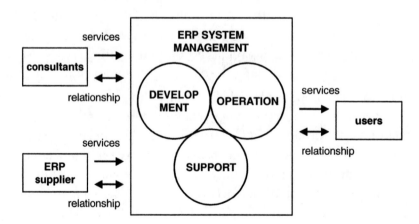

ERP systems will be analyzed. The model is completed with the aspects related to the actors involved, who may be internal (analysts and programmers) and external (suppliers, consultants and users) to the IT area. Figure 1 shows the schematic form of the management model.

Regarding development activities, the life cycle of ERP systems is quite distinct from the life cycle of internally developed systems. For instance, in relation to the process of maintenance, Pui-Ng, Chan and Gable (2001) point out that ERP systems undergo maintenance requested by the users (just as the systems developed internally) as well as that requested by the suppliers themselves in the form of patches (corrections of problems, small sized improvements or modifications required by law) and upgrades (new versions of the software).

With regard to the operational activities of the system, noteworthy are those related to its performance and availability. The knowledge needed to accomplish these activities, mainly in the case of performance tuning, may not be internally accessible. With respect to availability, the strong integration of ERP systems may lead to difficulties in "stopping the system" for the carrying out of maintenance and installation of corrections. Even the maintenance of specific modules may be troublesome because modifications in one module may demand simultaneous modifications in other modules.

Finally, the support activities entail training of users and response to their doubts related to use of the system. According to Pui-Ng, Chan and Gable (2001), such activities are more intense and difficult in the case of the ERP systems than in systems developed internally, mainly because of the limited knowledge on the internal functioning of the system.

The survey was exploratory and its objective was to examine how ERP systems transform the role of IT areas and expand the knowledge about key issues related to the management of such artifacts. For this purpose two cases of large sized Brazilian companies that implemented ERP systems more than two years ago were analyzed. This time interval was considered necessary for a company to overcome the stage of stabilization of the system and for the settlement of the functions connected to ERP management. The case study approach is justified because cases are useful in surveys whose purpose is to contextualize and deepen the study of a subject. According to Yin (1989), the utilization of more than one case in such study assures more substance to the results, in addition to permitting comparisons between two distinct situations.

A guide-list with open questions that sought to identify the more important management aspects of each company's ERP system was utilized for the interviews (see Appendix 1). Interviews were carried out in March and April of 2003. In the WMS company case, the IT manager, a system analyst and a key-user were interviewed. In the M&M company case one of the coordinators of the IT area was interviewed. Names of both surveyed companies are disguised. The reports of the cases studied are summarized below.

WMS Company Case

WMS is a multinational company that produces writing materials. In Brazil it has various plants and invoices US$100 million yearly, with some 3,000 employees.

Implementation History

WMS implemented the SAP R/3 system at 1998, in a *big-bang* mode, as the outcome of an implementation project begun in 1996, which lasted 18 months. The R/3 was implemented as a replacement for a complex of 26 systems developed internally. One of the main reasons was the need to reduce maintenance costs of the mainframes owned by the company and that also restricted the technological modernization of its systems. The company now has 180 users of the ERP system.

Soon after launch the system operation WMS endured a stabilization period, which lasted 30 months. This was because of settlement (adjustment) difficulties of the product to the Brazilian context and which was in its early stages of use in Brazil. This long period of stabilization hindered constant evolution of the system through new versions that SAP was making available. When this finally became possible, migration to a new and updated version resulted in a sizable "new project" that consumed some 10% of the value of the initial implementation project. This new project was concluded in 2002, closing an almost five-year long gap without updating.

Currently, the IT area has 31 persons, 13 dedicated to the development and configuration of functionalities of the R/3 (this includes two programmers of the ABAP R/3 language), 16 dedicated to support tasks, the IT manager and a secretary. Functional analysts are specialized per module of the R/3 system. The support area is responsible for the technical R/3 support and help-desk.

It is also responsible for the development and maintenance of the departmental systems developed in Access or Excel that meet the highly specific local functionalities not available or feasible in the R/3 system. The area is subordinated to the administrative and financial direction.

IT Management Change

In the former situation the concern was to manage the technical personnel for the development of programs and sometimes not integrated systems. In summary, the area systematically solved technical and localized departmental problems. The focus on IT professionals' training was mainly technical and directed towards the programming activities. There was no concern for the teaching of personnel dedicated to process analysis or development. Programming activity was first priority and took up all the staff's time, and therefore a focus on business procedures was impossible. According to the IT manager, "I intensely dedicated myself to the every day of programmers and analysts managing what each one did on a level of computer programs and not of organizational processes".

The R/3 introduction imposed a change of focus. It became necessary to train IT personnel to "think about company business processes and no longer about computer programs" and to "try to maximize the ERP system use in carrying out these processes". The most difficult part was the change required in the culture of the IT professionals. It was no longer important to program but to understand how to use the available functionality of the system to support business. However, this change "is still underway" since it is a slow transition from a culture of "system programmers" to "business analysts". In addition to training the professionals to change their way of thinking and acting, further changes were required in the profile of the IT area supervisors. It is interesting to note that the introduction of the new system did not cause IT personnel reduction. The professionals were assigned to other functions, possibly further contributing to the reported difficulties.

Another change was caused by the need to establish procedures for managing the outsourced tasks and resources. In the previous situation management was in charge of systems whose technology, architecture and development methodology was fully mastered by the company. The systems were independent and all people involved with it were part of the company. In this novel situation relations with the supplier and with consultants from whom "one must acquire knowledge not available in the company" must be managed. The company begins to rely on a series of conditions imposed by the supplier and which include specifications adherence and systematic introduction of corrections and upgrades. This requires a number of new qualifications from IT managers.

According to nterviews the new focus on business procedures definitely took place, but did not attain a satisfactory level. To some extent this is due to the delay in the stabilization of the system, which exhausted efforts of the IT professional in operational issues and corrective maintenances. It was also mentioned that this change of focus should not only take place in the IT area, but in the entire company. In some areas concern with the new system is restricted to the preparation of new reports or to the search for alternatives of implementation of very specific functionalities. The process and business vision is put aside. To summarize, notwithstanding that the new system has changed the focus of the IT area and of the users, it is only a passive agent of the process. Other actions are needed to complete the task.

ERP System Management

At WMS four activities carried out by the IT area are directly linked to the ERP system: (1) configuration, standardization and customization; (2) keeping the system in permanent operation; (3) management of the commercial and technical relations with suppliers and partners and; (4) research and improvement.

Configuration, standardization and customization of the system are carried out taking into account optimization of the processes, legislation changes and new requirements of the company. As a rule, changes are serviced by configuration and standardization. Customizing the system through development of new programs was cut back after the implementation of the new version. To keep the system in permanent operation entails the monitoring of software, hardware, networks, communication resources and databases. These activities are the most important and they consume most of the IT area resources. Management of the relations with outsourced parties encompasses negotiation of: new acquisition modalities, license grants, maintenance contracts and consultants hiring. These activities are carried out by the IT area manager and supervisors. Finally the research and improvement activity involves searching and studying the functionalities already available in the R/3 and not yet used by the company. This activity is carried out by the development team itself.

Management of the system also includes a help-desk procedure and a service to answer users' questions related to R/3 and which is handled by the functional analysts. Along the interviews was noted that users must be recycled some time after implementation end. This is due to the turnover of employees in the diverse areas, which reduces the quality of users' knowledge, insofar as it is transmitted from person to person. Many doubts submitted to the IT area are the outcome of the deterioration of knowledge in the user areas.

As a rule there is a considerable backlog of requests to be met by standardization or eventually by customization. In the opinion of the interviewees, to make changes in the old internal systems was much simpler and faster. Notwithstanding the backlog, actually user requests are understood as more addressed to processes and to business and not to details of screens or reports. Users also request and demand more, as a result of the new information requirements spurred by the current business dynamics of the company.

Relationship with Users

The ERP system changed the relationship between the IT area and users, who began to have a better interaction with the department. In the former situation users clung only to details such as formatting of screens and reports, because there was full freedom of development. In the current situation these details are in general pre-determined and the discussion becomes centered on processes and procedures. However, to make this possible, in addition to the great involvement of the users in the process of implementation, intense work was required with the users regarding behavior aspects. Thereby, the user's responsibility increases greatly with regard to the systems and in the current situation the co-responsibility between the IT departments and the users now prevails. Nevertheless this behavior is not homogeneous among users and is dependent on the profile of those involved.

There is not yet a committee of users to establish priorities of the IT area activities. Priority is assigned by the management itself as an outcome of the long period of stabilization when the user's committee was not relevant. Yearly, the IT area asks for a program of the users' requests and their priorities, which it endeavors to conciliate with the resources available. When there are conflicts, the system area meets with the departments to negotiate priorities. After R/3 implementation, the company kept the figure of the key users who act as centralizers of calls to the IT area, help in the clarification of doubts and solve small system problems. Evidently they play a role of multipliers of knowledge.

The difficulty of keeping abreast to the continued evolution of the ERP system in the computing area was also perceived due to the lack of user interest or time. As reported, people get accustomed to one way of doing things and are afraid to look for new different ways. When the IT area requests participation for some improvement activity the user may eventually not cooperate and the evolution does not take place. It was mentioned that improvement constitutes priority only in the IT area and that a recycling or retraining period for the users might contribute to motivate people to seek new alternatives for their work.

As a rule, in the case of the old internal systems it was easier to ascertain if a given user was or was not satisfied. It was also easier to identify the causes of dissatisfaction because the system had only one or few "owners". In the case of the ERP system, identification of satisfaction is no longer so direct, as the system is integrated and satisfaction of one user may be the dissatisfaction of another. Furthermore, it may be necessary to consider the satisfaction of the supplier and consultants. An integrated system is a complex system where it is difficult to impose the needs and preferences of one single person without taking the whole into account.

The company still does not use indicators of user satisfaction. As for technical indicators, such as access speed and amount of transactions handled, the company is surveying software alternatives. The availability of the system is not measured and for the time being this is not a problem. Programmed maintenance is also easily accommodated since there is no invoicing on Sundays during most of the year.

M&M Company Case

M&M is a Brazilian holding company of the mining and metallurgy areas. M&M has three business units in the branch of mining and processing of minerals. The company is comprised of various industrial plants in addition to the central office, has about 4,000 employees and invoices some US$300 million per year.

Implementation History

M&M implemented the Baan IV system in a project that started in 1998 and extended for over 10 months. M&M started operation of the system by means of the *big-bang* mode in two of the company's three business units. The chief difficulty faced by these units was related to the settlement of the package for the Brazilian context. A series of system problems related to the issuance of fiscal ledgers and to the remittance of information on collection to the banks made the launching of the operation rather complicated. The extent of settlement problems compelled the postponement of launching of the operation in the third unit and that is why problems in this unit were notably smaller.

The IT area is corporate and caters to the three business units of the company. The area is comprised of two teams: the infrastructure team, comprised of the coordinator and two more persons, and the Baan competence center team, comprised of the coordinator, four functional analysts (one for each implemented module) and a programming analyst. Coordinators are subordinate to the strategic planning and IT manager and the area has a total of 10 employees.

IT Management Change

Prior to implementation of the Baan system, IT had 39 persons who worked at the three business units; 22 were employees and 17 were outsourced. After the change the majority of the system analysts left the company, the operational employees were transferred to the help-desk outsourcing company and employees from user areas were utilized to set up the Baan competence center. The five participants of the Baan competence center, including the coordinator, came from the company's user areas.

The Baan competence center receives from the users requests related to the ERP system, performs the analysis of the solution alternatives and, whenever necessary, forwards the problems to Baan or consulting companies for the development of a solution. The company's proposal is to outsource the entire systems development that comprises programming and customizing of the Baan system. The objective is to keep the computing team focused on understanding the company's business and not on technology.

The company also outsourced the help-desk services and the datacenter. In the case of the help-desk, in addition to telephone support, the company keeps 12 people that belong to the supplier of the services, distributed in the manufacturing units. The company that supplies the datacenter services is a company belonging to the corporation. The servers of M&M are located in this company.

The interviewed coordinator believes that the change indeed shifted the focus of the area, "so much so that now the department is called Strategic Planning and Information Technology Department". The fact that all employees of the competence center come from user areas is, in principle, additional evidence that this shift of focus (from technology to processes and business) must really have taken place.

ERP System Management

The report states that some 40% of the system is customized. When there are legal modifications the supplier adds them to the standard package. Because the system is much customized, these modifications must be checked and often implemented again in the customized code. If the size of the modifications is small then implementation is carried out by the team's programming analyst him or herself; otherwise a consulting company is hired.

Apparently, management of these modifications in the customized code does not present a problem because the changes sent by the supplier are few. However, the company elected to only install and keep updated the modifications related to legal changes. For the remainder, which is non-obligatory, the company maintains the system not "updated" with respect to the supplier. Occasionally, this has brought about conflicts with the supplier and triggered more intense negotiations by the IT area. There is also a demand for migration to a new version of the system that should require considerable effort in a project assigned a duration of two years. Various other problems with the supplier were also reported, evidencing the importance of relationship management with the supplier.

The role of the Baan competence center is to receive and forward the requests for support and system improvements (calls always go through the help-desk and are referred from there to the center). Requests for support are of three kinds: functional support (such as how to carry out a given operation); support for operation faults (correction of operations incorrectly carried out by the users); and identification of system faults (bugs). Requests may be solved by the analysts themselves or forwarded to Baan. Contacts with Baan are only formulated by the IT area.

For the improvement requests a screening is performed to ensure that the request is not in conflict with the system's process models and to assess the possibility of implementation. At this stage the user is required to specify the benefits that will be achieved by the improvement. If approved, the request generates a detailed project and its cost is determined. If the IT budget for the year included this provision, then the request is complied with, based upon the IT budget. If it was not provisioned the user area may then have to wait for the following year to include the project in the IT budget; otherwise the user area may execute it immediately with the own budget.

All requests are treated as projects and they are developed with the support of consultants. There is intense user participation in the process during the stages of: approval of the functional design, approval of the technical design, tests, acceptance of the project and initial operation. The complete process is documented. The interviewee says that the backlog is not large because requests are not restrained. Once the need is detected and approved the development is immediately undertaken. If not approved it is returned to the user with a justification about the decision. It was also mentioned that the requirement of justification and specification of the expected benefits contributes to limit the number of requests.

Maintenance tasks of the ERP system related to infrastructure (such as backups and performance-tuning) are carried out by the outsourced datacenter company. Therefore, a significant part of the activity of ERP management ends up by being eliminated from the Baan competence center list of immediate concerns. This may contribute to the apparent success of the management model adopted by the M&M for its ERP system.

Relationship with Users

To allow that the reduced IT team may give support to a large number of users, there are keyusers in the industrial plants responsible for a given module and that are in charge of filtering and centralizing problems. As a rule, these users contact the Baan competence center to report problems or doubts that they were unable to deal with. The company has a total of 32 keyusers, distributed in the three business areas and along the various modules of the system. These users actively participate in the implementation process.

In case of employee turnover, the key users themselves do the training. The problem is aggravated when a key user leaves the company. Then individual new training is given by the IT area.

According to the report, the company has system use indicators geared to goals. There are service and user satisfaction goals, which are rated by questionnaires. There are also financial goals linked to the IT area budget. Monthly, the help-desk issues a report of satisfaction and service time supplied by the outsourced company, which has a service level agreement (SLA) with M&M.

Conclusion

A change of focus of the IT area becomes evident. In the two cases the area migrated from a technical approach of information systems to an approach of business processes supported by information systems. In the first case the company seeks a gradual transition to the new model, while in the second case the change was planned and carried out in a much more incisive manner. In both cases the differences are obvious: while in the first the conventional IT team is maintained, in the second a new team is elected, formed by professionals coming from the user area. This strategic difference is highlighted by the use of outsourcing in a much more assertive way in the second company.

In the two cases it is also apparent that the role of the users in the management of an ERP system is much more important and fundamental than in the case of internally developed systems. In the second company there is a major concern with the involvement of these users in the process and, apparently this really takes place. In the first one the change process took place in a more gradual manner and the IT area must continue to seek a greater involvement and participation.

Both companies faced severe settlement problems during the implementation of the ERP system, but they have certainly been overcome. In both cases currently, there are relationship problems with the supplier that demand the attention of the IT manager. Some of the difficulties apparently stem from the continued need of system updating that cannot always be strictly accomplished by the companies. Indeed, the two companies adopt alternative procedures to keep their updating efforts at levels consistent with their possibilities. Apparently companies that possess ERP systems also continue to be subject to the need of carrying out substantial upgrades requiring time and significant resources. Those are certainly important aspects of IT management that presumably were less significant at the time of internally developed systems.

Other noteworthy aspects are: the importance of user training, the figure of the key users, maintenance and development outsourcing, the adherence to the system's standards of availability and performance, the figure of the backlog, and so forth. These are aspects that usually can also be associated to conventional systems but that assume peculiar characteristics in the context of an integrated system. For instance the figure of the key user is now much more significant and must be explicitly taken into account in the system management. Furthermore, companies adopt different strategies in dealing with each aspect, yielding implications that possibly merit identification, understanding and dissemination. A more detailed contextual analysis of this myriad of details opens an interesting possibility for future research in the ambit of management of ERP systems.

References

Andressen, M. (2002). *The new IT crisis.* Retrieved December 11, 2002, from http://techupdate.zdnet.com.

Brooks, F.P. (1995). *The mythical man month* (20th Anniversary ed.). Addison Wesley.

Carr, N.G. (2003). A TI já não importa. *Harvard Business Review* (Brazilian ed.).

Chew, J. (2001). *Living with your enterprise apps.* Forrester Research Report.

Kayworth, T.R. (2002). Managing the corporate IS organization in the 21st century. *Proceedings of the AMCIS Minitrack Papers.*

Kern, H. (2002). Scrutinize shrink-wrapped software. Retrieved October 22, 2002, from http://techupdate.zdnet.com.

O'Brien, J.A. (2001). *Sistemas de informação e as decisões gerenciais na era da Internet.* São Paulo: Editora Saraiva.

Pui-Ng, C.S., Chan, T., & Gable, G. (2001). A client-benefits oriented taxonomy of ERP maintenance. *Proceedings of the IEEE International Conference on Software Maintenance.*

Yin, R.K. (1989). *Case study research: Design and methods.* London: Sage.

Appendix – Questionnaires for the Case Studies

IT Area

What is the makeup of the IT team?

Which are the activities carried out by the area within the company?

To what area is IT management subordinated?

ERP System Management

What is the meaning of ERP system management for the IT area?

Which are the activities related to this management?

Who performs them?

Which are the more important activities for the ERP system management?

Which are the more complex?

Which are the most burdensome?

Which are the main activities related to the evolution, maintenance and operation of the system?

IT Management Change

How did the ERP system use affect company's IT management?

Which were the benefits "promised" by the ERP system with regard to IT management?

Were they achieved?

Did the ERP system really expand the IT area focus in business?

Relationship with Users

Did the ERP system increase users' involvement in the definition of their information systems?

How did the ERP system use modify the framework of responsibilities between the IT area and users?

How did the ERP system change the relations of the IT area with the user areas?

Does the figure of the key-users still exist?

Which are the activities they perform?

How are the system's modifications carried out that may require the involvement of more than one area?

Relations with the Suppliers

Which are the motivating factors for the supplier in the evolution of ERP systems?

Do the interests of the suppliers clash with those of the company?

How are these conflicts resolved?

Which new types of services have been outsourced due to ERP system use?

Use of Indicators

Does the company use some type of indicator to assess ERP system management?

Which ones?

Which might or should be utilized?

Chapter XIII

A Critical Success Factor's Relevance Model for SAP Implementation Projects

José Esteves
Universidad Politécnica Catalunya, Spain

Joan Pastor
Universidad Internacional de Catalunya, Spain

Abstract

This chapter presents a unified model of Critical Success Factors (CSFs) for ERP implementation projects and the analysis of the relevance of these CSFs along the typical phases of a SAP implementation project. The Accelerated SAP implementation methodology (ASAP) is used as the SAP implementation reference method. Using Process Quality Management method, we derived a matrix of CSFs versus ASAP processes. Then, we evaluated the CSFs relevance along the five ASAP phases, specifically of those ones related with the organizational perspective. The main advantage of our approach is that we unified previous lists of CSFs for ERP implementation projects and we establish the CSFs relevance according to the implementation processes that should be made in a typical SAP implementation project. These findings will help managers to develop better strategies for supervising and controlling SAP or other similar ERP implementation projects.

Introduction

Despite the benefits that can be achieved from a successful Enterprise Resource Planning (ERP) systems implementation, there is already evidence of failure in ERP implementation projects (Davenport, 1998). Too often, project managers focus on the technical and financial aspects of a project and neglect to take into account the non-technical issues. To solve this problem, some researchers are using a Critical Success Factors (CSFs) approach to study ERP implementations. According to Rockart (1979), CSFs are "the limited number of areas in which results, if they are satisfactory, will ensure successful competitive performance for the organization". CSFs are based on the assumption that a limited amount of criteria, critical of the outcome of a project, can be identified, and that these criteria can be manipulated by managers (Wit, 1998). Thereby, they are a tool for forecasting and managing projects. The management of CSFs in ERP implementations is a thorny issue in ERP research. There is the practical and academic evidence that CSFs do not have the same importance along the various phases of an ERP implementation project (Esteves & Pastor, 2001). Markus and Tanis (2000) advert for the need to define success along the different phases of the ERP lifecycle. They argue that no single measure of ERP systems success is sufficient for all the concerns that organizations' executives might have about the ERP system experience, and that different measures are needed at different stages in the systems lifecycle. Thus, we attempt to develop a theoretical framework that describes this distribution along the ERP implementation phases. Several academic studies have been published related to CSFs identification but there is no evidence of studies related with operationalization and management of these CSFs.

We agree with Ward (1990) in that CSFs are not, in themselves, directly manageable. Rather than the CSFs, it is the processes that define what a management team "does," processes that can be owned, defined, measured and managed. Therefore, it is necessary to relate the CSFs to the SAP implementation project processes to provide an overall view of the importance of each process to the management of the CSFs in SAP implementation projects. These SAP implementation project processes are described in the implementation methodologies used. Broadly, a SAP implementation methodology covers the following: modeling business processes, mapping business processes onto the processes supported by the SAP system, perform the gap analysis, customizing the SAP system and finally, testing the customized SAP system before going live. Some SAP implementation methodologies have specific modules for knowledge management and change management.

This chapter is organized as follows. First, we present our unified model of CSFs that we used in our research and a brief description of the ASAP methodology. Then, we briefly describe the research framework followed. Next, we describe the findings, presenting the schema of CSFs relevance. Then, implications for practitioners and future research are outlined. Finally, some conclusions and further work are included.

Background

In order to study the relevance of CSFs along an ERP lifecycle, we made a literature review and we found four studies (Bergamaschi & Reinhard, 2000; Nah et al., 2001; Parr & Shanks, 2000; Somers & Nelson, 2001). Parr and Shanks (2000) studied CSFs relevance based in two ERP implementation case studies. However, only one of the case studies was considered a successful ERP implementation. Somers and Nelson (2001) described the impact of CSFs across the stages of a typical ERP implementation project based in a survey to 86 organizations. Bergamaschi and Reinhard (2000) analyzed the relevance of CSFs along the ERP lifecycle phases based in a survey to 43 organizations in Brazil. The study of Nah et al. (2001) defines in which phase of the ERP lifecycle each CSF may come into play, but authors include implementation stages in a unique phase denominated project phase. Our study extends the analysis of Nah et al. (2001) for the ERP lifecycle phases by focusing on implementation phase.

We found three main discrepancies in these studies: the first is related with the ERP lifecycle used, the second is related with the CSFs considered and the third is related with the research perspective. With regard to the ERP lifecycle, in all research studies, it is based in the particular researcher's definition and none of the studies tried to directly analyze the lifecycle of the branded implementation methodologies used in ERP implementation projects. All the implementation methodologies have as basis an ERP lifecycle. The adoption of an ERP implementation methodology is considered a CSF (Esteves & Pastor, 2000).

Second, the expression "implementation" is used in one case (Somers & Nelson, 2001) as referred to the whole process of adopting, selecting, implementing and using the ERP system. For us, the implementation phase consists of "the customization or parameterization and adaptation of the ERP package acquired according to the needs of the organization" (Esteves & Pastor, 2000). In relation to the definition of CSFs, each study used a different list of CSFs; some CSFs are the same but with different names, or different definitions encompass the same CSF. In order to solve these problems in our previous research we created a unified model of CSFs for ERP implementation projects (Esteves & Pastor, 2000). Later, we present this unified model.

Finally, all the studies used project managers and/or project team members perspective. In our case we opted to analyze CSFs relevance taking into account the ERP implementation processes underlying an ERP implementation project, which are detailed in all the ERP implementation methodologies. Since the focus of our research was a typical SAP implementation project, we opted for using the Accelerated SAP implementation (ASAP) methodology. The rest of the studies did not mention what type of ERP system they studied.

Unified Model of CSFs for ERP Implementation Projects

The CSF approach has been applied to many aspects and tasks of information systems, and more recently to ERP systems implementations, (e.g., Bancroft et al., 1998; Brown & Vessey, 1999; Clemons, 1998; Dolmetsch et al., 1998; Gibson & Mann, 1997, Holland et al., 1999; Nah et al., 2001; Parr et al., 1999; Somers & Nelson, 2001; Stefanou, 1999; Sumner, 1999). Based in a set of studies published by several authors, containing commented lists of CSFs in ERP implementations, we unified these lists and created a CSFs unified model for ERP implementation projects (Esteves & Pastor, 2000). The unified model is represented in Figure 1. The advantage of this model is that it unifies a set of studies related with lists of CSFs identified by other authors; the CSFs are categorized in different perspectives and each CSF is identified and defined.

Figure 1. Unified critical success factors model.

	Strategic	Tactical
Organizational	Sustained management support Effective organizational change management Adequate project team composition Good project scope management Comprehensive business process redesign Adequate project champion role Trust between partners User involvement and participation	Dedicated staff and consultants Appropriate usage of consultants Empowered decision makers Adequate training program Strong communication inwards and outwards Formalized project plan/schedule Preventive trouble shooting
Technological	Avoid customization Adequate ERP implementation strategy Adequate ERP version	Adequate infrastructure and interfaces Adequate legacy systems knowledge

In our view, the nature of the ERP implementation issues includes strategic, tactical, organizational and technological perspectives. Therefore, we propose that the CSFs model should have these four perspectives. The organizational perspective is related with concerns like organizational structure and culture and business processes. The technological perspective focuses on aspects related to the particular ERP product in consideration and on other related technical aspects, such as hardware and base software needs. The strategic perspective is related with core competencies accomplishing the organization's mission and long-term goals, while the tactical perspective affects the business activities with short-term objectives.

Organizational Perspective

Strategic Factors

Sustained management support. Sustained management commitment, both at top and middle levels during the implementation, in terms of their own involvement and the willingness to allocate valuable organizational resources (Holland et al., 1999). Management support is important for accomplishing project goals and objectives and aligning these with strategic business goals (Sumner, 1999).

Effective organizational change management. Organizational change refers to the body of knowledge that is used to ensure that a complex change, like that associated with a new big information system, gets the right results, in the right timeframe, at the right costs. The change management approach will try to ensure the acceptance and readiness of the new system, allowing the organization to get the benefits of its use. A successful organizational change approach relies in a proper integration of people, process and technology.

Good project scope management. This factor is related with concerns of project goals clarification and their congruence with the organizational mission and strategic goals. This includes both scope definition and subsequent scope control. Some components of this factor are: scope of business processes and business units involved, ERP functionality implemented, technology to be replaced/upgraded/integrated, and exchange of data.

Adequate project team composition. ERP projects typically require some combination of business, information technology, vendor, and consulting support. The structure of the project team has a strong impact in the implementation process. Two important factors are the integration of third-party consultants within the team and the retention within the organization of the relevant ERP knowledge.

Comprehensive business process reengineering. This is related with the alignment between business processes and the ERP business model and related best practices. This process will allow the improvement of the software functionality according to the organization needs. Managers have to decide if they do business process reengineering before, during or after ERP implementation.

Adequate project champion role. The main reason why this person is considered to be central to successful implementations is that s/he has both the position and the skills that are critical for handling organizational change (Parr et al., 1999). The role of the project champion is very important for marketing the project throughout the organization (Sumner, 1999).

User involvement and participation. User participation refers to the behaviors and activities that users perform in the system implementation process. User involvement refers to a psychological state of the individual, and is defined as the importance and personal relevance of a system to a user (Hartwick & Barki, 1994). User involvement and participation will result in a better fit of user requirements achieving better system quality, use and acceptance.

Trust between partners. During the implementation phase there are different partners involved, such as consultants and software and hardware vendors. An adequate partnership between them will ease achievement of the goals defined.

Tactical Factors

Dedicated staff and consultants. Usually, in many cases the time dedicated to the implementation project is shared with other activities. It is also important to ensure that the staff believes in the project success. Consultants should be involved in a way that helps the implementation process while also sharing their expertise with the internal staff involved. This is related with the recruitment and motivation of staff and consultants.

Strong communication inwards and outwards. Communication should be of two kinds: "inwards" to the project team and "outwards" to the whole organization. This means not only sharing information between the project team but also communicating to the whole organization the results and the goals in each implementation stage. The communication effort should be done in a regular basis during the implementation phase.

Formalized project plan/schedule. This means to have a well-defined plan/ schedule for all the activities involved in the ERP implementation, with an appropriate allocation of budget and resources for these activities. Evidence shows that the majority of projects fail to finish the activities on time and within budget. To ensure the project completion according with the plan/schedule, close monitoring and controlling of time and costs should be done, as well as implementation project scope and plan/ schedule review, whenever justified.

Adequate training program. The training plan should take into consideration both technical staff and end users, and its scope will depend on the type of implementation approach selected (see below). Some organizations use an in-house training approach while others prefer using training consultants.

Preventive trouble shooting. This factor is related with the problem and risk areas that exist in every implementation. Trouble-shooting mechanisms should be included in the implementation plan. Two important aspects are the adaptation and transfer of old data and the "go live" moment. The time and effort involved in the transfer of data from previous systems should not be underestimated.

Appropriate usage of consultants. Determining the number, how and when to use external consultants appropriate to the ERP implementation needs. The usage of external consultants will depend on the internal know-how that the organization has at the moment.

Empowered decision-makers. Project team members must be empowered to make quick decisions to reduce delays in implementation related with slow decision-making (Parr et al., 1999). Organizations should attempt to make decisions as rapidly as possible, as even small delays can have an impact on such a long-term project (De Bruin, 1997).

Technological Perspective

Strategic Factors

Adequate ERP implementation strategy. This includes management decisions concerning how the software package is to be implemented (Holland et al., 1999). There are different approaches to ERP implementation strategy, ranging from "skeleton" to "big-bang" implementations (Gibson et al., 1997). While "skeleton" implementations are phased and provide usable functionality incrementally, "big-bang" ones offer full functionality all at once at implementation end. The advantages and disadvantages of these extreme approaches should be measured, especially at a functionality level.

Avoid customization. Wherever and as far as possible, the ERP-hosting organization should try to adopt the processes and options built into the ERP, rather than seek to modify the ERP to fit the particular business practices (Parr et al., 1999). Thus, it is recommended that customization adheres to the standardized specifications that the software supports (Sumner, 1999). In this sense, a good business vision is helpful because it reduces the effort of capturing the functionality of the ERP business model and therefore minimizes the customization effort.

Adequate ERP version. An organization needs to determine which ERP version it will implement. Frequent upgrades can cause problems. This is particularly relevant when the organization has to wait for a future release that includes the functionality required (De Bruin, 1997).

Tactical Factors

Adequate infrastructure and interfaces. Usually, ERP systems do not provide all the functional requirements of an organization. Therefore ERP vendors have a complete program of interfacing with third-party products to leverage organizations with special expertise and products (Kale, 2000). There is the need to configure the interfaces according to the user's needs. Nowadays, there are some modeling tools that can help in all these tasks. Interfacing the different systems should be scheduled in such a way that the interfaces are operational when the ERP goes live. Before going live, validation tests should be applied.

Adequate legacy systems knowledge. Legacy systems are the business and IT systems prior to the ERP that encapsulate the existing business processes, organization structure, culture and information technology (Holland et al., 1999). They are a good source of information for ERP implementations and the possible problems that can be found during the implementation. Another aspect is to decide which legacy systems will be replaced and the need to interface with those legacy systems for which the ERP does not provide an adequate replacement. There is also the need to analyze the different transition strategies from legacy systems to the new ERP system.

The ASAP Implementation Methodology

In 1996, SAP introduced the Accelerated SAP (ASAP) implementation methodology with the goal of speeding up SAP implementation projects. ASAP was advocated to enable new customers to utilize the experience and expertise gleaned from thousands of implementations worldwide. This is specifically targeted for small and medium enterprises adopting SAP. The key phases of the ASAP methodology, also known as the ASAP roadmap, are:

• **Project preparation.** The purpose of this phase is to provide initial planning and preparation of SAP project. The steps of this phase help identify and plan the primary focus areas to be considered, such as: objectives, scope, plan and definition of project team.

- **Business blueprint.** The purpose of this phase is to create the business blueprint, which is a detailed documentation of the results gathered during requirements workshops/meetings. It will allow the implementation project team to clearly define their scope, and only focus on the SAP processes needed to run the organization business.

- **Realization.** The purpose of this phase is to implement business and processes requirements on the business blueprint. The objectives are final implementation in the system, an overall test, and the release of the system for production (live) operation.

- **Final preparation.** The purpose of this phase is to complete the final preparation, including testing, end user training, system management and cut over activities, to finalize the readiness to go live. The final preparation phase also serves to resolve all open issues.

- **Go live & support.** The purpose of this phase is to move from a pre-production environment to live production operation. A support organization must be set up for end users to provide long-term support. This phase is also used to monitor system transactions and to improve overall system performance. Finally the completed project is closed.

The structure of each phase is the following: each phase is composed of a group of work packages. These work packages are structured in activities, and each activity is composed of a group of tasks. An example of two work packages of ASAP, project kickoff and quality check, is described in Figure 4. For each task, a definition, a set of procedures, results and roles are provided in the ASAP roadmap documentation. According to a survey of Input company (Input, 1999), organizations have been more satisfied with SAP tools and methodologies than with those of implementation partners. Implementations where ASAP or Powered by SAP methodologies were used averaged only 8 months, compared to 15 months for standard implementations. In Dolmetsch et al. (1998), four case studies conducted in small to medium companies came to the eventual result that the implementation methodology ASAP supported the criteria for a successful SAP implementation by providing a transparent implementation process which allows the organization to make the most efficient use of consulting time.

Our Proposed CSF Relevance Model

CSFs can either be ongoing, or they can be temporal (Khandewal & Ferguson, 1999). Khandewal and Ferguson (1999) assert, notwithstanding the earlier statement that the CSFs can either be ongoing or temporal, that all CSFs can be defined in a way that they are temporal. For example, formal plan and schedule for the ERP implementation project can be defined as a temporal CSF. This CSF will then be considered having been achieved as soon as a project plan is developed. The assumption is that once the project plan is developed the ongoing updating of this plan would be an integral part of the project plan. All CSFs would thus belong to a point in time, although they may differ in their degree of temporality. Therefore, it is important to know these points in time where CSFs are more relevant. Next, we describe our research framework for evaluating CSFs relevance along SAP implementation phases and the relevance model obtained.

Research Framework for Evaluating CSFs Relevance

We have used the Process Quality Management (PQM) method (Ward, 1990) to relate the CSFs with the ASAP processes. The PQM method developed by IBM is "designed to assist the management team reach consensus on the most critical business activities, i.e., those whose performance will have the biggest impact on the success or failure of the enterprise" (Ward, 1990, p. 105). PQM uses the concept of CSFs (Rockart, 1979) to encourage management teams to focus their attention on the critical issues of the business, and then to base the IT strategy on these. Next, we describe the following steps of the PQM method, as we have applied them in our research case (see Figure 2):

- **First step: Define the mission.** We define the following mission: "To implement the ERP system, according to the organization's business and organizational needs" and then "to show that the ERP implementation will add value through the satisfaction of the organization requirements previously defined". This mission reflects the intention of the whole group of people involved in an ERP implementation project;

- **Second step: Define CSFs.** We will use the CSFs unified model proposed by Esteves and Pastor (2000);

Figure 2. Research framework.

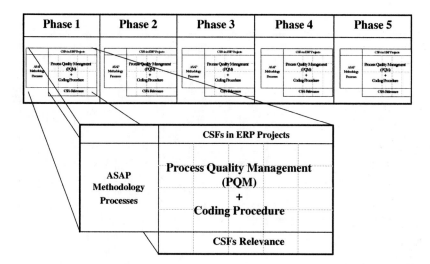

- **Third step: Define the processes.** In our case, the processes are those defined in the ASAP methodology;

- **Fourth step: Establish the relationship of CSFs versus ASAP processes.** This is done through the creation of the matrix presented in Figure 2 and Table 1. For each one of the five SAP implementation phases a matrix was created. Next, we describe how the matrix of CSFs versus ASAP processes was created.

According to Hardaker and Ward (1987), "the object is to single out the processes that have a primary impact on this particular CSF". What we are looking for are those essential activities and not all of them. The matrix in Table 1 has been built in the following way. We focused on each CSF and asked this question: Which ASAP processes must be performed especially well for us to be confident of achieving this CSF? Then, we looked at all the processes and decided which ones were important for that CSF. Each time we established a relationship between a CSF and a process, we marked a "1" in the corresponding cell of the matrix (see Table 1). A second process was used to validate and to get more reliability in the research. We used a coding procedure to analyze the ASAP documentation. The coding procedure consisted in coding line-by-line all the ASAP processes using a predefined list of codes, in this case the list

Table 1. Example of the matrix CSFs versus ASAP processes for project preparation phase.

	ASAP Processes (CSFs in ERP implementations)	Sustained management support	Effective organizational change	Good project scope management	Adequate project team composition	Comprehensive business process redesign	User involvement and participation	Adequate project champion role	Trust between partners	Dedicated staff and consultants	Strong communication	Formalize project plan/schedule	Adequate training program	Preventive trouble shooting	Usage of appropriate consultants	Empower decision makers	Adequate ERP implementation strategy	Avoid customization	Adequate ERP version	Adequate infrastructure and interfaces	Adequate legacy systems knowledge
W	**Project Kickoff**																				
A	Kickoff Meeting																				
T	Prepare for kickoff meeting						1					1									
T	Conduct kickoff meeting	1					1	1			1										
T	Company wide project introduction						1				1	1									
A	Project team standards meeting																				
T	Prepare for standard meeting						1					1									
T	Conduct standard meeting						1			1	1										
W	**Quality Check**																				
A	Perform quality check and approval																				
T	Conduct quality check						1														
T	Signoff project preparation phase	1					1														
	Number of CSFs occurrences	2	0	0	0	0	1	7	0	1	3	3	0	0	0	0	0	0	0	0	0

of CSFs. Next, we present part of the full matrix of CSFs versus ASAP processes built for the first phase of ASAP, the project preparation phase.

CSFs Relevance

Table 2 represents the CSFs relevance for each CSF in each phase. The values were calculated in the following way. We have built a matrix of CSFs versus ASAP processes such as the one in Table 1 for each implementation phase, and for each CSF we sum the number of occurrences of that CSF. For instance, the sum of 2 in the CSF Sustained Management Support means that we defined two relationships between this CSF and two ASAP tasks. Then, we converted the number of occurrences (raw scores) into a normative scale of 10 scores. In a scale of this kind, results from 1-3 are considered irrelevant, from 4-7 normal relevance, and 8-10 they are considered of high relevance. In our case, we see that almost all the factors are higher than 4. Thus, their relevance is normal or high in most cases. We do not pretend to say that a CSF with a low summation it is not important; what we say is that it is less relevant in that period of the project. CSFs have all the same importance,; therefore, all of them should be carefully respected and analyzed. The analysis of the table shows that:

- **In phase 1 (project preparation)**, the most relevant CSFs are sustained management support, project champion role and formalized project plan/schedule. We are at the beginning of the implementation project and it is very important to identify and plan the primary focus areas to be considered.

- **In phase 2 (business blueprint)**, the most relevant CSFs are project champion role, effective organizational change management and user involvement. The goal of this model is to create the business blueprint that is a visual model of the business' future state after which organizations have crossed the SAP finish line. It will allow the implementation project team to clearly define their scope, and only focus on the SAP processes needed to run the organization business.

- **In phase 3 (realization)**, the most relevant CSFs are adequate software configuration, project champion role, and user involvement. In this phase the configuration of SAP system begins; that is why the adequate ERP configuration factor is so important as well as the involvement of users. They help in the system parameterization.

- **In phase 4 (final preparation)**, the most relevant CSFs are project champion role and preventive troubleshooting and it is time to convert data and to test the system.

- **In phase 5 (go live & support)**, the most relevant CSFs are project champion role, sustained management support and strong communication inwards and outwards.

One of the main results from Table 2 is that organizational factors have more relevance along the SAP phases than technological ones. Once again, there is the need to focus more on people and process than on technology itself. This is not new, and other studies have proved the same aspect in other types of IS

Table 2. CSFs relevance along the ASAP implementation phases.

Perspectives		Critical Success Factors	SAP Implementation phases				
			1	2	3	4	5
Organizational Perspective	Strategic	Sustained management support	8	5	5	5	8
		Effective organizational change	6	8	5	5	6
		Good project scope management	5	4	4	4	5
		Adequate project team composition	4	4	4	4	4
		Comprehensive business process redesign	4	7	4	4	5
		User involvement and participation	5	8	10	8	6
		Project champion role	10	10	9	10	10
		Trust between partners	6	4	4	4	5
	Tactical	Dedicated staff and consultants	4	4	4	4	5
		Strong communication inwards and outwards	7	7	6	8	8
		Formalized project plan/schedule	8	7	7	7	5
		Adequate training program	5	5	5	7	5
		Preventive trouble shooting	4	4	8	8	7
		Usage of appropriate consultants	6	8	9	6	5
		Empowered decision makers	4	4	4	5	4
Technological Perspective	Strategic	Adequate ERP implementation strategy	5	4	4	4	4
		Avoid customization	4	4	5	4	4
	Tactical	Adequate ERP version	4	4	4	4	4
		Adequate infrastructure and interfaces	6	6	7	7	4
		Adequate legacy systems knowledge	4	4	4	4	4

implementation projects. This aspect is very important since as Felix and Harrison (1984) quoted, "technical problems can usually be detected and repaired before the system is put in jeopardy. The cost may be high in terms of either budget or schedule, but the repair can be made. Organizational and personnel problems often cannot be redressed, and continue to jeopardize the success of the system itself." Next, we describe each CSF along the ASAP phases, classified by organizational and technological perspectives.

Organizational Perspective

Sustained management support is more relevant at the beginning and at the end of the implementation. The reason is that at the beginning, senior management should help in the rollout of the project, analyze the business benefits, define the mission and scope of the project and provide the resources needed for the project. At the end, there is the need to encourage the system usage and help in the commitment of user involvement.

Effective organizational change management and **business process redesign** are more relevant in the second phase. In this phase the business blueprint is defined, and the business processes are analyzed, redesigned (some) and documented. There is the need to understand how the organization intends to run its business within the SAP system and the changes in the organization.

Adequate project team composition has the same relevance along all the phases since they play an important part in the whole project. ASAP methodology does not focus too much on this CSF since it assumes that the right people were chosen.

Good project scope management is relevant at the beginning when managers define the scope and in the last phase because the scope is usually revised and changed according to the results of the go live system tests.

Project champion role is relevant in all phases. It is less relevant in the third phase than in the others because this phase is dedicated to configuration tasks and here the role of the champion is to guarantee that everything goes according to the plan.

Trust between partners is relevant at the beginning when all the stakeholders involved in the project should share their goals and knowledge and at the end when they have to analyze and again share their knowledge to finish the project with success.

User involvement and participation is relevant in the phases where their know-how is important to achieve a good customization of the system to organizational needs. They participate in the definition of business requirements, help in the analysis of the ERP configuration and in conversion of data and the testing of the system.

Dedicated staff and consultants is more relevant in the last phase where there is the need to dedicate more effort in order for the system to go live and also be available to help users by answering their questions and reducing their doubts about the new system.

Appropriate usage of consultants is relevant especially in the second and third phases. On the second phase the knowledge of consultants is important to improve the business processes, and on the third phase consultants produce knowledge on the ERP system parameterization.

Empowered decision makers is more relevant in the second and fourth phases because there is the need to quickly make decisions related with the business processes redesign (second phase) and the adequate customization of ERP system (fourth phase) in order to accomplish project plan/schedule on time.

Adequate training program is more relevant in phase 4 because it is when the training program of end users starts, but in the previous phases there are also training concerns related with project team training and to prepare end-user training.

Strong communication inwards and outwards is more relevant at the first two phases where there is strong need of communication between senior management and the project team in the definition of project plan and scope, and in the last phase where there is the need of a strong communication with the whole organization to start the going live of the SAP system.

Formalized plan and schedule relevance decreases during the implementation project. The reason is that at the beginning it is important starting planning as early as possible. However, along the project, modifications to accomplish the results are expected.

Preventive troubleshooting is more relevant in the last three phases, especially in the fourth phase during which issues arise when the production system is being tested and old data converted to the new system.

Technological Perspective

Avoid customization is more relevant in phase 3, when the SAP system is configured and more than 8,000 tables must be parameterized. The software configuration should follow the business requirements defined in the previous phase.

Adequate ERP implementation strategy is more relevant at the first phase because it is in this phase that the SAP implementation strategy should be decided.

Adequate ERP version has the same relevance along all the phases. From the beginning until the end of the project implementation, SAP recommends that the project team follow the upgrade of SAP releases and should consider the adoption of new ones.

Adequate infrastructure and interfaces is more relevant in phases 3 and 4, when there is the need to configure the infrastructure for the production operation (go live). In these phases are also configured the interfaces with other systems, and the creation of reports and forms.

Adequate legacy systems knowledge is less relevant at the first phase because this phase is related with the preparation of project implementation. In phase 3 the need of knowledge of legacy systems is more relevant in order to minimize the effort of configuration, to help in conversion of data and the creation of interfaces.

Regarding the definition of the most relevant CSFs, we opted for accepting as the most relevant CSFs in each phase all the CSFs with a score up to 7 (see Figure 2). This CSFs relevance model suggests that organizational and project management factors have more relevance along the SAP implementation project phases. Once again, there is the need to focus more on people and process than technology itself. If we analyze the strategic and tactical perspectives, we evidence that strategic factors are the most relevant in the initial phases while the tactical factors gain relevance in the middle and final phases.

Figure 2. Most relevant CSFs model proposal for a typical SAP implementation project.

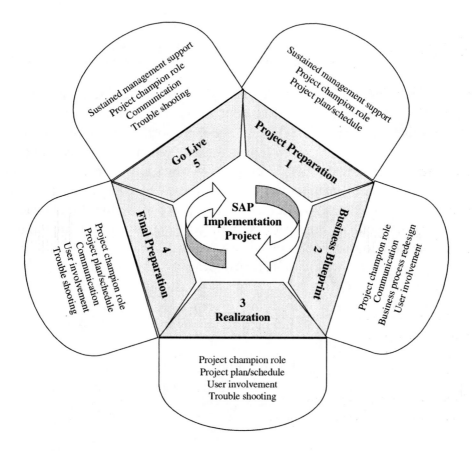

Implications for Practitioners

We think the CSFs relevance schema (Table 2) and the most relevant CSFs model (Figure 2) will be valuable documents for the management of CSFs because managers will know the variety of factors affecting a SAP implementation project success and their relative importance across SAP implementation stages. These CSFs relevance models provide guidance to practitioners in planning and monitoring a SAP implementation project with more emphasis in SAP system. The SAP implementation methodology is an important component of the SAP implementation strategy, and therefore it is necessary that CSFs should not only be identified, there is also the need to establish the relationship between these CSFs and the implementation project processes in order to verify if these processes support the accomplishment of CSFs. Finally, this knowledge may help in the allocation and management of project resources in each SAP implementation stage.

Implications for Further Research

We think the findings show the adequacy of our research approach in order to study CSFs relevance along SAP implementation phases. The CSFs relevance schema and the most CSFs relevant model proposal can help researchers focusing on why these CSFs are so relevant, and how managers and consultants deal with them. It would be also useful to know which are the determinants and precedents to achieve satisfactory results in these CSFs. Regarding the SAP implementation methodologies, the research approach used and the relevance model can be useful as tools to assess the adequacy of those SAP implementation methodologies. For instance, in the case of ASAP, we evidence that sustained management support is not so relevant during the middle phases. We think that ASAP should give more focus to this topic. The same happens to balanced team, which is a topic only referenced in the task of project team composition. Further research should also focus on how the ASAP processes support CSFs accomplishment.

In terms of our research design to study CSFs relevance, we think that our approach is useful since it helps to understand if implementation processes help to achieve CSFs and how to put them in practice.

Conclusions and Further Work

This chapter provides a CSFs unified model for ERP implementation projects, a schema of these CSFs relevance along the phases of the ASAP methodology and a most relevant CSFs model proposal. The CSFs unified model was built through a literature review and using open coding procedure from Grounded Theory method. The CSFs relevance schema was developed through the application of Process Quality Management method, based on the CSFs unified model for ERP implementation projects and the ASAP documentation.

It is important to point out that organizational factors have more relevance along the SAP implementation project phases. Once again, there is the need to focus more on people and process than technology itself. In our opinion, the proposed relevance findings are useful because:

- We have a clearer orientation of the relevance of each CSF along the SAP implementation project;

- With this knowledge, we can better control and monitor SAP implementation projects and drive them towards success or high levels of satisfaction.

We are now trying to validate these preliminary findings using the case study method and interviews with people of various roles involved in SAP implementation projects. We also want to analyze the implications of studying specific types such as higher education SAP implementation projects. Finally, we also will compare our findings with other studies of ERP implementation projects in general in order to identify similarities as discrepancies that may help improve our work.

References

Bancroft, N., Seip, H., & Sprengel, A. (1998). *Implementing SAP R/3* (2nd ed.). Greenwich: Manning Publications.

Brown, C., & Vessey, I. (1999). ERP implementation approaches: Toward a contingency framework. *International Conference on Information Systems.*

Clemons, C. (1998). Successful implementation of an enterprise system: A case study. *Americas Conference on Information Systems.*

Davenport, T. (1998, July-August). Putting the enterprise into the enterprise system. *Harvard Business Review*, 121-131.

De Bruin, P. (1997). *Unpublished 1997 Sapphire conference notes* in Gibson and Mann.

Dolmetsch, R., Huber, T., Fleisch, E., & Österle, H. (1998). *Accelerated SAP - 4 case studies* (pp. 1-8). University of St. Gallen.

Esteves, J., & Pastor, J. (1999). An ERP life-cycle-based research agenda. *1º International Workshop on Enterprise Management Resource and Planning Systems* (EMRPS), 359-371.

Esteves, J., & Pastor, J. (2000). Towards the unification of critical success factors for ERP implementations. *10ᵗʰ Annual BIT Conference.*

Esteves, J., & Pastor, J. (2001). Analysis of critical success factors relevance along SAP implementation phases. *Americas Conference on Information Systems.*

Felix, R., & Harrison, W. (1984). Project management considerations for distributed processing applications. *MISQ Quarterly, 8*(3), 161-170.

Gibson, J., & Mann, S. (1997). *A qualitative examination of SAP R/3 implementations in the Western Cape.* Research report, Department of Information Systems, University of Cape Town.

Hardaker, M., & Ward, B. (1987). How to make a team work. *Harvard Business Review, 65*(6), 112-120.

Holland, C., Light, B., & Gibson, N. (1999). A critical success factors model for enterprise resource planning implementation. *European Conference on Information Systems.*

Input. (1999). Buyers's guide to SAP services providers in the U.S. Input company. Available: http://www.input.com/buyers_guide

Khandelwal, V., & Ferguson, J. (1999). Critical success factors (CSFs) and the growth of IT in selected geographic regions. *Hawaii International Conference on System Sciences.*

Kwon, T., & Zmud R. (1987). Unifying the fragmented models of information systems implementation. In H. Boland (Eds.), *Critical issues in information research.* New York: Wiley.

Markus, L., & Tanis, C. (2000). The enterprise systems experience- From adoption to success. In RW. Zmud (Ed.), *Framing the domains of IT research: Glimpsing the future through the past.* Cincinnati: Pinnaflex Educational Resources, Inc.

Nah, F., Lau, J., & Kuang, J. (2001). Critical factors for successful implementation of enterprise systems. *Business Process Management Journal, 7*(3), 285-296.

Parr, A., Shanks, G., & Darke, P. (1999). Identification of necessary factors for successful implementation of ERP systems. *New information technologies in organizational processes, field studies and theoretical reflections on the future work* (pp. 99-119). Kluwer Academic Publishers.

Rockart, J. (1979). Chief executives define their own information needs. *Harvard Business Review,* 81-92.

Somers, T., & Nelson, K. (2001). The impact of critical success factors across the stages of enterprise resource planning implementations. *34th Hawaii International Conference on System Sciences.*

Stefanou, C. (1999). Supply chain management (SCM) and organizational key factors for successful implementation of enterprise resource planning (ERP) systems. *Americas Conference on Information Systems.*

Sumner, M. (1999). Critical success factors in enterprise wide information management systems projects. *Americas Conference on Information Systems.*

Ward, B. (1990). Planning for profit. In T.J. Lincoln (Ed.), *Managing information systems for profit* (pp. 103-146). John Wiles & Sons Ltd.

Wit, C. (1998). Proposal for a holistic research approach to studying the implementation of IT. *IRIS 21.*

Chapter XIV

A Comparative Analysis of Major ERP Life Cycle Implementation, Management and Support Issues in Queensland Government

She-I Chang
Queensland University of Technology, Australia

Guy G. Gable
Queensland University of Technology, Australia

Abstract

This chapter reports on a study of issues across the ERP life cycle from the perspectives of individuals with substantial and diverse involvement with SAP Financials in Queensland Government. A survey was conducted of 117 ERP system project participants in five closely related state government agencies. Through a modified Delphi technique, the study inventoried, synthesized, then weighted perceived major-issues in ongoing ERP life cycle implementation, management, and support. The five agencies each implemented SAP Financials simultaneously using a common implementation partner. The three Delphi survey rounds, together with a series of interviews and domain experts' workshops, resulted in a set of 10 major-issue categories with 38 sub-issues. Sub-issue weights are compared between strategic and operational personnel within the agencies in order to understand where the organizations should focus their resources in order to avoid, minimise, or eliminate these issues. Study findings confirm the importance of this finer partitioning of the data, and distinctions identified reflect the unique circumstances across the stakeholder groups. The study findings should be of interest to stakeholders who seek to better understand the issues surrounding ERP systems and to better realize the benefits of ERP.

Introduction

Organizations worldwide, whether public or private, are moving away from developing Information Systems (IS) in-house and are instead implementing Enterprise Resource Planning (ERP) systems and other packaged software (AMR Research, 1998; IDC Software Research, 2000; Price Waterhouse, 1995). ERP has been referred to as a business operating system that enables better resource planning and improved delivery of value-added products and services to customers. ERP systems have, in recent years, begun to revolutionise best practice business processes and functions. They automate core corporate activities such as manufacturing and the management of financial and human resources and the supply chain, while eliminating complex, expensive links between systems and business functions that were performed across legacy systems (Bingi et al., 1999; Gable et al., 1998; Klaus et al., 2000; Rosemann and Wiese, 1999).

Despite warnings in the literature, many organizations apparently continue to underestimate the issues and problems often encountered throughout the ERP life cycle, as evidenced by suggestions that: (1) more than 40% of large software projects fail; (2) 90% of ERP implementations end up late or over budget; and (3) 67% of enterprise application initiatives could be considered negative or unsuccessful (e.g., Martin, 1998; Davenport, 1998; Boston Consulting Group, 2000).

ERP life cycle-wide management and support are ongoing concerns rather than a destination. The pre-implementation, implementation, and post-implementation stages continue throughout the lifetime of the ERP as it evolves with the organization (Dailey, 1998). Unlike the traditional view of operational IS that describes a system life cycle in terms of development, implementation, and maintenance, examination of ERP implementations is revealing that their life cycle involves major iterations. Following initial implementation there are subsequent revisions, re-implementations, and upgrades that transcend what is normally considered system *maintenance*. As the number of organizations implementing ERP increases and ERP applications within organizations proliferate (Bancroft, 1998; Davenport, 1996; Hiquet et al., 1998; Shtub, 1999), improved understanding of ERP life cycle implementation, management, and support issues is required so that development, management, and training resources can be allocated effectively (Gable et al., 1998). A better understanding of ERP life cycle issues will also help direct the ERP research agenda.

Although ERP sales in 2000 declined for the main vendors (e.g., SAP, Baan, ORACLE, JD Edwards, Peoplesoft) due to post-Y2K curtailment in IT/IS activity and to saturation of large organizations, the outlook through to 2004 is for compound annual growth of 11.4% for license, maintenance, and related service revenue associated with enterprise resource management applications (IDC Software Research, 2000). This sustained interest in implementing and realising the benefits of ERP systems, and the consequent life cycle issues, provide the rationale for this study (this need is further outlined in Gable et al., 1997a, 1997b; Gable, 1998; Gable et al., 1998).

The paper proceeds as follows. First, the study background is described. Second, the research methodology is related. Third, study results are presented. Fourth, implications of the study findings are explored. Lastly, several broad conclusions are drawn.

Background of the Study

The Study Context

In 1983, the Queensland Government Financial Management System (QGFMS) was successfully implemented to provide a common financial management system to all Queensland government agencies. Over the years, the Government reaffirmed strong support for central coordination of financial information systems as a fundamental strategy underpinning sound financial management in the government budget sector. These activities created benefits associated with improved coordination and economies of scale. They include the provision of timely, current information on a government- or sector-wide basis and cost savings in the areas of training, relocation of staff, single-point market investigation, development, and support (*Financial Management Strategy,* 1994).

Nevertheless, QGFMS must continually evolve to support new initiatives aimed at improving the budget sector's effectiveness. Three related initiatives that continue to shape the Queensland Government budget sector environment are: program management, accrual accounting, and accrual output budgeting. These initiatives are being implemented across the departments under guidelines of *Managing for Outcomes* (MFO)–an integrated planning, budgeting, and performance management framework (*Financial Management Strategy*, 1998).

In 1995 an ERP system, SAP Financials, was chosen to become the "new generation" of QGFMS. The SAP system was selected based on the following requirements: the ability to quickly and easily adapt to changes in organizational structures and business environments; and the need for cash, accrual accounting, and year 2000 compliance. By the end of 1999 most Queensland Government agencies had completed their initial SAP Financials implementation.

Motivation for the Study

Although SAP Financials have now been established in some agencies for a considerable period, new issues associated with the system's ongoing support and evolution continue to arise. A standard accounting environment driven by central government (Treasury) regulation, combined with other centrally driven reporting requirements, as well as the same software (SAP) existing across all agencies, provided an excellent opportunity to study ERP-related issues. All key players (software vendors, implementation partners, and user organizations) involved in ERP life cycle implementation, management, and support can potentially benefit from a better understanding of these issues. ERP software vendors seek to redress negative perceptions that ERP implementation duration and costs are difficult to manage, and to improve ongoing customer support and satisfaction. Consulting firms seek to streamline implementation and share in the savings with clients. Both software vendors and consultants seek to increase the size of the ERP market through reduced costs and increased benefits to clients. Also, when software vendors and their implementation partners are more attuned to the issues identified, they will be well placed to further support clients throughout the ERP life cycle. Potential benefits to clients from identifying and analyzing ERP life cycle-related issues include: rationalised and more effective support from both the software vendor and implementation partner; improved ability to react to a changing environment; lower costs; and ERP systems that more accurately reflect business needs.

Information systems management community members (e.g., professional societies, educators, trainers, researchers), who seek to effectively serve their community, must also be aware of major ERP life cycle issues. Professional societies serve the community by arranging conferences, sponsoring guest lectures, and disseminating information through their publications. Educators and trainers need information on key issues to develop graduates with the necessary skills to address these concerns. Furthermore, researchers will be more successful in attracting sponsorship if they undertake studies that are closely aligned to the concerns of the marketplace.

Clearly there is a need for research aimed at identifying and explicating the specific client-centerd ERP life cycle implementation, management, and support issues experienced by different individuals in organizations in order to understand where the organization should focus their resources so that they will able to avoid, minimise, or eliminate these issues. The extensive deployment of ERP in private and public sector and the rapidly growing and changing portfolio of software applications on which the Queensland Government is dependent, magnify the imperative.

Methodology

Data Collection and Analysis

A three-round, non-anonymous Delphi-type open survey was conducted, using personalized e-mail with attached survey instruments. Chang and Gable (2000) critique the Delphi method in the context of IS key issues studies and its application within the context of the current study. The study involved three survey rounds: (1) "inventory" round, (2) "confirmation" round, and (3) "weights" round. Round-One sought to inventory the morass of issues perceived by the contacts. Subsequent to Round-One a "tentative set" of issue categories was synthesized. In Round-Two, a "preliminary set" was confirmed with respondents. Having established a "master set," in Round-Three respondents were asked to score or weight the issues in the master set, indicating their perceived relative importance.

In coding and synthesizing the survey responses from Round-One, several potential coding schemes were examined and tested. Attempts to map the data onto existing models (e.g., MIT90s framework, ERP life cycle) failed to provide a satisfactory level of discrimination between substantive issues. The strengths and weaknesses of potential coding methods and synthesis procedures are discussed in Chang et al. (2000). Qualitative data analysis techniques (Gadamer, 1977, 1985; Husserl, 1985; Lacity and Janson, 1994; Ramm, 1970; Tesch, 1991; Winograd and Flores, 1986) also served as a guide to coding and synthesis (e.g., how to deal with a large amount of non-numerical, unstructured, and rich data; how to ensure that when synthesized, those issues accurately reflect the respondents' concerns) that confront Delphi method researchers. Ultimately, an open coding approach was adopted to structure the issues identified in Round-One. The major strength of the open coding approach is that it is data driven – the categories so formed reflect the range of issues that were collected, rather than some pre-defined scheme. Because the categories are determined from the data themselves, respondents should comprehend them more readily in subsequent survey rounds.

To support the interpretation of study findings, an understanding of the contextual background of the Queensland budget sector and the study organizations in relation to their SAP Financials project was essential (i.e., organizational nature/background, major services/roles/responsibilities of the agency, history/initiatives of the financial management system, overview of agencies' SAP project). Thus, a series of interviews and domain experts' workshops that involved senior staff members from the respondent groups were conducted before, during, and after the Delphi survey rounds.

Study Population

During 1998 and early 1999, the study case (a group of five government agencies) proactively moved as a team and implemented the SAP Financials.

Individuals from the implementation partner (IP), a "big 5" Consulting Firm, and these five closely related government client agencies (agency A to E) were pre-identified and contacted for study participation. To qualify for study participation, they were required to possess substantial involvement with SAP Financials: at any level, in any role, in any phase of the life cycle, with any of the modules implemented. Employing formal "Survey Participants' Selection Guidelines," and through interviews of senior sponsors in each agency, 117 individuals were identified and included in the contact database. Note that the term "client" herein refers to employees of the agencies, who are "clients" of both the ERP vendor and the implementation partner. Owing to the full support of the Queensland Government in this study and to the assistance of key contacts in each organization, the 117 contacts selected approximate the 'population' of knowledgeable individuals (rather than a "sample").

Study Findings

Round 1–Inventory Round

In October 1999, a total of 117 "inventory" round questionnaires were distributed to individuals who had been substantially involved in the five government agencies' SAP Financials Project. Before the e-mailout, the survey questionnaire (Word attachment) and covering email were pre-tested for clarity and ease of understanding by several senior personnel in the government agencies. Minor cosmetic changes resulted. In all, 78 questionnaires were returned, yielding a 67% response rate. A total of 61 valid questionnaires were eventually obtained from the first-round survey (Table 1), providing a net response rate of 52%. More than two-fifths (44%) of the respondents were from Agency A, the lead agency on the implementation and a corporate services provider to the other agencies. Other agencies had comparatively fewer participants.

Respondents from the five agencies were further differentiated by organizational level of involvement, where (1) strategic = steering committee members, project sponsors, project managers, and (2) operational = business process team members, power users, help-desk team members, change-management team members. Approximately four-fifths (78%) of the respondents were involved at the operational level, the rest (22%) representing the strategic level.

Respondents were asked to identify any issues regarding implementing, managing, and supporting the SAP Financials throughout their life cycle in their 'home' agency. The 61 respondents identified 274 issues, or an average of 4.5 issues per respondent. Approximately 41% or 115 of the issues identified originated within Agency A. This is not surprising given the lead role played by this agency and given that 44% or 27 of the total respondents are from this agency. Approximately one-tenth of the issues identified were from the implementation partner. From within the agencies, approximately 28% of the issues identified were from the strategic level and 72% from various operational levels. In general, the number of issues identified by the various respondent groups was in proportion to the number of respondents in these groups. Table 2 shows responses by stakeholder groups.

Having identified 274 issues from 61 survey respondents, the study then sought to distill these issues into a summary set of major-issue categories and related sub-issues. This resulted in a "tentative set" of 12 major-issue categories, with 40 sub-issues pending further validity and reliability testing in Round-Two.

As a validity test, and in order to establish a summary set of major-issues representing the respondents' main concerns, a domain experts' workshop

Table 1: Inventory round survey responses.

Organization	#	%	Role	#	%	Level	#	%
IP	7	11	IP	7	11	Strategic	12	22
Agency A	27	44	Agency	54	89	Operational	42	78
B	12	20						
C	7	11						
D	2	3						
E	6	10						
Total	61	100	Total	61	100	Total	54	100

Table 2: Cross-tabulation of responses by stakeholder groups.

Organization	Issue #	Issue %	Response #	Response %	I/R	Role	Issue #	Issue %	Response #	Response %	I/R	Level	Response #	Response %	Issue #	Issue %	I/R
IP	26	10	7	11	3.7	IP	26	10	7	11	3.7	Strategic	75	28	12	22	6.3
Agency A	115	41	27	44	4.3	Agency	248	90	54	89	4.6	Operational	173	72	42	78	4.1
B	48	18	12	20	4.0												
C	34	12	7	11	4.9												
D	14	5	2	3	7.0												
E	37	14	6	10	6.2												
Total	274	100	61	100	4.5	Total	274	100	61	100	4.5	Total	248	100	54	100	4.6

was conducted soon after the "tentative set" of major-issues was derived during July 2000. Four out of five representatives from the government agencies and five research team members agreed to participate in this "synthesis" workshop. The workshop was organised to allow time for information sharing and discussion with the participants. The workshop yielded valuable insights and a greater level of understanding of SAP Financials issues in the agencies and resulted in a "preliminary set" of major-issues that were more relevant and meaningful to the study stakeholder groups, pending confirmation from all survey respondents.

Round 2–Confirmation Round

Having rationally synthesized and logically restructured the "preliminary set" of issue categories and related sub-issues through the coding and synthesis exercises and domain experts' workshop, in the second "confirmation" or interim survey round, the study sought respondents' comments on and confirmation of the "preliminary set" of major-issues. For each respondent from Round-One, a custom report was prepared. The report included the hierarchy of major- and related sub-issues in the "preliminary set." The report also clearly indicated the link between each of the respondent's original round-one issues and the related sub-issues with which they had been associated. A total of 61 Round-Two reports were distributed to individuals who had responded in the Round-One survey. Although participants were instructed that there was no need to formally respond if they agreed in principle with the "preliminary set" of major-issues, about one quarter of questionnaires were returned showing their further comments and agreement.

The comments on and confirmation of the issue categories from the domain experts' workshop and the Round-Two survey respondents, resulted in a minimally revised "master set" of 10 major-issue categories from M-1 to M-10 with 38 sub-issues from S-1 to S-38 (Appendix A). Figure 1 shows the incidence of the initial 274 issues from the 61 respondents across the 10 major-issue categories.

Using the incidence of overall citation as an early crude indicator of severity, it is noted that 63% (172) of all 274 initial issues cited pertain to: *OPERATIONAL-DEFICIENCIES* (67 issues); *KNOWLEDGE-MANAGEMENT* (55 issues); and *SYSTEM-DEVELOPMENT* (50 issues). We recognise that the number of sub-issues in other major-issue categories were relatively fewer,

Figure 1. Distribution of issues across the 10 major issue categories.

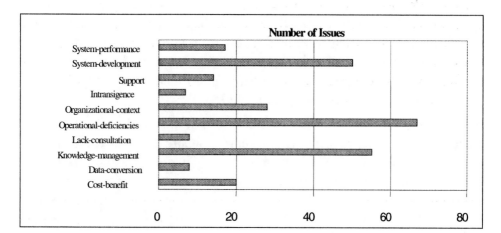

accounting to some extent for the lesser citations, and that not all issues listed are issues for all respondents (a further fallibility of citations as an indicator of issue severity). Nonetheless, the aim of the study was to be as inclusive as possible in this master set of issues, with further relative evaluation in the next "weights" round of the survey.

Round 3–Weights Round

During September-October of 2000, a total of 100 Round-Three question-naires were sent to Round-One contacts, excluding those who had indicated they would be unable to participate but including those who had not responded in the previous rounds. Respondents were asked to rate the importance of each of the 38 sub-issues on a scale from 1 to 10 where 1 means "not important" and 10 means "very important." Prior to its e-mailing, the survey was pre-tested for clarity and ease of understanding by several senior personnel in the government agencies. Slight changes were made.

Approximately one week after the due date, in an effort to boost the response rate, follow-up e-mail messages and phone calls were made to those who had not yet responded. When necessary, another copy of the questionnaire was e-mailed to those respondents who had "misplaced" the survey. The follow-up phone calls resulted in 15 additional returns. A total of 58 questionnaires were returned, yielding a 58% response rate. A total of 42 valid questionnaires were eventually obtained from the final round survey, providing a net response rate of 42%. Known reasons for non-response were: some respondents had discontinued their SAP responsibilities; others had left their organization; some were on holiday or maternity leave; several respondents did not wish to participate because of the time required to complete the questionnaires. The distribution of the survey respondents in this final-round survey by agency, role, and organizational level is shown in Table 3.

Table 4 shows the overall mean scores and rankings of the 10 major-issue categories from the "weights" round survey (where the mean for the major-issue is simply the average of the mean scores for its constituent sub-issues). A total of 1,134 valid scores for the 38 sub-issues were received from the 42 respondents (71% = 1,134 / (42*38)). The number of respondents varies between 29 and 34 across the sub-issues from which major-issue scores are derived.

Though *OPERATIONAL-DEFICIENCIES* ranked highest based on number of citations in the survey Round-One (see Figure 1), they have moved to fifth place based on Round-Three weights. This may suggest that though *OPERA-*

Table 3: Third-round survey responses.

Organization		#	%	Role	#	%	Level	#	%
	IP	6	14	IP	6	14	Strategic	11	26
Agency A		15	36	Agency	36	86	Operational	25	74
	B	7	17						
	C	3	7						
	D	3	7						
	E	8	19						
Total		42	100	Total	42	100	Total	36	100

Table 4: Overall ranking of major issue.

M-#	Mean	Std Dev	Rank	Major Issue Categories
3	6.19	2.53	1	Knowledge-management
9	6.00	2.34	2	System-development
8	5.79	2.68	3	Support
2	5.69	2.97	4	Data-conversion
5	5.62	2.73	5	Operational-deficiencies
4	5.58	2.53	6	Lack-consultation
1	5.25	2.86	7	Cost-benefit
6	5.06	2.70	8	Organizational-context
7	4.79	2.84	9	Intransigence
10	4.28	2.82	10	System-performance
Overall	5.57	2.67		

TIONAL-DEFICIENCIES were prominent in many respondents' conscious-ness during Round-One, subsequently when listed alongside other sub-issues in Round-Three, they were felt by respondents to be somewhat lower in importance than the earlier relative incidence of citations implied. Note that frequency of citation was known from the outset to be a much cruder indicator of issue importance than weights. Many may feel that something is an issue, while at the same time universally believing it to be a relatively lesser issue. Regardless, with a mean score of 5.62, *OPERATIONAL-DEFICIENCIES* are yet marginally above the scale mid-point (5.5), suggesting that these at a minimum, are perceived to be moderately important issues. Even *SYSTEM-PERFORMANCE* issues with a mean score of 4.28, more than a full point below the scale mid-point, and ranked last (10th) based on weights, should not be overly discounted. These too are issues cited by multiple respondents in Round-One, and here in Round-Three scored as moderately important. *KNOWLEDGE-MANAGEMENT* major-issues have moved from second place based on citations to first place based on weights. *SYSTEM-DEVELOP-MENT, SUPPORT*, and *DATA-CONVERSION* are ranked second through fourth respectively based on weights.

The detailed mean scores and ranks of the 38 related sub-issues (Appendix A) and comparisons between the strategic and operational personnel within agencies are discussed in the following section.

Analysis

In an attempt to understand areas of consensus and disagreement between the stakeholder groups, in addition to reviewing ranks of the sub-issues based on overall-agency mean scores, this section presents a comparison between strategic vs. operational personnel across the agencies. The number of IP (consultant) respondents was too few to yield meaningful comparison between the IP and the agencies, and the agencies were not surprisingly interested in agency perspectives. (Note that IP versus agency perspectives are being compared in a follow-up study of all agencies of Queensland Government nearing completion as of this writing. This larger study will also facilitate cross-agency comparisons.) The results of the "weights" round survey for these demographic groupings are presented in Appendix A. The sub-issues are numbered S-1 to S-38 in rank-order based on overall agencies' mean scores.

A rank of 1 is ascribed to the sub-issue with the highest computed mean score, and a rank of 38 is ascribed to the sub-issue with the lowest mean score.

A total of 36 valid agency responses were eventually obtained from the "weights" round – 30% (11) strategic respondents and 70% (25) operational respondents. Figure 2 is a line-chart of strategic and operational mean scores on the 38 sub-issues. Analysis of variance (independent sample t-test) identified only one significant difference: S27 – *organization appears unable or unwilling to be responsive to requests for changes in the system to resolve operational problems.* Operational personnel rated this sub issue higher (mean=5.60 yielding a rank of 24) than strategic personnel (mean=3.17, rank=37). Regardless, for neither group was this sub-issue ranked in the top 10 of the sub-issues. Furthermore, although strategic personnel may be expected to be more concerned about management-related issues while operational personnel focus on operations-related issues, it is observed that there is broad consensus between these two groups, with only the one significant difference identified.

It is noted that six sub-issues are ranked in the top-10 (S30, S13, S12, S21, S7, S9) based on both strategic and operational respondent weights (again suggesting broad concurrence of views – see Appendix A). These areas of agreement between strategic and operational respondents are discussed next, followed by brief discussion on issues of relatively greater concern to strategic

Figure 2. Strategic and operational personnel mean scores on 38 sub issues.

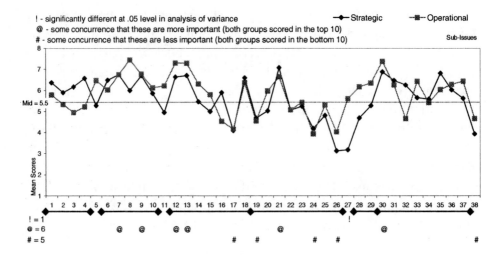

respondents, those of relatively greater importance to operational respondents, and those of relatively lesser importance to both respondent groups.

Issues of Relatively Greater Importance to Both Respondent Groups

The *SYSTEM-DEVELOPMENT* – related issue, *complexity of SAP means few, if any, people understand SAP beyond a single module, making overall design decisions very difficult* (S30) was the number one issue overall. Survey respondents suggested that complexity and the integrated nature of SAP make it difficult to configure without being aware of potential consequences for other modules. Furthermore, they indicated that in-depth understanding of SAP is difficult to obtain within a short period of time and that the lack of sufficient understanding has an enormous impact on ability to use the system efficiently and effectively. Recent research too suggests that lack of ERP product knowledge has been a major concern in the late 1990s (Davenport, 1998; Markus et al., 2000) for many organizations. Most organizations use consultants to facilitate the implementation process. Consultants may have experience in specific industries, comprehensive knowledge about certain modules, and may be better able to determine which suite will work best for a given organization (Davenport, 2000; Piturro, 1999; Thong et al., 1994). Evidence from workshop participants, however, suggested that although several knowledgeable experts in particular modules of SAP were involved, no one seemed to have a broad knowledge and expertise across SAP. This resulted in significant concerns for decision makers who had to decide on a complete business design rather than a module by module design. Other issues identified also reflect consequences of insufficient knowledge of SAP.

Two *OPERATIONAL-DEFICIENCIES* – related issues, *developing reports is difficult in SAP (S12)* and *not all required reports were available at implementation time (S13)* were ranked second and third based on overall agency scores (ranked seventh and fifth for strategic respondents and ranked third and fourth for operational respondents). SAP was vastly different, in both presentation and functionality, to the previous QGFMS of which the agencies had deep experience, extending over the period 1983 to 1998. During this 15-year period, the agencies undertook significant customisation, particularly in reporting and in enhancing their business processes. With the advent of SAP, the agencies were faced with abandoning a system they had been using for 15 years and forfeiting the knowledge, development, and sophistication of reporting that had developed over that period. They were unprepared for SAP standard reports. Furthermore, survey respondents indicated that it was easier to develop reports on the old system (e.g., because the table names and field names were in English rather than German, as was the case with the then SAP standard report system). Differences in system operation were also perceived to impact on the accuracy and efficiency of operations and ease of use of the system. Some agencies found that the standard ERP reports do not offer the presentation and flexibility to which users are accustomed. This has resulted in some clients buying separate tools or developing their own in-house reporting system. It must be noted that views expressed at the workshops on reporting were sometimes diametrically opposed, with those who were more intimate with SAP reporting touting its advantages. This again suggests problems with knowledge of the product, rather than with the product itself.

The *ORGANIZATIONAL-CONTEXT* – related issue, *implementation across multiple agencies led to sub-optimisation of the system configuration (S21)*, was ranked most important by strategic respondents (5th overall and 7th by operational respondents). When government is considering the adoption of an ERP package, management may have opportunity to choose between a single system across all of government, versus allowing each department to choose its own system and to bear responsibility for changing their processes to fit the system or the system to fit their processes. A main guiding management principle on the SAP Financials implementation in Queensland Government was to maximize commonality across the agencies. Workshop participants believed that, to have allowed greater latitude to the individual agencies would have significantly added to the cost and duration of implementation, and that unique agency systems would constrain their ability to benefit from vendor software maintenance and upgrades. Researchers also suggest that "configuration" should only be requested when essential, or when the competitive advantage derived from using non-standard processing can be clearly demonstrated (Appleton, 1997; Holland and Light, 1999; Janson and Subramanian, 1996; Parr and Shanks, 2000; Escalle and Cotteleer, 1999). Nonetheless, differences in business orientation, organization size, and related requirements may argue for unique processes. It is clear from the rank ascribed to this sub-issue that many felt important compromises had been made to achieve the level of standardisation sought.

Two *KNOWLEDGE-MANAGEMENT* – related issues, *insufficient resources and effort put into developing in-house knowledge (S7)* and *shared knowledge among project team members was a problem – agency staff did not understand SAP and implementation personnel did not cover the diversity of circumstances encountered in normal daily operations (S9)*, rank fourth and fifth for the strategic respondents and sixth and fifth based on the operational respondent scores. Survey respondents felt that insufficient long-term planning had been undertaken for maintaining a knowledgeable and skilled in-house SAP team. The acquisition and maintenance of skilled personnel proved both difficult and expensive. Workshop participants further suggested that when SAP is implemented, it is important to retain the knowledge and skills gained by staff involved on the project and to ensure that sufficient ongoing training is provided within the agencies so that this is then converted to organizational knowledge. Grover et al. (1995) found that failure to commit required financial, human, and other resources is commonplace in reengineering projects and highly likely to be a problem with other related projects, like ERP implementation. According to the SAP Financials Project Business Case, skill transfer from contractors/consultants to permanent staff was a prime objective of the project. However, the ability to share knowledge among project team members was found to be a problem.

Several implementation concerns arose during the project when agency staff had insufficient knowledge of the workings of SAP, and the implementation partner had too little knowledge of the agency requirements. Workshop participants believed that continuing development of internal skills in SAP, and ensuring that appropriate primary and secondary functional support is in place for each SAP module, is key to addressing the *KNOWLEDGE-MANAGE-MENT* – related issues raised by the workshop participants. Thus, it is suggested that dedicated resources for sharing experiences and knowledge gained are critical to realize the benefits associated with ERP (Davenport, 2000; Gable et al., 1998; Robinson and Dilts, 1999).

Though not amongst the overall top-10 sub-issues, broad consensus is noted on the *OPERATIONAL-DEFICIENCIES* – related issue S18 – *security is difficult to maintain in SAP resulting in some users being granted too much access and others not having access to data they need* (ranked eighth and 11th by strategic and operational respondents). SAP security is considered complex and resource-intensive to maintain. Survey respondents suggested that there is a requirement for better definition of security management. Furthermore they indicated that with so many different security profiles in the new system, it is difficult for smaller agencies to comply with segregation requirements when implementing ERP. It is very important for the project team to consider how to handle security. The system must have proper access controls and partitioning so that unauthorised users cannot access information. In addition to general system security, other activities (e.g., data warehousing and e-commerce add-ons, and outsourcing of the ERP maintenance) require extra security controls (Riet et al., 1998).

Issues of Relatively Greater Importance to Strategic Personnel

The *SYSTEM-DEVELOPMENT* – related issue S35, *requested system functionality was sacrificed in order to meet implementation deadlines*, was ranked third most important by strategic respondents, but only 19th by operational respondents. While sacrifices were undoubtedly made to keep the project on track, workshop participants indicated that the weekly cost of continuing the implementation project was very high, and that this was not widely understood across the agencies. The feeling was that tradeoffs are unavoidable, and that those made were well informed and well considered.

A further *KNOWLEDGE-MANAGEMENT* – related issue S6, *difficult to retain people with SAP skills due to market pressure to leave*, is ranked among the top-10 (10th) by strategic respondents (ranked 20th by operational respondents). A stable team of SAP skilled personnel is necessary for the smooth implementation and running of the SAP system. Nonetheless, personnel with SAP experience were much sought after in the marketplace, particularly in the late 1990s, thereby further complicating the task of building a strong base of SAP knowledge within the agencies. The study found little evidence of special incentives for SAP skilled personnel in agencies, at a time when employee turnover was relatively high. These difficulties with finding and retaining skilled ERP people, staffing the project team, and maintaining staffing post-implementation have been recognised in prior studies (Bryan, 1998; Markus et al., 2000; Niehus et al., 1998; Somers and Nelson, 2001).

The *COST-BENEFIT* – related issue, *SAP implementation benefits do not justify costs (S4)*, is ranked ninth by strategic respondents, yet 29th by operational respondents. Survey respondents claimed with hindsight that the value for money obtained from any SAP implementation has to be carefully evaluated. They suggested that the implementation costs increase as the degree of customisation increases, and the cost of hiring consultants can consume a substantial proportion of the implementation budget. A recent survey of

Fortune 1000 companies regarding ERP customisation policies indicates that 41% of companies re-engineer their business to fit the application, 37% choose applications that fit their business and customise only marginally, and only 5% customise the application to fit their business (Davis, 1998). As suggested earlier, because customisation is usually associated with increased information systems costs, longer implementation time, and the inability to benefit from vendor software maintenance and upgrades (Janson and Subramanian, 1996), it should only be requested when essential.

Many researchers suggest that a key benefit of ERP is the seamless integration of information flowing through the organization (Bryan, 1998; Shang and Seddon, 2000; Somers and Nelson, 2001; Sumner, 2000). To successfully achieve this benefit, the business processes and functions must be integrated (Davenport, 2000). Although it is likely that many benefits will not be realized for some time post-implementation, workshop participants indicated that the agencies have been able to accomplish tasks with SAP that would not have been possible with the previous system. With the aim of increasing benefits from the SAP investment, a continuous improvement process and benefits realisation program was established across the government agencies after "go live" of the system.

Though not among the top-10, it is noteworthy that the four "costs"-related sub-issues (S1, S2, S3, S4) are all ranked relatively higher by strategic respondents (12th, 18th, 14th, ninth) than by operational respondents (23rd, 27th, 31st, 29th). Clearly, and understandably, strategic respondents are more attuned to costs of the new system than are operational respondents. Having said this, the overall rankings of these four sub-issues (19th, 25th, 28th, 22nd) puts them all in the bottom half of the sub issues (moderately important).

Issues of Relatively Greater Importance to Operational Personnel

Operational personnel viewed the *KNOWLEDGE-MANAGEMENT* – related issue, *training provided was inadequate and did not cover the diversity of circumstances encountered in normal daily operations (S8)*, as most important overall (ranked 16th by strategic respondents). This concern would be close to the consciousness of staff who are responsible for the day-to-day running of the system or handling month- and year-end processes. Survey respondents suggested that significant problems were encountered with interfaces, business-area balancing, legal consolidations, and controlled and administered reporting, which were not well-documented, nor was adequate training provided. Several studies have suggested that when implementing an ERP package, training is an important component and should be a high priority (Bryan, 1998; Crowley, 1999; Ross, 1999; Wilder and Davis, 1998). Organizations in the current study are realising the need for improved training, not only in the software, but also in the new job function. Workshop participants suggested that the government agencies have already taken action, soon after "go live" (e.g., making a large investment in staff training and ongoing support of the SAP system), to minimise reliance on external contractors and to build in-house expertise. A performance planning and development program within the agencies (which looks at staff training over time) was implemented to manage this issue with in-house skills development, and to ensure all staff receive appropriated SAP training prior to the pending upgrade project.

The *DATA-CONVERSION* – related issue S5, *errors were found in data converted from former QGFMS*, is ranked 8th most important by operational respondents (ranked 24th by strategic respondents). A fundamental requirement for the effectiveness of the ERP system is the availability and timeliness of accurate data. Somers and Nelson (2001) suggest that management of data entering the ERP system represents a critical issue throughout the implementation process. Data conversion problems can cause serious implementation delays and cost overruns (Neihus et al., 1998; Holland and Light, 1999). Survey respondents stated that the new fields did not always encompass the old-field data during data conversion testing. They further indicated that a substantial number of transactions were posted to a "blank business area" before anyone realized the extent of the problem. Data adopted from prior systems must be mapped into the correct fields and subsequently maintained. *DATA-CONVERSION* can be an overwhelming process, especially if organizations do not understand what should be included in the new systems and what needs to be omitted. Workshop participants indicated that this issue has been addressed but needs to be considered more carefully in any future conversion exercise.

Two *SYSTEM-DEVELOPMENT* – related issues, *too little effort put into redesigning the underlying business processes, resulting in a system that represented a "technology swap" that failed to capture many of the benefits of SAP (S37)* and *inadequate system testing left many errors in the implemented system (S33)* are ranked ninth and 10th most important by operational respondents (24th and 21st respectively by strategic respondents). Implementing an ERP system involves re-engineering existing business processes to meet the best business process standard (Davenport, 2000; Markus et al., 2000). One major benefit of ERP comes from re-engineering the organization's way of conducting business. However, workshop participants indicated that the costs and benefits of aligning with an ERP model can be very high because it is difficult to gain agreement to the new process from all who are affected. Furthermore, they suggested that some existing business processes are so specific to the agency(ies) that they need to be preserved or appropriate steps taken to customise them.

Clear goals and objectives are critical in any ERP implementation. Owing to the Y2K deadline, the then looming GST and the uncertain costs/benefits of business re-engineering, management chose to pursue a "technology swap" for the five agencies. Workshop participants too felt that it was easier and appropriate to first complete the project, secure the system, and resolve problems, and then seek to realize the benefits. Nonetheless, a surprising number of transactions failed on implementation due to insufficient testing and lack of time. A general finding is that too much was relegated to "being fixed later" in an effort to meet "go live" deadlines. Workshop participants suggested that the areas experiencing the most problems tended to relate to functionality that was added to SAP to meet a specific business requirement. It is clearly necessary to ensure comprehensive testing during user acceptance testing and to ensure sign-off of test results.

Issues of Relatively Lesser Importance to Both Respondent Groups

Strategic and operational personnel concur on the relatively lesser importance of the five sub-issues *ORGANIZATIONAL-CONTEXT*: *S19 – differences in work ethic among project personnel*, *S24 – political issues had negative impact on the project*, and *S26 – timing of implementation was inappropriate because of change underway in the public sector*; *OPERATIONAL-DEFICIENCIES*: *S17 – SAP lacks some functionality of QGFMS*; *SYSTEM-PERFORMANCE*: *S38 – system performance is inadequate to meet operational requirements*. The fact that only one of the eight sub-issues associated with the *ORGANIZATIONAL-CONTEXT* major-issue was rated in the top-half of the rankings (S7), and five of these eight are rated in the bottom-10 by both operational and strategic respondents, is strong evidence that agencies did not perceive *organizational context* as a primary concern overall.

Conclusion

This research began with the proposition that for those who implement, manage, and support ERP systems, there is benefit in knowing the major ERP life cycle issues and the relative importance of these issues as they affect various stakeholder groups. It was noted that numerous studies of IS issues have been conducted for the benefit of private sector organizations, but that there has been little study of public sector organizations. Accordingly, a modified Delphi-type survey, together with a series of interviews and domain experts' workshops, were conducted to establish a set of major-issues and related sub-issues that were confirmed as relevant to the study stakeholder groups. Ultimately, while findings are expected to be particularly valuable to organizations implementing ERP, an improved understanding of ERP life cycle implementation, management and support issues is expected also to benefit other types of systems and the complete range of consulting firms' and software vendors' services, as well as broader IS research.

Acknowledgments

This study was conducted by the Information Systems Management Research Center (ISMRC), Queensland University of Technology (QUT), in collaboration with SAP Australia and with the full support of the Queensland Government. The study is funded by an Australian Research Council "Strategic Partnership with Industry for Research and Development" (SPIRT) collaborative grant between ISMRC and SAP Australia titled "Cooperative ERP Lifecycle Knowledge Management."

References

AMR Research. (1998). *AMR Research Predicts Industrial Enterprise Applications Market Will Reach $72.6 Billion By 2002. AMR Research.* www.amrresearch.com/press/981102.htm, 1997.

Appleton, E. L. (1997). How to survive ERP. *Datamation, 43*(3) 50-53.

Bancroft, N. H. (1998). *Implementing SAP R/3: How to Introduce a Large System into a Large Organization* (second edition). London: Manning/Prentice Hall.

Bingi, P., Sharma, M. & Godla, J. (1999). Critical factors affecting an ERP implementation. *Information Systems Management.* Summer, *16*(3), 7-15.

Boston Consulting Group. (2000). *Getting Value from Enterprise Initiatives: A Survey of Executives.* www.bcg.com/news/enterprise_report, 31/03/2000.

Bryan, M. (1998). ERP Mayday: Why ERP could sink your business? *MIS Australia*, November, 48-54.

Chang, S.-I. & Gable, G. G. (2000). A critique of the Delphi method in the context of IS key issues studies. *Proceedings of the Pacific Asia Conference on Information Systems 2000*, Hong Kong, 1-3 June, 1168-1181.

Chang, S.-I., Gable, G. G., Smythe, E. & Timbrell, G. (2000). Methods for distilling IS key issues using a Delphi approach. *Proceedings of the 11ᵗʰ Australasian Conference on Information Systems*, Brisbane, 6-8 December, 1-11.

Crowley, A. (1999). Training treadmill–A rigorous plan of end-user education is critical to whipping ERP systems into shape. *PC Week Online,* January.

Dailey, A. (1998). SAP R/3: Managing the life cycle. *GartnerGroup Symposium/Itxpo 98*, 28-30 October, Brisbane Australia.

Davenport, T. E. (1996). Holistic management of megapackage change: The case of SAP. *Proceedings of the AIS Americas Conference on Information Systems, 51a-51c,* August 16-18.

Davenport, T. H. (1998). Putting the enterprise into the enterprise system. *Harvard Business Review*, 121-131, July-August.

Davenport, T. H. (2000). *Mission Critical: Realizing the Promise of Enterprise Systems*. Boston, MA: Harvard Business School Press.

Davis, J. (1998). Scooping up vanilla ERP. *Infoworld, 20*(47), 23 November, 57.

Escalle, C. X. & Cotteleer, M. J. (1999). Enterprise resource planning, Technology Note. *Harvard Business School*. HBS case #9-699-020, February 11.

Financial Management Strategy. (1994). *Financial Management Strategy in Queensland Government, 1994*. Queensland Treasury, Public Document.

Financial Management Strategy. (1998). *Financial Management Strategy in Queensland Government, 1998*. Queensland Treasury, Public Document.

Gable, G. G. (1998). Large package software: A neglected technology. *Journal of Global Information Management, 6*(3), 3-4.

Gable, G. G., Scott, J. & Davenport, T. (1998). Cooperative EWS life-cycle knowledge management. *Proceedings of the Ninth Australasian Conference on Information Systems*, 227-240, 29 September–2 October, Sydney, Australia.

Gable, G.G., van Den Heever, R., Erlank, S. & Scott, J. (1997a). Large packaged software: The need for research. *Proceedings of the 3rd Pacific Asia Conference on Information Systems*, 381-388. Brisbane, Australia, 1-5 April.

Gable, G.G., van Den Heever, R., Erlank, S. & Scott, J. (1997b). Using large packaged software in teaching: The case of SAP R/3. *Proceedings of the AIS Americas Conference*, 15-17. Indianapolis, USA, 15-17 August.

Gadamer, H. G. (1977). The scope of hermeneutic reflection. In Linge, D. E. (Ed.), *Philosophical Hermeneutics*, 3-104. Berkeley, CA: University of California Press.

Gadamer, H. G. (1985). The historicity of understanding. In Mueller-Vollmer, K. (Ed.), *The Hermeneutics Reader: Texts of the German Tradition from the Enlightenment to the Present*, 256-292. New York: Continuum.

Grover, V., Jeong, S. R., Kettinger, W. J. & Teng, J. T. (1995). The implementation of business process reengineering. *Journal of Management Information Systems, 12*(1), 109-144.

Hiquet, B. D., Kelly, A. F. & Kelly-Levey and Associates. (1998). *SAP R/3 Implementation Guide: A Manager's Guide to Understanding SAP.* USA: Macmillan Technical Publishing.

Holland, C. & Light, B. (1999). Critical success factors model for ERP implementation. *IEEE Software*, May/June, 1630-1636.

Husserl, E. (1985). The phenomenological theory of meaning and of meaning-apprehension. In Mueller-Vollmer, K. (Ed.), *The Hermeneutics Reader: Texts of the German Tradition from the Enlightenment to the Present*, 165-186. New York: Continuum.

IDC Software Research. (2000). Enterprise Resource Management Application Market Forecast and Analysis, 2000-2004. *IDC Software Research,* 22326 (June).

Janson, M. A. & Subramanian, A. (1996). Packaged software: Selection and implementation policies. *INFOR, 34*(2), 133-151.

Klaus, H., Rosemann, M. & Gable, G. G. (2000). What is ERP? *Information Systems Frontiers, 2*(2), 141-162.

Lacity, M. C. & Janson, M. A. (1994). Understanding qualitative data: A framework of test analysis methods. *Journal of Management Information Systems, 11*(2), 137-160.

Markus, M. L., Axline, S., Petrie, D. & Tanis, C. (2000). Learning from adopters' experiences with ERP: Problems encountered and success achieved. *Journal of Information Technology, 15*(4), 245-265.

Martin, M. H. (1998). An ERP strategy. *Fortune, 137*(2), 149-151.

Nelson, R. R. & Cheney, P. H. (1987). Training end users: An exploratory study. *MIS Quarterly, 11*(4), 547-559.

Niehus, J., Knobel, B., Townley-O'Neill, R., Gable, G. G. & Stewart, G. (1998). Implementing SAP R/3 at Queensland departments of transport and main roads: A case study. In Baets, W. R. J. (Ed.), *Proceedings of the 6th European Conference on Information Systems*, 1486-1500, June. Aix-en-Provence, Granada: Euro-Arab Management School.

Parr, A. & Shanks, G. (2000). A model of ERP project implementation. *Journal of Information Technology, 15*(4), 289-304.

Piturro, M. (1999). How midsize companies are buying ERP. *Journal of Accountancy, 188*(3), 41-48.

Price Waterhouse. (1995). Information Technology Survey. London: Price Waterhouse.

Ramm, B. (1970). *Protestant Biblical Interpretation*. Ann Arbor, MI: Cushing-Malloy.

Riet, R., Janssen, W. & Gruitjer, P. (1998). Security moving from database systems to ERP systems. *Proceeding of 9ᵗʰ International Workshop on Database and Expert Systems Applications DEXA*. Vienna, Austria.

Robinson, A. G. & Dilts, D. M. (1999). OR & ERP: A match for the new millennium? *OR/MS Today, 26*(3), 30-35.

Rosemann, M. & Wiese, J.(1999). Measuring the performance of ERP software–A balanced a core card approach. *Proceedings from the 10th Australasian Conference of Information Systems (ACIS)*. 1-3rd December, Welington, New Zealand.

Ross, J. W. (1999). Dow corning corporation: Business processes and information technology. *Journal of Information Technology, 14*(3), 253-266.

Shtub, A. (1999). *Enterprise Resource Planning (ERP): The Dynamics of Operations Mangement (2nd ed.)*. The Netherlands: Kluwer Academic Publishers Group.

Somers, M. T. & Nelson, K. (2001). The impact of critical success factors across the stages of enterprise resource planning implementations. *Proceedings of the 34th Hawaii International Conference on System Sciences*, 1-10.

Sumner, M. (2000). Risk factors in enterprise-wide/ERP projects. *Journal of Information Technology, 15*(4), 317-328.

Tesch, R. (1991). Software for qualitative researchers: Analysis needs and program capabilities. In Fielding, N. G. and Lee, R. M. (Eds.), *Using Computers in Qualitative Research*, 16-37. London: Sage.

Thong, J. Y. L., Yap, C. S. & Raman, K. S. (1994). Engagement of external expertise in information systems implementation. *Journal of Management Information Systems, 11*(2), 209-231.

Wilder, C. & Davis, B. (1998). False starts strong finishes. *Information Week*, 41-53, 30 November.

Winograd, T. & Flores, F. (1986). *Understanding Computers and Cognition*, 143-162. Reading, MA: Addison-Wesley.

Appendix A. Sub-issue mean scores and ranks by major issue, by stakeholder group

	Category		Agency (N=36)		Strategic (N=11)		Operational (N=25)		
	S-#	M-#	Mean	Rank	Mean	Rank	Mean	Rank	
Top 10	30	9	7.21	1	6.88	2@	7.38	2@	Complexity of SAP means few, if any, people understand SAP beyond a single module, making overall design decisions very difficult
Top 10	13	5	7.10	2	6.70	5@	7.29	4@	Not all required reports were available at implementation time
Top 10	12	5	7.09	3	6.63	7@	7.30	3@	Developing reports is difficult in SAP
Top 10	8	3	7.07	4	6.00	16	7.44	1	Training provided was inadequate and did not cover the diversity of circumstances encountered in normal daily operations
Top 10	21	6	6.80	5	7.07	1@	6.65	7@	Implementation across multiple agencies led to sub-optimisation of the system configuration
Top 10	7	3	6.75	6	6.75	4@	6.75	6@	Insufficient resources and effort put into developing in-house knowledge
Top 10	9	3	6.74	7	6.70	5@	6.77	5@	Shared knowledge among project team members was a problem - agency staff did not understand SAP and implementation personnel did not understand age
Top 10	18	5	6.44	8	6.59	8	6.36	11	Security is difficult to maintain in SAP resulting in some users being granted too much access and others not having access to data they need
Top 10	31	9	6.34	9	6.47	11	6.25	15	Frequency of SAP upgrades places a large burden on system maintenance
Top 10	35	9	6.33	10	6.82	3	6.04	19	Requested system functionality was sacrificed in order to meet implementation deadlines
	36	9	6.20	11	6.02	15	6.29	14	The project team was disbanded when the system was handed over despite many issues remaining unresolved
	37	9	6.19	12	5.63	21	6.43	9	Too little effort put into redesigning the underlying business processes, resulting in a system that represented a 'technology swap' that failed to capture many
	6	3	6.18	13	6.48	10	6.02	20	Difficult to retain people with SAP skills due to market pressure to leave
	33	9	6.17	14	5.65	20	6.42	10	Inadequate system testing left many errors in the implemented system
	5	2	6.15	15	5.29	24	6.47	8	Errors were found in data converted from former QGFMS
	14	5	6.05	16	5.46	23	6.31	13	Operational deficiencies that impact the accuracy and efficiency of operations and the ease of use of the system
	29	8	6.04	17	5.27	25	6.35	12	Support personnel are inadequately trained
	10	3	6.04	18	5.85	19	6.12	18	System documentation is inadequate, particularly with respect to system design and controls
	1	1	5.99	19	6.37	12	5.79	23	Complexity (and therefore cost) of SAP far exceeds the requirements of some agencies
	11	4	5.91	20	4.95	30	6.22	16	Lack of consultation with operational level users meant that operation requirements were not met
	28	8	5.76	21	4.69	32	6.17	17	Ongoing support for the SAP system is inadequate
	4	1	5.65	22	6.57	9	5.22	29	SAP implementation benefits do not justify costs
	20	6	5.65	23	5.03	28	5.97	21	Diversity of government systems makes integration difficult
	15	5	5.58	24	5.00	29	5.79	22	Persistent minor errors and operational issues have not been rectified
	2	1	5.51	25	5.90	18	5.33	27	Complexity of SAP drives costs beyond reasonable limits
	34	9	5.47	26	5.58	22	5.42	26	Issues that arose during, or result from, the development phase of the SAP system
	23	6	5.38	27	5.24	26	5.44	25	Lack of ownership/responsibility by agency personnel at the project level
	3	1	5.38	28	6.17	14	4.96	31	Costs of SAP exceed those of QGFMS without commensurate benefit
Bottom 10	32	9	5.27	29	6.25	13	4.66	32	Frequency with which requirements changed caused problems for developers
Bottom 10	25	6	5.16	30	4.81	31	5.30	28	Poor communication between agencies
Bottom 10	22	6	5.07	31	5.07	27	5.07	30	Lack of leadership at senior levels
Bottom 10	27	7	4.99	32	3.17!	37	5.60!	24	Organisation appears unable or unwilling to be responsive to requests for changes in the system to resolve operational problems
Bottom 10	16	5	4.97	33	5.90	17	4.53	35	SAP is not sufficiently integrated with other systems
Bottom 10	19	6	4.59	34	4.69	32#	4.55	34#	Differences in work ethic among project personnel
Bottom 10	38	10	4.49	35	3.93	36#	4.66	33#	System performance is inadequate to meet operational requirements
Bottom 10	17	5	4.14	36	4.08	35#	4.16	36#	SAP lacks some functionality of QGFMS
Bottom 10	24	6	4.00	37	4.19	34#	3.93	38#	Political issues had a negative impact on the project
Bottom 10	26	6	3.76	38	3.13	38#	4.03	37#	Timing of implemention was inappropriate because of change underway in the public sector

! - significant difference at .05 level in analysis of variance. @ - some concurrence that these are more important (scored in the top 10). # - some concurrence that these are less important (scored in th

Chapter XV

Organizational Knowledge Sharing in ERP Implementation:
Lessons from Industry

Mary C. Jones
University of North Texas, USA

R. Leon Price
University of Oklahoma, USA

Abstract

This study examines organizational knowledge sharing in enterprise resource planning (ERP) implementation. Knowledge sharing in ERP implementation is somewhat unique because ERP requires end users to have more divergent knowledge than is required in the use of traditional systems. Because of the length of time and commitment that ERP implementation requires, end users are also often more involved in ERP implementations than they are in more traditional ERP implementations. They must understand how their tasks fit into the overall process, and they must understand how their process fits with other organizational processes. Knowledge sharing among organizational members is one critical piece of ERP implementation, yet it is challenging to achieve. There is often a large gap in knowledge among ERP implementation personnel, and people do not easily share what they know. This study presents findings about organizational knowledge sharing during ERP implementation in three firms. Data were collected through interviews using a multi-site case study methodology. Findings are analyzed in an effort to provide a basis on which practitioners can more effectively facilitate knowledge sharing during ERP implementation.

Introduction

Enterprise resource planning (ERP) is a strategic tool that helps companies gain a competitive edge by streamlining business processes, integrating business units, and providing organizational members greater access to real-time information. Many firms are using ERP systems to cut costs, standardize operations, and leverage common processes across the organization. ERP allows firms to have a more convergent view of their information by integrating processes across functional and divisional lines using a centralized database and integrated sets of software modules (Scott and Kaindl, 2000; Zheng et al., 2000).

However, the convergence that ERP affords at the organizational level often results in a divergence of the knowledge required at the individual level (Baskerville et al., 2000). ERP imposes a new framework on the organization (Robey et al., 2002). It requires end users to have broader knowledge than is required in the use of traditional systems. They must understand how their tasks fit into the overall process and how their process fits with other organizational processes (Lee and Lee, 2000). Thus, knowledge sharing is one critical piece of ERP implementation. An organization begins to build the foundation during implementation on which end users can understand enough about the ERP framework to realize its benefits (Robey et al., 2002). Because of the time commitments and the extensive knowledge sharing that must take place during ERP implementation, end users are often more involved in the implementation than they are in more traditional implementations. In some cases, ERP implementations are managed and led by end users and end user managers, and IT staff serves primarily as technical advisors (Jones, 2001). Unfortunately, there is usually a significant gap in knowledge among these implementation personnel, and people do not easily share what they know (Constant et al., 1994; Jarvenpaa and Staples, 2000; Osterloh and Frey, 2000; Soh et al., 2000).

This study was undertaken to examine how firms ensure that organizational knowledge is shared during ERP implementations. One objective is to identify facilitators of organizational knowledge sharing. Another is to synthesize findings into lessons about knowledge sharing during implementation that other firms can apply in their own ERP implementations.

Theoretical Background

Knowledge sharing in ERP implementation is somewhat unique because ERP redefines jobs and blurs traditional intra-organizational boundaries (Lee and Lee, 2000). Knowledge must be shared across functional and divisional boundaries, and the knowledge required during ERP implementation entails a wider variety of experiences, perspectives, and abilities than traditional information systems implementations (Baskerville et al., 2000; Robey et al., 2002). Knowledge sharing is challenging because much knowledge is embedded into organizational processes (Davenport, 1998). The way people actually do their jobs is often different from the formal procedures specified for even the most routine tasks (Brown and Duguid, 2000). It is also challenging because there are gaps between what people do and what they think they do (Brown and Duguid, 2000). Some tasks are so routine, and people have done them for so long, that many of the steps involved are subconscious (Leonard and Sensiper, 1998). However, there is a variety of factors that can facilitate knowledge sharing during ERP implementation.

In order to present a coherent and logical view of knowledge sharing, we identify factors that influence knowledge sharing that are linked by a common conceptual underpinning, which allows individuals to share observations and experiences across traditional boundaries. Most ERP implementation activities center around the ERP implementation team (Baskerville et al., 2000). ERP implementation teams typically consist of organizational members from a variety of functional areas and organizational divisions. Each team member must understand what the others do in order to effectively map processes during the implementation (Baskerville et al., 2000). Team members must work to achieve this level of understanding. The knowledge sharing required does not come automatically with team membership; it must be facilitated. Thus, facilitation of knowledge sharing on the team is one factor examined.

The team must also interact with end users to gather relevant information about processes and to keep end users and user managers informed about changes to expect when the ERP is implemented (Robey, Ross, and Boudreau, 2002). Ideally, there is an intensive exchange of knowledge between the team and these users that they represent (Baskerville et al., 2000). Inadequate knowledge sharing between these two groups leads to unsuccessful implementation (Soh et al., 2000). One key to a smooth ERP implementation is effective change management (Andriola, 1999; Harari, 1996). Because of the complexity and cost of ERP, it must be visibly planned and implemented (Hammer, 1990). One way to communicate plans, share knowledge with end users, and gather knowledge from end users is through careful change management (Clement, 1994). Therefore, change management is another knowledge sharing factor examined.

A large part of change management is training. Those affected by the implementation should receive training to develop new and improved skills to deal with new challenges brought about by the change (Andriola, 1999). Users must gain knowledge about the business rules and processes embedded in the ERP software (Lee and Lee, 2000). They also must understand the integrative nature of ERP in order to use it effectively. ERP requires end users to understand that they are no longer working in silos, and whatever they do now impacts someone else (Welti, 1999). Entire departments must be retrained with this in mind (Caldwell and Stein, 1998; Al-Mashari and Zairi, 2000). Training on transactions and on the integrative nature of ERP is another factor examined.

Most firms hire external consultants (integration partners) that know the ERP software to help them through the implementation (Soh et al., 2000). This involves knowledge sharing because the organizational implementation team seeks ways for the know-how and skills possessed by integration partner staff (IPS) to be shared with them so that they are not lost when the IPS leaves (Al-Mashari and Zairi, 2000). This goes beyond written documentation and training manuals. For example, consultants are assigned to work side by side with organizational team members so that the members can learn what the consultants know about the package that can not easily be written down (Osterloh and Frey, 2000). One source of failure in ERP implementation is the IPS who works alone, and fails to share knowledge with organizational members (Welti, 1999). When the IPS fails to share what they know, the firm often has trouble supporting the ERP after they leave. Thus, it is important that the firm capture as much of the IPS's knowledge as possible before they transition off the team.

Transition of IPS knowledge is another knowledge sharing factor examined. In summary, several factors that may influence knowledge sharing are examined. These are facilitation of knowledge sharing on the implementation team, change management activities, type of training end users receive (i.e., transactional or integrative), and use of formal knowledge transfer from integration partner staff when they leave the organization.

Finally, the extent to which a firm is beginning to alter its core knowledge competency after SAP implementation is examined. The active sharing of organizational members' knowledge is linked to a firm's ability to alter its core knowledge competencies (Kogut and Zander, 1992; Grant, 1996; Hine and Goul, 1998). Altering knowledge competency involves sharing knowledge across the organization in a way that preserves existing knowledge competencies and at the same time absorbs new knowledge that expands and strengthens those competencies (Stein and Vandenbosch, 1996). An innovation that impacts the entire organization and facilitates major changes in a firm's processes, as ERP does, provides an opportunity for firms to do this (Brown and Vessey, 1999). Evidence of this alteration is found in fundamental changes in the way a firm performs its core processes. ERP benefits are the result of ongoing efforts to continuously improve processes (Ross, 1999). At the time of data collection, these firms were still too early in their use of ERP to have realized extensive change. They were, however, making efforts to integrate processes and thereby alter core knowledge competency. Thus, change in core knowledge competency in this study is assessed as the extent to which processes were being changed as a result of ERP, rather than the extent to which they had changed.

Methodology

Data were collected as part of a larger study using a multiple case study of firms in the petroleum industry that had implemented SAP R/3. Focusing on a single package helps minimize bias that might be introduced into findings across packages. However, because the focus is on knowledge sharing, rather than on technical aspects of the package itself, findings should be generalizable to implementation of other ERP software in other industries. The CIO or top IS executive of 10 firms in the industry were contacted to determine if they had implemented or were implementing SAP, and if so, whether they would agree to participate in the study. In some cases, a division of the firm was included rather than the whole firm. Because of size, structure, or geographic dispersion, some firms have conducted completely separate implementations in divisions around the world, with little or no communication between the implementation teams. In those cases, the division seemed to be a more appropriate case site than the entire organization. We collected data from those that did agree to participate, and that met two other criteria. We eliminated firms that had implemented only one or two modules with no plans to implement more. We also eliminated firms that had not implemented across the organization or the specific division in which we were interested. Each firm in the study implemented the major modules of SAP including FI/CO (financial accounting and controlling), AM (fixed assets management), PS (project systems), PM (plant maintenance), SD (sales and distribution), MM (materials management), and PP (production planning). These criteria helped to ensure that the case sites were comparable, and that differences in findings were not due to the scale of implementation.

In order to minimize bias that the researchers might introduce into the process of analyzing findings, a rigorous and structured approach to analysis was followed (Yin, 1989). For example, the interviewer took notes and taped each interview. Tapes and notes were transcribed by a third party, reviewed by the interviewer, and respondents were asked for clarification on points that seemed vague or missing. The transcriptions were then summarized, reviewed by another researcher to help ensure that the transcriptions flowed well and made sense. Finally, the primary contacts in each firm reviewed summaries to help ensure that what was recorded represented actual events and perceptions. A case study database consisting of interview notes, documentation provided by respondents, tables summarizing findings, and an exact narrative transcription of all interviews were used. The questions from the interview guide are provided in Appendix A. A within case analysis was performed where data were extracted using the interview questions as a guide to get a clearer picture of knowledge sharing in each firm. Then, a cross-case analysis was performed in which knowledge sharing across the firms was compared.

Because of the size of the project teams, interviewing a sample of key members was deemed more manageable than attempting to interview each member. In addition, many members had left the firm, or moved out of the areas in which they had originally worked. Thus, we asked each of the top IS executives to identify key members of their SAP project team that were still involved with SAP in some way, including support and post-implementation process redesign. This method of identifying respondents has been demonstrated to be acceptable because professionals in a field have been shown capable of nominating key respondents that have a consistent set of attributes appropriate for a study such as this (Nelson et al., 2000). A series of semi-structured interviews were conducted with 8 to 10 members of each firm. The number of interviewees was chosen based on the concept of theoretical saturation, where "incremental learning is minimal because the researchers are observing phenomena seen before" (Eisenhardt, 1989, p. 545). In these interviews, the researchers often heard the same examples from most of the respondents in a site regardless of functional background, when they came on the team, or their job at the time of the interview. In addition, the respondents often used the same phrases to express their perceptions. This was true of respondents who were not located at the same physical locations at a site or who were not all on the team at the same time. Thus, it was deemed that additional interviews would not yield significantly different insights. For example, all the respondents at USWhole used the phrase "psychological effort" when referring to how they approached the project. They indicated one guiding tenant of their project was that the implementation was as much a "psychological effort as a technical effort." In another example, the phrase "the accountants always cleaned up after everyone" came up in most interviews at each case site.

The interviews lasted between one and two hours each over a period of seven months between July 2000 and February 2001. Each person was interviewed once in person for one to two hours, and then was contacted by e-mail or by telephone for additional information or clarification. In addition to the face-to-face interviews, the researchers also preceded and followed up the interviews with e-mail and telephone calls for background information, clarification, and points not covered in the interviews.

Respondents included both information systems staff and business/functional staff. Some had been on the team from the beginning, while others joined at various points in the project. These people represented a variety of perspectives on SAP, including some who were pleased with it, some who hated it, and others who were indifferent. They also represented a variety of levels in the firm ranging from CIO and/or project manager to lower level employees, and included people from such functional areas as accounting, purchasing, refineries, sales and distribution, and a variety of engineering functions (Table 1).

Profile of Companies

USWhole is the U.S. division of one of the world's leading oil companies. It includes upstream (exploration & production), downstream (marketing, refining, and transportation), and chemical segments. The firm has exploration and production interests in many countries, with a large concentration in the U.S., and it markets its products worldwide. USWhole performed five SAP implementations for each of its major business units, including a small pilot test site, and corporate headquarters. It began its SAP project in early 1995, and completed its first implementation in March 1996. The final two implementations were completed simultaneously in July 1998. There are approximately 15,000 SAP users in USWhole.

E&P is the North American exploration and production division of an international petroleum company that has annual revenues in excess of US$90 billion. This particular division is engaged in the exploration and production of crude oil and natural gas worldwide, and accounts for approximately US$6.8 billion of the corporation's revenue. Although SAP has been implemented in various units of the parent company throughout the world, each project has been a separate activity from all the others. The teams, scope, budget, and timelines have been managed separately, and SAP has been designed and configured

Table 1. Profile of respondents.

Company	SAP Team Role for each respondent (1 respondent per line)
USWhole (Multiple roles for many members)	Responsible for SAP configuration; reengineering processes; managed quality assurance & testing; change management IT team leader; applications development lead; general leadership with 3 others of Chemical & Downstream implementations Managed configuration & upgrades throughout the company Project manager Project manager
E&P	Service delivery manager; Managed transition plan from production to operations and oversight of the conversion Technical leader for FI/CO; was also on HR design team Functional expert in project systems and asset management Team member; worked with conversion of legacy systems & investment management data to SAP Leader for transition from development to support Site implementation manager
Chemicals	Logistics team leader Team leader of all financial modules of SAP Director of the order-to-cash process. Dealt with customer service, accounts receivable, credit and some sales accounting. Team leader for sales and operations planning Change management leader. Responsible for communications and training materials Business implementation leader Manager of the support group Co-project manager Co-project manager

Table 2. Corporate profile.

Corporate Identity	Revenue (U.S. $)	Began SAP	Implementation Date	Number of Users
USWhole	*	1995	1996-1998	15,000
E&P	6.8 Billion	1996	1998	3,000
Chemicals	4 Billion	1996	1998-1999	5,000

* USWhole requested that this not be revealed

differently for each, with very little or no collaboration among the units. Therefore, focusing only on E&P's application in this firm seems to provide a unit of analysis that is comparable to that in the other sites. E&P began its project in 1996, using a big bang implementation where all modules were implemented at one time, and finished the implementation in mid-1998, for approximately 3,000 users.

Chemicals is the chemical division of an international petroleum company with annual revenues of approximately US$16 billion. Chemicals accounts for approximately one-fourth of its parent company's revenue, with annual revenues of approximately US$4 billion. It is a leading chemical manufacturer with interests in basic chemicals, vinyls, petrochemicals, and specialty products. Its products are largely commodity in nature, in that they are equivalent to products manufactured by others and are generally available in the marketplace. They are produced and sold in large volumes, primarily to industrial customers for use as raw materials. Chemicals began its SAP project in late 1996, with the first of nine implementations in January 1998. The implementations occurred approximately every two to three months until all implementations were finished in December 1999. There are approximately 5,000 SAP users in Chemicals. A summary of profiles is provided in Table 2.

Data Analysis

In the sections that follow is a description of knowledge sharing factors in each firm, including facilitation of knowledge sharing on the team, change management/training, and transition of IPS knowledge. The extent to which firms had changed or were beginning to change their core knowledge competencies

Table 3a. Summary of facilitation of knowledge sharing on the team.

Company	Facilitation of knowledge sharing on the team
USWhole	deemphasized titles, rank, and seniority on the team; emphasis on codifying how things worked and comparing written descriptions
E&P	lots of socialization after work; team members got to know each other and were supportive of each other; viewed each other as experts in their respective areas focused on a common purpose; some tension between IT and integration partner yet subsided as the project required heavy time and energy commitments; proactively sought ways to minimize the impact of the tension
Chemicals	team organized by process; deemphasized seniority and rank by providing the same bonus to all on the team actively; involved a variety of key users early in the process to ensure that they gathered knowledge from the right people

through changes in processes as a result of the SAP implementation is also discussed. A summary of points covered is provided in Tables 3a, 3b, and 3c. Table 3a provides a summary of facilitation of knowledge sharing on the team. Table 3b provides a summary of change management and training activities, and IPS knowledge transition activities. Table 3c provides a summary of changes in core knowledge competency.

USWhole

Facilitation of Knowledge Sharing on the Team

Teams at USWhole had a negative connotation prior to the SAP project. They were often used as dumping grounds for weak employees. This was a major obstacle to overcome in facilitating knowledge sharing on the SAP implementation team. Top management strongly supported SAP, so the project managers were able to ask for and get the "best people in most cases" for the implementation team. They sent people back to their units if they did not work

Table 3b. Summary of change management/training for end users and transition of IPS knowledge.

Company	Change Management	Training	Transition of IPS Knowledge
USWhole	**Team communicated with end users about how SAP would change their jobs;** **Identified end users to be change agents within the units,** **Relied on change agents to communicate as well**	**Identified power users among end users to train;** **Power users helped train other users;** **Focused largely on transactions** **Limited focus on integration**	**Worked with IPS throughout the project;** **Documented lessons learned at the end of each go-live;** **Used no formal transfer process at the end**
E&P	**Team went to change management training;** **Followed a change management strategy;** **Focused on communicating project status to the company;** **Made sure end users who were not directly part of the team had input into the project**	**Identified power users among end users to train;** **Power users helped train other users;** **Focused largely on transactions** **Limited focus on integration**	**Used formal transfer process with checklists on how to configure and on which things triggered what;** **Transferred knowledge from IPS to 3rd party consultant, then from that consultant to E&P support team**
Chemicals	**Focused on helping end users understand how their jobs would change after SAP** **Focused on how end users would use SAP**	**Identified power users among end users to train;** **Power users helped train other users;** **Focused on integration in addition to transactions**	**Built knowledge transfer into the contract with the IPS;** **Focused on how they solved problems & where they looked for answers;** **Team members gradually took on more responsibility so they could learn what the integration partner knew**

out. Thus, they put together team members that had reasonably good knowledge about their own processes. USWhole facilitated knowledge sharing on the team by eliminating seniority and functional distinctions. For example, senior people worked alongside hourly workers on the team, and if the lower level employees had an idea or wanted to try something, the senior people listened to them, and in some cases took direction from them. As one person

Table 3c. Summary of changes in core knowledge competency.

Company	Changes
USWhole	Gradually eliminating silo behavior; Some units adapted better than others, thus have seen more changes than others; Adaptation across the firm seems to be occurring; "it's not like I do a job anymore, but I perform a step in a process"
E&P	Slowly moving away from silo behavior; People are beginning to understand the integration points better, particularly in the financials area; Adaptation limited by corporate budget cuts unrelated to SAP; Are still in the learning cycle, but changes are ongoing
Chemicals	Majority of Chemicals units have embraced the concept of common processes, particularly in financials and purchasing; Have completed development of a common master file for parts, and units are designing purchasing around families of parts; Processes in general are now more well defined and better understood across functions within and across divisions

said, before this project "a lower level person wouldn't say what they thought in front of a more senior person. But with the shared goal of getting the project done quickly, they did." Lower level people also challenged senior people if they didn't agree or thought there was a better way of doing something. USWhole provided a structure to the team that allowed people to share knowledge openly and freely. This helped to resolve conflicts and to map processes to SAP effectively.

As one person said, "the bad thing was to have an idea and not express it." USWhole also relied heavily on codifying knowledge, and writing down how processes worked. For example, "If someone said we can't do it this way, we said, 'Why can't you? Is it really unique?' We'd get them to list what they do and to look at what others have listed, and identify the commonalities." USWhole used several approaches to facilitating knowledge sharing on the team, including codifying knowledge, structuring the team to remove barriers to knowledge sharing, and proactively seeking to overcome the stigma associated with teams.

Change Management/Training

USWhole had a strong change management team from the beginning of the project to communicate with the rest of the organization about project status, issues, ideas, managing expectations, and training. As one said, "It's all about change management. That's the name of the game." Another person indicated that "we had to break down cultural barriers (to common processes) through communication." The team shared their knowledge about SAP with the users in order to do so. They used several verbal and written communication means to reach users at all levels of the organization. The change management team helped users and managers understand how SAP would impact them, gathered feedback on user perceptions, concerns, and issues, and helped overcome resistance to change.

USWhole used a power user concept for training users. They identified users in each of the business units that were influential in their units and that were interested in SAP, and trained them extensively in how to do transaction processing as well as in how processes were changing and being integrated. However, there was more emphasis on the 'how-to' than on process changes. Users largely learned the latter on the job as they began to use the system. As power users shared their knowledge with other users, knowledge about how to use SAP began to permeate the organization. However, this was more difficult in some streams than in others. For example, one unit had old technology, and went from "1960's technology to 1990's technology in one fell swoop. Some had never used a mouse before, and one guy was moving his mouse over the screen to choose an icon." Thus, it was harder for them to learn how to use the new system even at the most basic level.

Transition of IPS Knowledge

Because of the sheer size of the project, USWhole had several integration partners. They did not use a formal knowledge transfer process when IPS left, but they did document how to configure and perform all major activities, and they documented lessons learned with each implementation. USWhole people worked with each integration partner throughout the project so that the knowledge transfer took place over time. In addition, although integration partners may have been different for each business unit, the core team from USWhole was the same throughout. Thus, knowledge gained in one implementation was not lost, but rather, was enhanced as the project progressed.

Changes in Core Knowledge Competency

Team members gained knowledge about the organization as a result of SAP as they learned about the "linkages and inefficiencies between processes." However, the organization has had mixed results in altering core knowledge competencies to change the way they perform processes. "Different streams have adapted differently." The downstream operations are the most complex to do in SAP, and this stream had experienced the least change in the past. In the beginning, it had the greatest difficulty in adapting to integrated, common processes. "Downstream adapted very poorly early on." The chemicals division was used to change because it operates in an "acquisition and trade environment." It also was running SAP R/2, so it was more familiar with the integrated process approach. Thus, it has had an easier time adapting. Similarly, "upstream is primarily accounting based, so with the changing economy they grew used to change," and this stream has adapted to the changes more readily. Thus, USWhole has experienced mixed results in its efforts to alter core knowledge competencies, but is continually working toward change.

One explanation for this is that USWhole did not recognize early enough differences in the streams' abilities to adapt to change. Their change management approach was not tailored to each stream, and even though they received feedback from each, if a stream was resistant, it may not have shared enough of what it knew so that the team could make the transition more effective. Although USWhole worked hard, to ensure effective knowledge sharing took place on the team, its efforts to ensure knowledge sharing between the team and the rest of the organization may not have been strong enough to impact change in core processes.

E&P

Facilitation of Knowledge Sharing on the Team

E&P used informal team building activities to help solidify team member relationships in an effort to foster knowledge sharing. Team members frequently socialized together after work, and at the end of major milestones, the company treated the entire team at various dinners, parties, and other outings. The team was also solidified because team members "knew the legacy systems on the business and technical side, and they were highly capable and credible in their areas." They viewed each other as experts in their areas, and thus, were willing to listen to and learn from each other.

However, E&P had a somewhat unique obstacle to knowledge sharing to overcome in its implementation. The information technology (IT) division of the parent company is managed as a separate company, and must contract with E&P and in competition with other outsourcing vendors for jobs. The IT company bid to be the integration partner on the SAP project, yet the E&P project leader chose another firm to be the primary integration partner because it had more experience with SAP. However, the IT staff had extensive knowledge about and experience with the E&P legacy systems that SAP replaced. In some cases, the IT staff had as much or more knowledge about how processes worked than the E&P business unit employees. Thus, they were selected to be part of the SAP team in order not to lose their knowledge. At first, there was some tension between IT staff and the IPS because the IT staff felt that they should have been chosen as the primary integration partner. However, there was a strong corporate culture of working in teams, thus this tension was minimized, and team members focused primarily on the common purpose of completing the project rather than on themselves. In addition, as new people came on the team throughout the project, they were not aware of the earlier tension, which also helped to dissipate it. As one said "we didn't have time to draw lines in the sand. We were concerned with meeting deadlines, and we all had the same goal —making SAP work."

Change Management/Training

E&P had a change management team in place whose responsibility was to make sure that current project status was communicated to all company employees, and to make sure that people not directly tied to the project felt like they also had some ownership. There was particular emphasis on this communication because "our experience on these large implementations has a very checkered past." E&P had implemented "fairly well conceived" large systems in the past where the change management people did not handle the change well. As a result, organizational members did not like the systems, and sometimes the systems were perceived as becoming the "butt of a lot of jokes." Thus, senior management placed a high priority on managing change in the SAP project, and a large piece of the budget was devoted to it. The change management team went through change management training classes, and the integration partner "brought in a very strong change management plan." The "change management piece was very mature, very well thought out, very strong." The change management team handled all communication, using a variety of written and verbal communication techniques ranging from e-mail to town hall meetings. "We got some good input (through this communication) that helped us restore some things that may have caused trouble later on."

Training was done using the power user concept. The emphasis in training was more on how to perform transaction processing than on the way processes were changing or the integrative nature of processes. The project budget provided for the latter aspect of training after implementation to give the users a chance to first understand how to use the system for basic transactions. However, the budget for all training at E&P, not just SAP, was cut, and they did not get to do as much of that as they wanted. This hurt the change management team's ability to share knowledge with the organization. One site was able to do more training because they had some additional resources that they could use. Even though "it wasn't much more training, you can really see the difference in how much better they are able to take advantage of SAP than other locations are."

Transition of IPS Knowledge

When it came time to transition the IPS off the team, the original tension regarding choice of partner began to resurface. Although most of the team members had either gotten past it or were unaware of it throughout the project, the project manager still had reservations about the firm's internal IT capabilities to support SAP after implementation. He wanted to hire the integration partner to continue working with the firm indefinitely as the SAP support team, even though this was a more expensive long run option. Because of the expense and the tension the decision created, senior management overrode the project manager's decision and hired the IT division to do long-term support. To ensure that the transition was smooth, they removed the project manager from the project and transferred him laterally to another part of the organization that had nothing to do with SAP. They appointed an experienced, senior IT manager to oversee the transition of knowledge from the integration partner to the team, and to manage the establishment of the support team. This was a strong, proactive attempt to overcome an obstacle that could have negatively impacted the rest of the project.

Another choice that helped minimize effects of this situation is that E&P hired another consulting firm with experience in SAP to help transition the IPS off the team and ensure that their knowledge was not lost to E&P. Because the support team members had worked throughout the SAP project, they already understood the processes quite well, but were missing technical information such as how to configure particular processes, or where to look for certain technical or operational information. The integration partner transferred their knowledge to the third-party consultant, and then the third-party consultant transferred that knowledge to the E&P support team. In their knowledge transfer model, "it was transferring SAP knowledge from one SAP experienced group to another SAP experienced group, then that group transitioned the knowledge to us in a way we could understand." While some knowledge was surely lost because of the varying perceptions, experiences, and communication barriers involved in getting second-hand or third-hand knowledge, this may have been the best way E&P could gain integration partner knowledge, given the situation in which they were working. Thus, E&P took strong steps to minimize knowledge loss when it recognized a potential problem with knowledge sharing.

Changes in Core Knowledge Competency

The extent to which E&P has integrated the results of its knowledge sharing to alter core knowledge and processes is somewhat lacking in consistency. One person indicated that for a long time "people didn't really try to exploit SAP; they just tried to get their jobs done." However, several months after implementation that began to change. The support team is "getting more requests from people looking at how to use SAP to change the business." Part of that is because budget cuts and layoffs that occurred about the time SAP was implemented (not SAP related), created a strain on employee's time and motivation to learn something new. The pressure on the budget has eased, yet the emphasis on cost cutting remains. Thus, end users have renewed their efforts to find opportunities to run the business more cost effectively. They are asking the SAP support team questions about how to identify and make use of these opportunities in SAP. They have also begun to understand that what they do in their process now affects someone else in another process, and are looking for ways to take advantage of that. The SAP support team continues to encourage people to exploit SAP opportunities. E&P has continued sharing knowledge and seeking ways to exploit old certainties and exploring new possibilities long after implementation. Thus, changes to the core knowledge competency are ongoing. Users are now trying to use SAP to change the way they perform processes and are thus beginning to alter core knowledge competencies. One explanation for this may be the efforts E&P made throughout the implementation to facilitate knowledge sharing on the team and with the rest of the organization. These knowledge sharing efforts helped make the organization ready to facilitate change in processes, and that readiness lasted through corporate budget cuts.

Chemicals

Facilitation of Knowledge Sharing on the Team

Chemicals' project manager said that "one of the things I always tell my folks is that SAP is a team sport. If you don't play as a team, you can't win." One of the things in place to discourage individual hoarding of knowledge was that each member of the team received the same bonus at the end of an implementation regardless of rank in the organization, and the bonus was based on the quality of the work, and how well the implementation deadlines were met. Thus, there was incentive for each member to work with others to accomplish a common goal. "We had a foxhole mentality" whereby team members were united around a common cause.

The team was also organized by process, rather than by function or SAP module, to facilitate knowledge sharing. Chemicals built overlap between modules and functions into the project, and often two or more groups worked together on a particular piece. For example, logistics is in the SD (sales and distribution) module, but Chemicals broke it out and had a subteam manage the logistics process separately from the sales and distribution people. Much of that data was also in the order-to-cash process performed by the customer service area. Thus, the logistics group had to work closely with the order-to-cash group to make sure that the logistics pieces fit. They also did cross-team training to help ensure that people working on one piece understood how their piece impacted others. Although this approach required more effort in many cases than a module-oriented approach they believed that "if you get too module oriented, you get too focused on the modules you're working on," and lose sight of the big picture, which is the processes. Thus, the SAP team was organized to focus on the transfer of knowledge across functions, processes, and units, and to eliminate silo behavior within the team and between the team and the organization. Although they did not use formal team-building activities, "everyone on the team had to rely on everyone else," because no one person or group knew all the things it took to do the project.

The SAP team also decided to bring the key end users across plants into implementation planning meetings where each team gave a basic overview of how each process would work in SAP, which included SAP terminology and basic concepts. They went through an exhaustive set of detailed questions about how processes worked and how they did their jobs. They built these questions over time, based on the integration partner's experience, and on what they learned with each implementation. Thus, by the last few implementations, they had developed a set of questions that allowed them to cover almost every conceivable part of the business processes. "We'd talk about the pros and cons of each decision these plant people made. And we'd try to make people understand what it actually meant, and document the decision. We'd distribute minutes of the meeting and have people either agree or not with what we'd decided on." This allowed the business people in multiple plants to share knowledge and make decisions about common processes across the plants. As a result, there was more uniformity of processes across plants, and there was a better understanding of how to handle exceptions or things that had traditionally been 'workarounds' in the legacy system. "We had some consultants who said our method was non-standard and shouldn't be used, but it worked well for us."

Change Management/Training

Chemicals had a very strong change management process in place, and although they had a formal team in place for this, much of the change management was an overall SAP team responsibility rather than that of just one subgroup. "We had never worked so hard on cultural readiness," one person said. "We worked really hard on communications," through email, memos, 'lunch and learns,' and television monitors with an animated video presentation that ran continually in the cafeterias in plants. The on-site planning meetings were also viewed as an important part of change management. "We had decision makers from every functional group in the plants in each design and implementation," which went a long way toward the cultural readiness on which change management was focused.

Although there was some use of the power user concept for training, the team members who implemented also trained the users on site during the implementation using materials the change management group had developed. Training involved the transactional based skills and a "heavy focus on the integration points" to help people understand "where they fit in the chain of events and why their piece was important and how it had downstream processes." They originally thought that the training would be more focused on the how-to, transactional skills, yet when they realized that "if we were going to get the wins we hoped were there, it was predicated on everybody doing their job." Thus, the training role changed considerably. "We spent more time and money around training than we originally planned, and we had planned to train much heavier than we had in any previous system."

Transition of IPS Knowledge

Chemicals built knowledge sharing into their contract with the integration partner. Team members focused both on how the partner solved problems and on where they looked for answers. This provided them with not only "how-to" knowledge, but also with more experiential knowledge about how to solve problems. Another way that Chemicals ensured knowledge sharing with its integration partner is that team members took on more responsibility as the implementation progressed so they could learn what the integration partner knew, and so they could develop shared SAP experiences with the partner.

Changes in Core Knowledge Competency

Chemicals has made substantial progress toward integrating what it had learned through the knowledge sharing in the SAP project into its core knowledge, and its processes have begun to change. "A lot more people are aware of the integration and dependencies among processes....Our business processes have become much more well-defined and understood." They are beginning to see substantial financial savings from leveraging common processes across units. For example, the purchasing process is now uniform throughout all the plants, and Chemicals has negotiated better prices on parts by buying the same part for all plants through fewer suppliers. To do this, the plants had to work together to change their nomenclature for parts to create a common master file of parts across plants, which was a major hurdle to cross because of the vast number of parts involved. Chemicals hired a consulting firm that had experience with this type of task to help them. The firm now has a uniform on-line catalog of parts and vendors. Buyers are now called alliance owners who "negotiate contracts, approve changes from vendors, and monitor the business flow with the vendors" across Chemicals for a particular family of parts rather than buying all the parts for a given plant. "We're still not over the hump on all of these (standards). The process works, but there's room for improvement."

One explanation for this is the strong knowledge sharing facilitators that Chemicals built throughout the implementation. It began from a process focus in which functional boundaries were removed, and team members from a variety of processes had to work together and share their knowledge. This process focus also engaged end users from across the organization to ensure that their knowledge about processes was incorporated into the implementation. In addition, users that were not directly involved in the implementation were trained not only on transactions, but also on the integrative nature of performing processes in ERP. Based on this evidence, Chemicals had the strongest knowledge sharing during implementation and seems to have been able to move more quickly than the other two firms in altering core knowledge competencies through changing the way they perform processes.

Lessons Learned

The firms that have had success with knowledge sharing during the implementation process are making great strides toward taking advantage of ERP to change the way they perform key processes. Although it is too early for these companies to have realized substantial benefits, they have mechanisms in place that put them well on the road to doing so. They have formed cross-functional, cross-unit networks of employees to alter core knowledge competencies by standardizing nomenclature, leveraging common processes, and eliminating silo behavior between units. These networks have arisen out of the knowledge sharing that took place during the implementation project among team members, other organizational members, and integration partners. Thus, there are several valuable lessons from these findings (see Table 4 for a summary).

One lesson learned is that when firms start to implement an ERP, they should identify organizational facilitators of and obstacles to knowledge sharing, and proactively seek to overcome the obstacles. For example, team members at E&P recognized a potential problem in the tension between two organizational units, and made a conscious decision to minimize it, thus successfully ensuring it was not passed on to new team members. One of Chemicals' goals was to engage a large number of the appropriate end users in the implementation to ensure that they captured the right knowledge. Chemicals and USWhole both worked to overcome traditional barriers to knowledge sharing such as rank, seniority, titles, and physical workspace. Barriers or obstacles that a firm has had in the past on large scale projects will not disappear by themselves, and ignoring them in an ERP project may magnify them. These firms took actions that were different from, if not counter to, organizational norms and patterns in order to ensure that the ERP implementation could successfully integrate processes and eliminate silos.

Lesson two is that firms should focus on integration from the beginning of the ERP project. Because ERP requires integration of processes in the end, the transition from silos is easier if the entire implementation effort is built around this integration. Implementing by module may feel more natural because it's how organizational members are used to working. However, it only prolongs the inevitable change to integrated processes necessary to realize significant ERP benefits. For example, Chemicals sought to overcome the divisions among functional areas and business units from the very beginning of its project. Chemicals' employees were educated about integration of processes from the beginning of the project because they were involved in integrated groups as they worked with the SAP team to map out processes and as they were trained to use SAP. Furthermore, the firms that primarily focused on "how-to" training said that they regret not having realized the importance of focusing on integration points with users earlier.

Lesson three is that firms should learn from the past and not be afraid to acknowledge prior project weaknesses or failures. For example, E&P recognized that it had not been good at change management in the past, and took steps to correct this weakness. USWhole recognized that its management of teams in the past was not good, and took deliberate steps to build a strong SAP team.

Lesson four is that firms should focus on knowledge sharing both on the team and with the rest of the organization. For example, USWhole may not have recognized the differences in the ability of its streams to adapt to changes brought about by SAP early enough because it did not tailor its change management activities to the different streams. As a result, different streams adapted differently, and the team had to work harder with some than others to begin to affect change in processes. On the other hand, E&P and Chemicals worked hard to facilitate knowledge sharing among all relevant stakeholders in

Table 4: Summary of lessons learned.

Identify and eliminate obstacles to success e.g., cultural barriers such as stigma associated with teamwork or tensions between units;   structural barriers that promote silo behavior or inhibit knowledge sharing between levels
Focus on integration from the beginning of the project e.g., implement by process rather than by module;   focus training on integration points in addition to how to process transactions
Focus on finding the best solutions to problems e.g., don't 'sweep problems under the rug' and hope to fix them later;   resist pressures to meet deadlines simply to mark milestones

Build organizational knowledge sharing throughout the project
 e.g., foster knowledge sharing among team members with formal & informal activities;
   encourage knowledge sharing between team and other organizational members;
   minimize knowledge lost when consultants or other team members leave through formal roll- off procedures

Learn from the past e.g., acknowledge prior project weaknesses and look for ways to do better;   recognize prior strengths and build on those

their implementations. Both organizations have begun to change core processes and alter core knowledge competencies.

Thus, the findings from this study provide several lessons firms may apply in their own ERP implementations. Even firms that already have implementations in progress or that are struggling to make ERP work after the initial implementation can apply these lessons to their own situations. ERP is a long term solution, and once implemented, it is difficult, if not impossible, to go back to the way things were prior to ERP. Thus, it is never too late to look at other firms' success stories to find what we can learn from them.

Limitations of the Study and Directions for Future Research

One limitation of the study is that only one industry and one package was examined. Although this helps to minimize bias that could be introduced across industries and packages, there is a trade-off between generalizability of findings and minimizing bias. Minimizing bias helps eliminate many factors that might confound the results and provides a clearer view of the phenomenon of interest. Selection of appropriate case sites controls extraneous variation and helps define the limits for generalizing findings (Eisenhardt, 1989). If consistent results are found across similar case sites, then we can be surer that the theory that led to the case study originally will also help identify other cases to which results are analytically generalizable (Eisenhardt, 1989; Yin, 1989). However, using one industry ignores difficulties or challenges in implementation that may be unique to a given industry. One avenue for future research is to examine these constructs in this study across industries and using different ERP packages to determine whether industry or package mediate the findings in this study.

Another limitation is the number of respondents interviewed. Although many of the same phrases were heard from respondents, indicating that theoretical saturation had been reached, one direction for future research is to examine the phenomena of interest in this study using a larger sample size in order to be more sure that the responses obtained in this study do represent the broader views and perceptions of the project team. In addition, the unit of analysis in this study is restricted to the implementation team. Although most knowledge sharing during the implementation revolved around this team, future research that explores the perceptions of other organizational members or of the integration partner staff could be useful. One avenue for this future research is to compare responses to determine whether knowledge sharing is perceived differently between the team, other organizational members, and the integration partner staff.

Contributions of the Study

This study contributes to what is known about knowledge sharing in ERP implementations in several ways. First, it identifies, categorizes, and discusses several factors that facilitate knowledge sharing during ERP implementation. Second, it links knowledge sharing to attempts to change core knowledge competencies. Third, it provides several lessons for practitioners that they can use in their own ERP implementations. Practitioners engaged in ERP implementation can use these findings both to determine what may work best for them and to identify their own facilitators of knowledge sharing. Fourth, this study provides directions for future research by identifying limitations of the current study and suggesting ways that future research could examine those limitations to further extend what we know about knowledge sharing in ERP implementation.

Author Note

This paper supported by NSF Grant SES 000-1998

References

Al-Mashari, M. & Zairi, M.(2000). The effective application of SAP R/3: A proposed model of best practice, *Logistics Information Management*, *13*(3), 156-166.

Andriola, T. (1999). Information technology—The driver of change, *Hospital Material Management, 21*(2), 52-58.

Baskerville, R., Pawlowski, S., & McLean, E.(2000). Enterprise resource planning and organizational knowledge: Patterns of convergence and divergence, *Proceedings of the 21st ICIS Conference*, Brisbane, Australia, 396-406.

Brown, C. & Vessey, I. (1999). ERP implementation approaches: Toward a contingency framework, *Proceedings of the 20th Annual International Conference on Information Systems*, Charlotte, NC, December 12-14, 411-416.

Brown, J.S. & Duguid, P. (2000). Balancing act: How to capture knowledge without killing it, *Harvard Business Review*, May-June, 73-80.

Caldwell, B. & Stein, T. (1998). Beyond ERP - New IT agenda - A second wave of ERP activity promises to increase efficiency and transform ways of doing business, *InformationWeek*, (November), 30, 34-35.

Clement, R.W. (1994). Culture, leadership, and power: The keys to organizational change, *Business Horizons, 37*(1), 33-39.

Constant, D., Kiesler, S., & Sproull, L, (1994). What's mine is ours, or is it? A study of attitudes about information sharing," *Information Systems Research, 5*(4), 400-421.

Davenport, T.H. (1998). Putting the enterprise in the enterprise system, *Harvard Business Review*, July-August, 121-131.

Eisenhardt, K.M. (1989). Building theories form case research, *Academy of Management Review, 14*(4), 532-550.

Grant, R.M. (1996). Prospering in dynamically competitive environments: Organizational capability as knowledge integration, *Organization Science*, *7*(4), 375-387.

Hammer, M. (1990). Reengineering work: Don't automate, obliterate, *Harvard Business Review*, *68*(4), 104-112.

Harari, O. (1996). Why did reengineering die, *Management Review, 85*(6), 49-52.

Hine, M.J. & Goul, M. (1998). The design, development, and validation of a knowledge-based organizational learning support system, *Journal of Management Information Systems, 15*(2), 119-152.

Jarvenpaa, S.L. & Staples, D.S., (2000). The use of collaborative electronic media for information sharing: An exploratory study of determinants, *Journal of Strategic Information Systems*, 9, 129-154.

Jones, M.C. (2001). *The Role of Organizational Knowledge Sharing in ERP Implementation*, Final Report to the National Science Foundation Grant SES 0001998.

Kogut, B. & Zander, U.(1992). Knowledge of the firm, combinative capabilities, and the replication of technology, *Organization Science*, *3*(3), pp. 383-397.

Leonard, D. & Sensiper, S. (1998). The role of tacit knowledge in group innovation, *California Management Review*, *40*(3), 112-132.

Nelson, K.M., Nadkarni, S., Narayanan, V.K., & Ghods, M.(2000). Understanding software operations support expertise: A revealed causal mapping approach, *MIS Quarterly, 24*(3), 475-507.

Osterloh, M. & Frey, B.S. (2000). Motivation, knowledge transfer, and organizational forms, *Organization Science, 11*(5), 538-550.

Robey, D., Ross, J.W., & Boudreau, M-C. (2002). Learning to implement enterprises systems: An exploratory study of the dialectics of change, *Journal of Management Information Systems, 19*(1), 17-46.

Ross, J. (1999). Surprising facts about implementing ERP, *IT Pro*, July/August, 65-68.

Scott, J.E. & Kaindl, L. (2000). Enhancing functionality in an enterprise software package, *Information and Management*, 37, 111-122.

Soh, C., Kien, S.S., & Tay-Yap, J. (2000). Cultural fits and misfits: Is ERP a universal solution? *Communications of the ACM, 43*(4), pp. 47-51.

Stein, E.W. & Vandenbosch, B. (1996). Organizational learning during advanced systems development: Opportunities and obstacles, *Journal of Management Information Systems*, *13*(2), 115-136.

Welti, N. (1999). *Successful SAP R/3 implementation: Practical management of ERP projects*, Addison-Wesley: Reading, MA.

Yin, R. K.(1989). *Case Study Research: Design and Methods*, Sage Publications: Newbury Park, CA.

Zheng, S., Yen, D.C., & Tarn, J.M., (2000). The new spectrum of the cross-enterprise solution: The integration of supply chain management and enterprise resources planning systems," *Journal of Computer Information Systems*, Fall, 84-93.

Appendix A: Semi-structured Interview Guide

Team vs. Individual Efforts

1. Do you usually work on a project team or do you primarily work alone on projects?

2. Do you think you are more rewarded for individual activities or for work on teams? How important is project teamwork to your company?

3. Are teams primarily made up of people from the same functional areas or from across functions?

4. How would you describe the culture of the firm?

Process vs. Product (Deadline) Orientation

1. How much focus was there on meeting deadlines and finishing the project under budget?

2. How well were deadlines met?

3. When deadlines weren't met, what was the reason?

4. How did your team determine whether the goals were valid and being met?

5. How did your team learn about opportunities SAP could provide your firm?

6. Do you think this learning process occurred throughout the implementation?

Organizational Knowledge Sharing During the Project

1. How were the SAP project team members selected?

2. How were differences in perspectives melded together?

3. Was this easy or difficult?

4. Was there ever a time when differences couldn't be resolved? (if so, how was that handled?)

5. How did your team seek input from others in the company on areas where you were uncertain?

6. How did your team seek to keep others in the company informed about company goals and progress on SAP?

7. Do you think this was ever seen as simply another IT project?

8. How much did your group rely on outside consultant expertise?

9. How did you make sure that you had learned enough from them so that you could carry on after they left?

10. Was there much transition off your SAP team? How was it managed?

11. How were new people coming on the team brought up to speed?

12. During SAP team meetings, were people encouraged to express their ideas, even if they weren't fully formed yet? And did they express these ideas? Can you give some examples?

13. Was there ever anything in the implementation process you felt just wasn't right, but couldn't exactly explain why? If so, did you express this? Why or why not?

14. Was there anything you assumed to be true about SAP that you later changed your mind about?

Incorporation of New Knowledge into Core Knowledge Competencies

1. Do you believe that the organization is different now than before SAP implementation? If not, why; if so, how?

2. Have the processes changed or are they being changed because of SAP?

3. How has SAP changed the way you think about your job or the company?

4. What are some things that you learned about the business processes at the company that you didn't know before the SAP implementation?

About the Authors

Linda K. Lau is an assistant professor of Computer Information Management Systems at the College of Business and Economics of Longwood University (USA) since 1994. She worked briefly as a financial consultant with Salomon Smith Barney from 1999-2000. She received her PhD in Management Information Systems from Rensselaer Polytechnic Institute in 1993, and her Master's of Business Administration and Bachelor of Science in Industrial Technology from Illinois State University in 1987 and 1986, respectively. She is a member of the Editorial Board for *SAM Advanced Management Journal,* and an ad-hoc reviewer for the *Information Resources Management Journal* (IRMJ) and the *Journal of Global Information Management* (JGIM). Her current research areas include enterprise resource planning, distance learning, and Web development. She has published several articles in journals and conference proceedings, and she also edited a book entitled *Distance Learning Technologies: Issues, Trends and Opportunities,* with Idea Group Inc. in 2000.

*   *   *   *   *

Colin G. Ash is the associate head of the School, Management Information Systems at Edith Cowan University in Perth, Western Australia. His current research interest relates to the virtual empowerment that organisations can realise through the effective implementation of e-business applications with ongoing ERP enterprise resource planning systems. Colin has published extensively in the area of e-business development and implementation, with over 50 research papers.

Graham Blick has 35 years of working experience in a variety of industries including agriculture, education, mining and utilities. He has worked and lived in four continents. Graham is a graduate of Monash University, Melbourne, Australia. Currently he is pursuing Doctorate in Business Administration at the Graduate School of Business, Curtin University, Australia. His research interests are in technology based change management process, benefit realization of ERP systems, and information management. Graham is a fellow of Australian Institute of Management and Australian Human Resource Institute.

Janice M. Burn is foundation professor of Information Systems and head of School, Management Information Systems at Edith Cowan University in Perth, Western Australia. She previously worked in Hong Kong and the UK. Her research interests relate to global e-business transformation, collaborative commerce for small business, e-health and e-government. She has gained a number of grants for international projects and she has published five books and over 150 research papers.

She-I Chang has five years experience lecturing in Information Management in the Department of Business Administration at Kao-Yuan Institute of Technology (Taiwan). He is currently a PhD candidate at ISMRC/QUT (Australia), his research focusing on ERP systems, with a particular emphasis on the issues, challenges, and benefits associated with ERP life cycle-wide implementation, management, and support. He also has methodological interest in the Delphi survey methodology. He has presented and published this research at ICIS, ECIS, PACIS, and ACIS.

Sue Conger has a BS in psychology from Ohio State University, an M.B.A. in finance and cost accounting from Rutgers University, and a PhD in computer information systems from the Stern School of Management at New York University. Her texts include *Planning and Designing Effective Web Sites* (with Richard O. Mason) published in 1998, and *The New Software Engineering* published in 1994. Dr. Conger's recent research is on e-government and e-business, particularly in the ERP area, and innovative use of IT. The research presented in this text on SAP in the enterprise was spawned by joint interest with Dr. Laura Meade, a University of Dallas (USA) colleague, and access to Celanese Corporation, an SAP user where her husband worked for over 20 years.

José Esteves is a doctoral student in the IS doctoral program of the Technical University of Catalonia, Barcelona, Spain. He is a computer engineer, has a master in IS, and a diploma in business administration. His research interests include ERP systems, knowledge management and qualitative research. He can be reached by e-mail at jesteves@lsi.upc.es.

Jane Fedorowicz, the Rae D. Anderson Chair of Accounting and Information Systems, holds a joint appointment in the Accountancy and Computer Information Systems departments at Bentley College (USA). Professor Fedorowicz earned MS and PhD degrees in Systems Sciences from Carnegie Mellon University. She currently serves as Vice President of Chapters and Affiliated Organizations for the Association for Information Systems (AIS). She also serves as the Northeast regional representative for the Emerging Technologies Section of the American Accounting Association, and was co-general chair for the 2001 Americas Conference for Information Systems. Professor Fedorowicz has published over 60 articles in refereed journals and conference proceedings. The American Accounting Association recognized Professor Fedorowicz with the 1997 Notable Contribution to the Information Systems Literature Award, and she was selected as Bentley College's Scholar of the Year for 2000.

Susan Foster is a lecturer in the School of Information Systems at Monash University, Australia. She has qualifications in information technology, teaching, and psychology. She has a strong interest in change management and has written a number of papers and books chapters related to this. She is an affiliate member of the ERP Research Group.

Guy G. Gable directs the Information Systems Management Research Center (ISMRC), Queensland University of Technology (QUT), Australia. Dr. Gable, having worked in enterprise systems practice and academe in North America, Asia, and Australia, championed the 'Enterprise Systems (ERP) in curriculum and research' initiative at QUT, which leads the way in the Asia Pacific region. He is Chair of the Australasian Universities Application Hosting Center Board of Management. His doctorate is from University of Bradford, England, and his MBA from the University of Western Ontario, Canada. He is 1st Chief Investigator or Team Leader on three in-progress ARC collaborative (Linkage-Projects) grants involving > $1M in total resources. He has published over 70 refereed journal articles and conference papers and books (e.g., *Manage-*

ment Science, Journal of Strategic Information Systems, Information & Management, European Journal of Information Systems) and is on the editorial boards of eight journals–*Journal of Strategic Information Systems* (since '92), *Australian Journal of Information Systems* (since '94), *Computers & Security* (since '94), *Journal of Global Information Management* (Oct '97), *Journal of Software Maintenance* (since Dec '97), *Information Systems Frontiers* (since Jul '98), *Electronic Commerce Research and Applications* (since Nov '00), *Information Systems and e-Business Management* (since Nov '00). Dr. Gable has a particular interest in Knowledge Management practices of large consulting firms. His doctoral thesis on "Consultant Engagement Success Factors" won the ICIS'92 doctoral thesis award. Other areas of research in which he is active include: life cycle-wide ERP knowledge management, ERP maintenance management, research project management, ERP benefits realisation, and process modeling success factors.

Ulric J. (**Joe**) **Gelinas, Jr.**, is an associate professor of Accountancy at Bentley College (USA). He received his MBA and PhD degrees from the University of Massachusetts. He is co-author of *Accounting Information Systems, 5th ed.*, *Business Processes and Information Technology,* and founding editor of the *Journal of Accounting and Computers.* He participated in the development of *Control Objectives for Information and Related Technology (COBIT)* by participating in the COBIT Expert Review and by authoring portions of the *Implementation Tool Set.* He is a recipient of the Innovation in Auditing and Assurance Education Award from the American Accounting Association. Dr. Gelinas has published articles in *Issues in Accounting Education, Information Systems Audit & Control Journal, Technical Communications Quarterly, IEEE Transactions on Professional Communication, Annals of Cases on Information Technology* and other outlets.

George Hachey is an associate professor of Finance at Bentley College (USA). BS and MS, Georgetown University; MBA, University of Rhode Island; PhD, University of New Hampshire. Currently developing interdisciplinary business courses and implementing enterprise software such as SAP into the finance curriculum. Is campus coordinator for SAP's University Alliance. Is currently teaching Performance Measurement and Evaluation, the capstone course in the Corporate Finance Accounting major that he co-developed with Dr. Catherine Usoff. Formerly academic coordinator for Bentley's Estonia

Program, which received substantial financial support from USAID and USIA. Developed Bentley's International Relations major. Authored various articles on capital markets and international finance with particular emphasis on the Eurocurrency market and financial futures. Has published in the *Journal of Money, Credit and Banking,* the Journal of International Money and Finance, Business and the Contemporary World, and the Journal of Real Estate, Finance and Economics. Formerly taught at University of Rhode Island, University of New Hampshire and Merrimack College.

Paul Hawking is senior lecturer in Information Systems at Victoria University, Melbourne, Australia. He has contributed to the *Journal of ERP Implementation and Management, Management Research News* and contributed many conference papers on IS theory and practice. He is responsible for managing the university's strategic alliance with SAP and is coordinator of the university's ERP Research Group. Paul is immediate past chairperson of the SAP Australian User Group.

Mary C. Jones is an associate professor of information systems at the University of North Texas (USA). She received her doctorate from the University of Oklahoma in 1990. Dr. Jones has published articles in such journals as Information and Management, Information Resources Management Journal, European Journal of Information Systems, Journal of Computer Information Systems, and Behavioral Science. Her research interests are in the management and integration of emerging electronic commerce technologies and in organizational factors associated with enterprise-wide systems.

John Loonam is a PhD candidate at Trinity College Dublin, Ireland. He researches in the fields of organisation development and information technology, with particular interest in executive management, organisational, and enterprise systems. His doctoral research marries both fields of inquiry, focusing upon the nature of top management support for enterprise systems initiatives.

Joe John McDonagh is the Director of Executive Education at Trinity College, Dublin, Ireland. He works in the fields of organization development and information technology, specializing in executive leadership and the management of IT-enabled business change. He teaches Senior Management at

Trinity College Dublin and at a number of business schools in Europe and America. He works on research, consultancy and executive development with many European and American multinationals as well as providing advice to government. He publishes widely on the management of large-scale IT-enabled business change. Recent and forthcoming publications are to be found in *Handbook of Action Research, Issues of Human Computer Interaction, Information Technology and e-Business in Financial Services,* and *Public Administration Quarterly,* among others.

Joan Pastor is an associate professor and Dean of the IT school of Universidad Internacional de Catalunya, Barcelona, Spain. He holds a degree in computer science and a PhD in software. He is also leading the "Twist" group on IS qualitative research, addressing topics like ERP procurement and implementation. He can be reached by e-mail at jap@unica.edu.

R. Leon Price is a Conoco Teaching Fellow at the University of Oklahoma, USA. Dr. Price has published many articles and papers, one of which the Academy of Management Review named as one of their seven outstanding articles of the year. Other publication outlets include Behavioral Science, Information Resources Management Journal, Journal of Computer Information Systems, and Information Executive. His research interests are in the management of information technologies.

Mohammed Quaddus received his PhD from the University of Pittsburgh, MS from University of Pittsburgh and Asian Institute of Technology. His research interests are in information management, decision support systems, group decision and negotiation support systems, multiple criteria decision making, systems dynamics, business research methods and in the theories and applications of innovation diffusion process. Dr. Quaddus has published in a number of journals and contributed in several books/monographs. In 1996 he received the Researcher of the Year award in Curtin Business School, Curtin University of Technology, Australia. Currently he is an associate professor with the Graduate School of Business, Curtin University of Technology, Australia. Prior to joining Curtin, Dr. Quaddus was with the University of Technology-Sydney and with the National University of Singapore. He also spent a year at the Information Management Research Centre, Nanyang Technological University, Singapore.

Andrew Stein is a lecturer in the School of Information Systems in the Faculty of Business and Law at Victoria University, Melbourne, Australia. He has contributed to the *International Journal of Management, Journal of Information Management, Journal of ERP Implementation and Management* and contributed many conference papers on IS theory and practice. His research interests include enterprise systems, e-procurement applications, e-marketplace business models and reverse auction systems. He is a member of the university's ERP Research Group.

Cesar Alexandre de Souza is a doctoral student at the School of Economics and Administration of the University of São Paulo (FEA-USP), Brazil. He has previously received his Masters in Business Administration from the same institution. His previous career path includes being an industrial engineer from the Polytechnic School of USP, professor and researcher at the Business Administration Course of the São Judas Tadeu University (USJT), Brazil, and a business consultant on information technology management and ERP systems implementation.

Catherine Usoff is an associate professor of Accountancy at Bentley College (USA). She earned her undergraduate degree in Accounting at Boston College, and MBA and PhD degrees from the Ohio State University. Dr. Usoff co-teaches a year-long business process course in the cohort Information Age MBA program into which she has integrated SAP and a process modeling software. She has supervised several student teams performing comprehensive business process analysis projects in leading companies. Dr. Usoff has presented several research papers at national conferences and has published in *Advances in Accounting Education* and the *Managerial Auditing Journal*.

David C. Wyld currently serves as a professor of Management at Southeastern Louisiana University (USA), where he teaches business strategy and heads the College of Business & Technology's Strategic e-Commerce Initiative. He has been widely published in leading journals in business and management, and recently, he was named editor of the *Journal of the Academy of Strategic e-Commerce*. He has been awarded with the Distinguished Researcher award for Southeastern Louisiana University and has won several best paper awards at leading academic conferences. He has conducted graduate executive education courses and consulted with a wide variety of industrial and public sector clients.

Ronaldo Zwicker received his PhD in Business Administration at the School of Economics and Administration of the University of São Paulo (FEA-USP), Brazil. He earned his Masters in Applied Mathematics from the Institute for Mathematics and Statistics of USP. He was a chemical engineer at the Polytechnic School of USP. He is a professor and researcher of the Administration Department of the FEA-USP. He is also a business consultant.

Index

Advances in Software Maintenance Management:
Technologies and Solutions

Macario Polo, Mario Piattini and Francisco Ruiz
University of Castilla–La Mancha, Spain

Advances in Software Maintenance Management: Technologies and Solutions is a collection of proposals from some of the best researchers and practitioners in software maintenance, with the goal of exposing recent techniques and methods for helping in software maintenance. The chapters in this book are intended to be useful to a wide audience: project managers and programmers, IT auditors, consultants, as well as professors and students of Software Engineering, where software maintenances is a mandatory matter for study according to the most known manuals - the SWEBOK or the ACM Computer Curricula.

ISBN 1-59140-047-3 (h/c) • US$79.95 • eISBN 1-59140-085-6
• 310 pages • Copyright © 2003

"*Software organizations still pay more attention to software development than to maintenance. In fact, most techniques, methods, and methodologies are devoted to the development of new software products, setting aside the maintenance of legacy ones.*"

Macario Polo, Mario Piattini, and Francisco Ruiz
University of Castilla—La Mancha, Spain